340.2 COM

COMPARATIVE LAW YEARBOOK

The Center for International Legal Studies is a non-profit and non-stock organization incorporated under the laws of the State of California and with headquarters in Salzburg, Austria. The Center is devoted to the promotion of international legal education, research, information exchange and understanding. It coordinates and supervises various law seminars in Europe and sponsors research in areas of Comparative and International Law.

The Center is assisted by a Board of Advisors consisting of Mr. Harry Arkin, Attorney-at-Law, Denver, Colorado; Professor Rona Aybay, Aybay and Aybay, Istanbul, Turkey; Professor R. Bernhardt, Director, Max-Planck-Institut, Heidelberg, Germany; Professor Frank Ellsworth, Faculty of Law, University of Chicago, Chicago, Illinois; Professor H.-G. Koppensteiner, Faculty of Law, Salzburg University, Salzburg, Austria; Judge Erich Korf, District Court of Siegburg, Germany; Professor Ferenc Mádl, Faculty of Law, Eötvös Loránd University, Budapest, Hungary; Justice Gustaf Petrén, Supreme Administrative Court, Stockholm, Sweden; Dr. Peter Prettenhofer, Attorney-at-Law, Vienna, Austria; Professor S.F. Richter, Austro-American Institute of Education, Vienna, Austria; Mr. Robert Salkin, Attorney-at-Law, Los Angeles, California, and Mr. Bruce Zagaris, Attorney-at-Law, Washington, D.C.

The editor of the *Comparative Law Yearbook* is Professor Dennis Campbell, Director, Center for International Legal Studies. Dr. William Tower and Ms. Judith Foot are assistant directors of the Center.

The *Comparative Law Yearbook* prints matter it deems worthy of publication. Views expressed in material appearing herein are those of the authors and do not necessarily reflect the policies or opinions of the *Comparative Law Yearbook,* its editors or the Center for International Legal Studies.

Manuscripts should be sent to the editor, *Comparative Law Yearbook,* Center for International Legal Studies, Box 19, A-5033 Salzburg, Austria.

Comparative Law Yearbook

Issued by
The Center for International Legal Studies

Volume 7, 1983

1984 **MARTINUS NIJHOFF PUBLISHERS**
a member of the KLUWER ACADEMIC PUBLISHERS GROUP
DORDRECHT / BOSTON / LANCASTER

Distributors

for the United States and Canada: Kluwer Boston, Inc., 190 Old Derby Street, Hingham, MA 02043, USA
for the UK and Ireland: Kluwer Academic Publishers, MTP Press Limited, Falcon House, Queen Square, Lancaster LA1 1RN, England
for all other countries: Kluwer Academic Publishers Group, Distribution Center, P.O. Box 322, 3300 AH Dordrecht, The Netherlands

Library of Congress Cataloging in Publication Data

Library of Congress Catalog Card Number 79-649337.

ISBN 90-247-2966-1 (this volume)
ISBN 90-247-3002-3 (series)
Volumes 1 – 3 were published by Sijthoff & Noordhoff

PRINTED IN THE NETHERLANDS

Table of Contents

Part I

SYMPOSIUM

Abortion Law and Public Policy

Introduction

Susan Rust Bulfinch, Attorney-at-Law and Intern,
1983-1984, Commission of Human Rights, Council of
Europe, Strasbourg, France

Since the United States Supreme Court rendered its decision in the landmark abortion case *Roe* v. *Wade*[1] in 1973, the high courts of most of the leading Western countries have experienced similar constitutional debates regarding the right to seek and have an abortion. This Introduction briefly outlines the current state of the law concerning abortion in the United States, the United Kingdom, Canada, Germany (the Federal Republic), France, and Italy.

These Western democratic countries have liberalized to some extent the strict penal sanctions previously imposed upon those persons wishing to have or willing to perform abortions. All of the high courts have recognized the two ends of the spectrum on the issue of abortion − the protection of the fundamental interest of the fetus and the possibly conflicting interests of the woman. Each country, through its developing legislation, has sought to balance the protection of both.

In 1977, the European Commission of Human Rights submitted its report in the case of *Brüggemann and Scheuten* v. *the Federal Republic of Germany.*[2] The applicants complained in large part that their right to respect for private and family life was violated by the Government in that they were not free to have an abortion carried out in the event of an unwanted pregnancy. They alleged a violation of Article 8 of the European Convention on Human Rights[3] among others, as a result of the judgment of the Federal Constitutional Court in Germany on 25 February 1975.[4] The Court ruled that the Fifth Criminal Law Reform Act which had been adopted in 1974 was void insofar as it provided for the termination of pregnancy during the first twelve weeks without requiring any particular reason for it. The Commission of Human Rights interpreted the language of Article 8 as meaning 'that not every regulation of the termination of unwanted pregnancy constitutes an interference with the right to respect for the private life of the mother, in that Article 8, paragraph 1, could not be interpreted as meaning that pregnancy and its termination are, as a principle, solely a matter of the private life of the mother; and that therefore the ... legal rules in force in German law ... do not interfere with their right to respect for their private life'.[5] The Committee of Ministers on 17 March 1978 decided that there had

Comparative Law Yearbook, Volume 7, 1983. ISBN 90-247-2966-1.
© *1984, Martinus Nijhoff Publishers, Dordrecht. Printed in the Netherlands*

been no violation of the Convention by the Federal Republic of Germany in the application submitted by Brüggemann and Scheuten.[6]

By refusing to accept abortion as a human right under the Convention, the Commission of Human Rights recognized that attitudes, political traditions, and ethical judgments concerning abortion and the rights of the unborn differ among the member states of the Council of Europe. Effective enforcement of human rights on the international level requires a commonality of values and shared ideals. With respect to abortion, no such consensus exists at the present time.

It is not the purpose of this discussion to elucidate upon the procedures of each country's constitutional courts, nor to develop in detail the history underlying the decriminalization of many abortion laws. The fact alone that more than one abortion case has been considered by the European Commission of Human Rights[7] is suggestive of the timeliness and importance of the issues surrounding the subject of privacy and correlative measures adopted for the regulation of abortion practices.

The Common Law Jurisdictions

United States

It was during the 19th century in the United States when many state legislatures enacted criminal abortion laws. The Texas statute, at issue in *Roe* v. *Wade,*[8] exemplified what was typical of the time making it a criminal offense to ' "procure an abortion", as therein defined, or to attempt one, except with respect to "an abortion procured or attempted by medical advice for the purpose of saving the life of the mother" '.[9] The issue before the Supreme Court in *Roe* v. *Wade* was the constitutionality of the state abortion statute permitting abortions only to save the life of the mother.

Based on case precedent from *Union Pacific Railroad Co.* v. *Botsford,*[10] to *Griswold* v. *Connecticut,*[11] wherein the Court read into the Bill of Rights the right to privacy, there had been a slowly evolving right to personal privacy rooted in the First Amendment. This right, however, was not determined by the Court to be absolute. In a plurality decision, the Court stated:

> [A] State may properly assert important interests in safeguarding health, in maintaining medical standards, and in protecting potential life. At some point in pregnancy, these respective interests become sufficiently compelling to sustain regulation of the factors that govern the abortion decision. The privacy right involved, therefore, cannot be said to be absolute ...
>
> ...

We, therefore, conclude that the right of personal privacy includes the abortion decision, but that this right is not unqualified and must be considered against important state interests in regulation.[12]

The Court held that the 'compelling' point for the state's important and legitimate interest in the health of the mother is at the end of the first trimester, approximately the twelfth week of pregnancy. From this period through the twenty-fourth week of pregnancy or the second trimester, a state may regulate the procedures for abortion as reasonably relate to the preservation and protection of the health of the mother. During the third trimester, a state may regulate and even proscribe abortion except where it is necessary to save the life or health of the mother. It is only during the third trimester that the state has full regulatory power to prohibit abortion.

Although a woman has the right in the United States to terminate her pregnancy during the first trimester, this right is limited to some extent to those women who can afford one. In light of more recent Supreme Court decisions, *viz., Maher* v. *Roe,*[13] state legislation prohibiting the use of state and federal welfare funds for non-therapeutic abortions has been held to be a constitutionally permissible restriction. The Court held that mere governmental failure to fund abortions did not violate a substantive constitutional right.

United Kingdom

Prior to 1803, the termination of any pregnancy in England was punishable as a common law misdemeanor. In 1861, the Offences against the Person Act was passed. Sections 58 and 59 in particular formed the basic prohibitory regulation against abortion practice.[14] It was an offense to procure or attempt to procure an abortion. Anyone who violated the statute was guilty of a felony.

The Act subsequently has been the subject of various judicial decisions. Perhaps the most noteworthy of all, from an historical as well as a legal-sociological viewpoint, is the case of *R.* v. *Bourne.*[15] This 1938 case depicted the lawfullness of abortion to preserve not only the woman's life but also her mental health. The defendant, Dr. Bourne, was acquitted by a jury for terminating the pregnancy of a woman on the basis that she would become 'a mental wreck' were she required to carry out her term of pregnancy.

The post-war passion for social change succeeded in implementing the Abortion Act 1967.[16] It is a fairly permissive abortion law for it permits abortions if the risks to the physical or mental health of the woman or her children are greater than those of terminating her pregnancy. The law states that, in determining whether continuation of the pregnancy would constitute a risk to her health, "account may be taken of the pregnant woman's actual or reasonably foreseeable environment."[17] The language of the Act thus combines both a mental health indicator with a social and economic indicator to balance the effect of another child not only on the woman but also on her children.

The more recent legislative reforms were directed with the passage of the Abortion Act 1967 applicable to England, Scotland, and Wales but not to Northern Ireland. Subsequent to its enactment, however, there was continued opposition to the Act. In June 1971, the Lane Committee[18] was established, with the primary purpose to review the operations of the 1967 Act. This Committee produced a three volume report in April 1974. Based in large part on the unanimous conclusions produced by the report, no new amendments were proposed.

Canada

The governing statute permitting therapeutic abortions in Canada is provided in Section 251 of the Criminal Code.[19] Essentially abortion is prohibited in Canada, but if specific conditions are met a legal abortion may be procured under Section 251(4). These include the obtaining of approval of a majority of the members of the therapeutic abortion committee for the approved hospital where the abortion is to occur and such approval must be in the form of a written certificate stating that the pregnancy will likely endanger the life of the woman or her health.

Although the legal statute makes provisions for abortions in certain specified circumstances, the availability for having them is limited to the means provided by the provinces. For example, what is the effect of the situation where a hospital has not made provisions for a therapeutic abortion committee? This was in part one of the issues considered by the Supreme Court in Canada in the well-known case of *Morgentaler* v. *R*.[20] The defendant in the case was acquitted on the charge of performing an illegal abortion based on the common law defense of necessity.

> This common law defence of necessity, when applied to abortion, would require two elements to be established: necessity in the sense that the operation was urgent to save the mother's life or health; and necessity in the sense that it was not possible to follow the Section 251 procedure for obtaining approval. That is, the requirements of Section 251 and the difficulty of fulfilling them may in themselves help to create the situation of necessity which justifies disregarding them.[21]

A comparable study to the Lane Committee's report in England was conducted in 1975 in Canada by the Committee on the Operation of the Abortion Law. Professor Robin Badgley chaired the Committee comprised of two other female members.[22] In January 1977, the Committee presented its report, but interestingly enough, no recommendations for amending the law were given. Moreover, the report commented on the absence of due process given to applicants who had been refused an abortion by the therapeutic abortion committee.[23] There was also general acknowledgment of the discrepency in uniformity of the requirements under which the abortion committees would decide on each application. As of 1 May 1978, however, Sections 251–252 of the Criminal Code have been in force.

The Civil Law Jurisdictions

The Civil Law countries – the Federal Republic of Germany, France, and Italy – have followed a strict interpretation of each country's constitutional protections and in comparison with the common law countries have been slow to decriminalize abortion laws.

The Federal Republic of Germany

The current law regarding the termination of pregnancy is governed by Sections 218 to 220 of the German Penal Code.[24] Originally, the criminal code in Germany was based upon the Prussian Penal Code of 1851 which was then adopted by the German Reich in 1871. Similar to the history of abortion legislation in the United States, the United Kingdom, and Canada, abortion was prohibited.[25] Yet, the Supreme Court (*Reichsgericht*) in a 1927 decision held that an abortion procured for medical reasons, that is, to preserve the life and health of the mother, would not be punishable under the law.[26] During the 1950s and 1960s, a more comprehensive review of abortion laws and policies took place eventually leading to the major reform of abortion laws in the Abortion Reform Act of 1974.[27]

It is the Fifth Criminal Law Reform Act of 18 June 1974 that contains the major revisions of the penal code and above all decriminalized abortion which was carried out by a doctor with the consent of the woman within 12 weeks after conception.[28] In principle, the penalty was maintained but it was only during the second and third trimesters that special reasons were required to justify the termination of a pregnancy.

The liberalization of the criminal sanctions against abortion, however, was short-lived. Once promulgated, the statute was challenged on constitutional grounds by the governments of Baden-Württemberg, Saarland,

Bavaria, Schleswig-Holstein, and Rhineland-Pfalz. The Abortion Reform Act was declared null and void by a vote of 6 to 2 by the First Senate of the Federal Constitutional Court on 25 February 1975.[29] The Court held that the 'developing life' in the womb had independent legal value protected by Article 2 of the Basic Law of the German Constitution.[30]

Accordingly, the Court directed that the law be amended. On 12 February 1976 the West German Parliament (*Bundestag*) enacted the Fifteenth Criminal Law Amendment Act (*Fünfzehntes Strafrechtsänderungsgesetz*).[31] The Act was promulgated on 21 May 1976 and is currently in force in the Federal Republic of Germany.

France

The first section of Article 317 of the French Penal Code provides:

> Any person who causes or attempts to cause an abortion on a pregnant or putatively pregnant woman, regardless of her consent, by means of food, beverages, prescriptions, manipulations, force, or by any other means whatsoever, shall be punished by jailing from one to five years and by fine of 1,800 to 60,000 Francs.[32]

The enforcement of Article 317 was temporarily suspended on 17 January 1975 by Act Number 75–17.[33] During this five-year suspended period, there was no punishment for abortions. In France, the conditions under which abortions may be procured are governed by provisions of the Public Health Code. Prior to 1975, these legislative measures were contained in a decree issued on 5 October 1953, specifically Article L. 162–1–4.[34] Article 162–1 allowed a woman to freely seek the services of a doctor to perform an abortion until the end of the tenth week of pregnancy.[35] The new Act, L. 176, or the Voluntary Termination of Pregnancy Act, amended the provisions allowing a woman to terminate her pregnancy before the end of the tenth week but only if she is fully informed of the risks involved in the abortion procedure and the means of assistance available to her pre- and post-delivery.[36]

In a major decision of 15 January 1975, the *Conseil Constitutionnel* held that the provisions of the law regarding the voluntary termination of pregnancy were not contrary to the Constitution.[37] The tenth week remains the legal time limit after which abortions are prohibited unless there is certification by two physicians that the pregnancy is seriously endangering the woman's health or that there is a strong indication that the unborn child is suffering from a serious disease or incurable condition.

Italy

The constitutionality of Article 546 of the Italian Penal Code prohibiting all abortions was considered by the Italian Constitutional Court in the case of *Carmosina et al.*[38] Article 546 articulated the necessity elements required for a legal abortion. The legislature, however, had not adequately examined the conditions which would justify the procurement of an abortion. For example, there was no recognition of the need for an abortion to protect the life and/or health of the mother.

In its decision on 18 February 1975, the Court declared Article 546 unconstitutional as it prohibits an abortion when the continued pregnancy involves serious risk of injury or danger to the health of the mother which cannot be prevented otherwise. The vagueness of the provisions under the code could no longer be tolerated.

On 21 January 1977, a new Abortion Bill was adopted by the Chamber of Deputies. Essentially, this bill was more lenient than Article 546 by providing additional reasons for the termination of a pregnancy. Under the bill, a woman could decide to terminate her pregnancy within the first 90 days (first trimester) if there should be indications of serious danger to her physical or mental wellbeing. Such reasons include not only her health but also economic, social, or family reasons. A termination was also justified in cases of rape or incest or danger of a malformity. After the first trimester, an abortion was only justified if there was a present danger to the woman's life or health.[39] The bill was rejected by a narrow majority of the Senate in June of 1977 but subsequently introduced again in the Chamber of Deputies.

After considerable deliberation, the Italian government passed the Law on the Social Protection of Motherhood and the Voluntary Termination of Pregnancy on 22 May 1978.[40] In a referendum held in 1981, the law was overwhelmingly approved.

Conclusion

The result of a more realistic and flexible attitude towards abortion legislation and the decriminalization of previously held rigid statutes has had a profound effect in many Western countries. For example, the Badgley Committee, commenting on Canada's 1969 legislation, stated that:

> The number of deaths of women for Canada resulting from attempted self-induced or criminal abortions, which averaged 12.3 each year between 1958 and 1969, dropped to 1.8 deaths annually from 1970 to 1974.[41]

There is an overriding similarity that exists in most of the abortion laws in the Western countries discussed in this article. The Constitutional Courts have identified two legitimate governmental interests which provide the foundation for abortion regulation during certain stages of pregnancy: the mother's health for the stage subsequent to the end of the first trimester and the life of the fetus for the stage subsequent to viability. Not all jurisdictions, especially in the Federal Republic of Germany as compared to the United States, recognize and accept the same definition of conception. Yet, the developing trend in the law regarding the termination of pregnancy is to balance the social, economic, and family interests of the woman with the political and legal interests of the fetus. The following chapters dealing with the United States, Austria and Germany trace developments in the abortion law and policy in those countries since the decisions of their high courts approximately a decade ago.

Notes

1. *Roe* v. *Wade*, 410 U.S. 113 (1973); see also *Doe* v. *Bolton*, 410 U.S. 179 (1973)
2. Application Number 6959/75. The European Commission of Human Rights was created as an impartial, international body to which complaints could be filed alleging that a member state had failed to secure for persons within its jurisdiction the rights set forth in the convention. For further reference see Petzold, *The European Convention on Human Rights,* 4th edn. (1981).
3. Article 8 of the Convention provides:
   (1) Everyone has the right to respect for his private and family life, his home and his correspondence.
   (2) There shall be no interference by a public authority with the exercise of this right except such as is in accordance with the law and is necessary in a democratic society in the interests of national security, public safety or the economic well-being of the country, for the prevention of disorder or crime, for the protection of health or morals, or for the protection of the rights and freedoms of others.
4. Fully published in Entscheidungen des Bundesverfassungsgerichts (BVerfGE), Volume 29, pp. 1–95.
5. Report of the European Commission of Human Rights adopted on 12 July 1977, p. 148. See also *Decisions and Reports* Number 10, p. 122.
6. Resolution DH (78) 1 of the Committee of Ministers adopted on 17 March 1978.
7. Although other applicants have submitted applications alleging a violation of the Convention based on the leniency or restrictiveness of their Government's abortion laws, the Commission has declared most applications inadmissible. *X* v. *Austria,* Application Number 7045/75 was deemed to be *ratione personae* incompatible with the provisions of the Convention. In *X* v. *Norway,* Application Number 867/60, the Commission noted that it is competent to examine the compatibility of domestic legislation with the Convention only with respect to its application in a concrete case and is, therefore, not competent to examine *in abstracto* its compatibility with the Convention. The Commission found the petition inadmissible because the Norwegian petitioner, who declared that he acted in the interest of third persons, could not claim to be himself the victim of a violation under the Convention.

8. Supra n. 1.
9. 410 U.S. 154: quoted in 'Constitutional Decisions on Abortion,' *Comparative Constitutional Law* (1976), Chapter 12, p. 564.
10. 141 U.S. 250 (1891).
11. 381 U.S. 479 (1965).
12. Supra n. 9, p. 567.
13. 432 U.S. 464 (1977). See also *Harris* v. *McRae,* 448 U.S. 297 (1980).
14. See *International Digest of Health Legislation,* Vol. 30(3), 1979, p. 401:

Section 58 of the 1861 Act

Every woman, being with child, who, with intent to procure her own miscarriage, shall unlawfully administer to herself any poison or other noxious thing, or shall unlawfully use any instrument or other means whatsoever with the like intent, and whosoever, with intent to procure the miscarriage of any woman, whether she be or not be with child, shall unlawfully administer to her or cause to be taken by her any poison or other noxious thing, or shall unlawfully use any instrument or other means whatsoever with the like intent, shall be guilty of felony ...

Section 59 prescribes that:

Whosoever shall unlawfully supply or procure any poison or other noxious thing, or any instrument or thing whatsoever, knowing that the same is intended to be unlawfully used or employed with intent to procure the miscarriage of any woman, whether she be or be not with child, shall be guilty of a misdemeanor ...

15. 1 K.B. 687 (1939), 3 All E.R. 615 (1938).
16. The workings of the English abortion law are discussed in depth in the three volume *Report of the Committee on the working of the Abortion Act*, commonly referred to as the Lane Report (London: Her Majesty's Stationery Office (1974)).
17. Isaacs, 'Reproductive Rights 1983: An International Survey,' 14 *Colum. Hum. R. L. Rev.* 311 (1983), p. 346.
18. The Committee was so named because it was chaired by Mrs. Justice Lane of the English High Court. The Committee was comprised of fifteen members, ten of whom were women.
19. Section 251 provides the following:

(1) Every one who, with intent to procure the miscarriage of a female person, whether or not she is pregnant, uses any means for the purpose of carrying out his intention is guilty of an indictable offence and is liable to imprisonment for life.

(2) Every female person who, being pregnant, with intent to procure her own miscarriage, uses any means or permits any means to be used for the purpose of carrying out her intention is guilty of an indictable offence and is liable to imprisonment for two years ...

(4) Subsections (1) and (2) do not apply to

(a) a qualified medical practitioner, other than a member of a therapeutic abortion committee for any hospital, who in good faith uses in an accredited or approved hospital any means for the purpose of carrying out his intention to procure the miscarriage of a female person, or

(b) a female person who, being pregnant, permits a qualified medical practitioner to use in an accredited or approved hospital any means described in paragraph (a) for the purpose of carrying out her intention to procure her own miscarriage, if, before the use of those means, the therapeutic abortion committee for that accredited or approved hospital, by a majority of the members of the committee at which the case of such female person has been reviewed,

(c) has by certificate in writing stated that in its opinion the continuation of the pregnancy of such female person would or would be likely to endanger her life or health, and

(d) has caused a copy of such certificate to be given to the qualified medical practitioner ...

Criminal Code, R.S.C. 1970.
See also n. 21 infra, pp. 7, 8.

20. *Morgentaler* v. *R.* (1976) 1 S.C.R. 616, (1974) C.A. 129, 42 D.L.R. (3d) 444.
21. Sommerville, 'Reflections on Canada's Abortion Law: Evacuation and Destruction – Two Separate Issues,' 31 *Univ. of Toronto L.J.* 1 (1981), p. 10.
22. As a consequence, the report has come to be known as the Badgley Report.
23. The Badgley Report is discussed further in 'Abortion Laws in Commonwealth Countries' *International Digest of Health Legislation,* Volume 30(3), 1979.
24. Sections 218 and 219 provide the following:

§218
Interruption of Pregnancy

(1) Anyone who interrupts a pregnancy after the 13th day following conception shall be punished by incarceration up to three years or fined.

(2) The punishment shall be six months to five years if the actor
1. acts against the will of the pregnant woman, or,
2. wantonly causes the danger of death or serious impairment of health to the pregnant woman.

The court can set up a supervision authority. (§68, Par. 1, No. 2).

(3) If the pregnant woman commits the act, the punishment is incarceration up to one year or a fine.

(4) The attempt is punishable. The woman shall not be punished for an attempt.

§218a
Freedom from Punishment for Interruption
of Pregnancy in the First Twelve Weeks

An interruption of pregnancy performed by a physician with the consent of the pregnant woman is not punishable under §218 if no more than twelve weeks have elapsed since conception.

§218b
Indications for Interruption of
Pregnancy After Twelve Weeks

An interruption of pregnancy performed by a physician with the consent of the pregnant woman after the expiration of twelve weeks after conception is not punishable under §218 if, according to the judgment of medical science:
1. The interruption of pregnancy is indicated in order to avert from the pregnant woman a danger to her life or the danger of serious impairment to the condition of her health insofar as the danger cannot be averted in a manner that is otherwise exactable (reasonably expected) from her, or
2. Compelling reasons require the assumption that the child will suffer from an impairment of its health which cannot be remedied on account of an hereditary disposition or injurious prenatal influences which is so serious that a continuation of the pregnancy cannot be exacted (reasonably expected) of the pregnant woman; and not more than 22 weeks have elapsed since conception.

§218c
Interruption of Pregnancy Without Instruction
and Counseling of the Pregnant Woman

(1) He who interrupts a pregnancy without the pregnant woman:

1. first having, on account of the question of the interruption of her pregnancy, presented herself to a physician or to a counseling center empowered for the purpose and there been instructed about the public and private assistance available for the pregnant women, mothers and children, especially such assistance which facilitates the continuation of the pregnancy and eases the condition of mother and child, and

2. having been counseled by a physician,

shall be punished up to one year incarceration or by a fine if the act is not punishable under §218.

(2)The woman upon whom the operation is performed is not subject to punishment under Paragraph one.

§219
Interruption of Pregnancy
Without Expert Opinion

(1)Anyone who interrupts a pregnancy after the expiration of twelve weeks after conception without a competent counseling center having confirmed that the prerequisites of §218b No. 1 or No. 2 are satisfied, shall be punished with incarceration up to one year or by fine if the act is not punishable under §218.

(2) The woman upon whom the operation is performed is not subject to punishment under Paragraph one.

Taken from Jonas and Gorby, 'West German Abortion Decision: A Contrast to *Roe* v. *Wade*,' 9 *John Marshall J. Prac. and Proc.* 551 (1976), pp. 612, 613.

25. German Penal Code of 1871, Section 218.
26. Judgment of 11 March 1927, 61 RGSt (Entscheidungen des Reichgerichts in Strafsachen) 242. See also Kommers, 'Abortion and Constitution: United States and West Germany,' 25 *Amer. J. Comp. Law* 250 (1977).
27. Fifth Law of 18 June 1974; *Bundesgesetzblatt,* Part I, 21 June 1974, Number 63, pp. 1297–1300. 1974 BGBl. I 1297.

Amendment of the Penal Code

1. Sections 218 to 220 of the Penal Code shall be replaced by the following provisions:

Termination of Pregnancy

218. (1) Any person who terminates a pregnancy later than the 13th day after conception shall be sentenced to up to three years' imprisonment or to a fine.

(2) The penalty shall be imprisonment for a period of between six months and five years if the offender:

1. has acted against the wishes of the pregnant woman; or

2. by acting without due care, has endangered the life or caused a risk of severe injury to the health of the pregnant woman.

The court may order judicial surveillance [Führungsaufsicht] (item 2 of sub-section 1 of Section 68).

(3) If the act has been committed by the pregnant woman, the penalty shall be imprisonment for a period of up to one year or a fine.

(4) An attempt to commit the aforesaid act shall be punishable. The woman shall not be punished for attempting to commit the act.

Lawfulness of Pregnancy Terminations During the First 12 Weeks

218a. The termination of pregnancy performed by a physician with the consent of the pregnant woman shall not be punishable under Section 218 if not more than 12 weeks have elapsed since conception.

Indications for Pregnancy Terminations After the 12th Week

218*b*. The termination of pregnancy performed by a physician with the consent of the pregnant woman after 12 weeks have elapsed since conception shall not be punishable if, according to the findings of medical science:

1. a. pregnancy termination is indicated in order to avert a risk to the life of the pregnant woman or a risk of serious damage to her state of health, insofar as the said risk cannot be averted by any other means that the woman can be expected to accept; or

2. imperative reasons exist for presuming that, as a consequence of a hereditary predisposition or harmful influences prior to birth, the child would suffer from irremediable injury to its state of health of such gravity that the pregnant woman be required to continue the pregnancy to term, and not more than 22 weeks have elapsed since conception.

Termination of Pregnancy Without the Provision of Information and Advice to the Pregnant Woman

218*c*. (1) Where the act is not punishable under Section 218, a sentence of up to one year's imprisonment or a fine shall be imposed on any person terminating a pregnancy in cases where the pregnant woman has not:

1. consulted a physician or a duly authorized counselling center beforehand concerning the question of the termination of her pregnancy, and received from one of these sources information concerning the public and private assistance available to pregnant women, mothers, and children, particularly as regards assistance which would render the continuance of the pregnancy and the situation of the mother and child less onerous; and

2. been advised by a physician.

(2) The woman on whom the operation is performed shall not be punishable under subsection 1.

Termination of Pregnancy in the Absence of an Expert Appraisal

219. (1) Any person who terminates a pregnancy after twelve weeks have elapsed since conception without a competent center having previously confirmed that the conditions laid down in items 1 or 2 of Section 218*b* are fulfilled shall be sentenced to up to one year's imprisonment or to a fine, where the act is not punishable under Section 218.

(2) The woman on whom the operation is performed shall not be punishable under subsection 1.

Publicity for Pregnancy Terminations

219*a*. (1) A sentence of up to two years' imprisonment or a fine shall be imposed on any person who, at a public gathering or by the dissemination of written material, audio-visual materials, pictures, or presentations, with the object of personal gain or in a grossly offensive manner, offers, anounces, recommends, or publicizes:

1. his own services or the services of other persons for performing or abetting the performance of a pregnancy termination; or

2. products, articles, or procedures suitable for the termination of pregnancy, reference being made to their suitability for this purpose.

(2) Item 1 of sub-section 1 shall not be applicable where physicians or authorized counselling centres (Section 281*c*) are informed as to which physicians, hospitals, or establishments are prepared to perform abortions under the conditions laid down in Sections 218*a* and 218*b*.

(3) Item 2 of sub-section 1 shall not be applicable where the activity in question is addressed to physicians or persons entitled to deal in the products or articles mentioned in item 2 of sub-section 1, or is carried out in the form of a published announcement in specialized medical or pharmaceutical journals.

Circulation of Products for Pregnancy Terminations

219b. (1) Any person who places in circulation products or articles suitable for the termination of pregnancy with the intention of abetting unlawful acts within the meaning of Section 218 shall be sentenced to up to two years' imprisonment or to a fine.

(2) Participation by a woman preparing to terminate her pregnancy shall not be punishable under sub-section 1.

(3) Products or articles to which the aforesaid act relates may be confiscated.

Refusal to Perform Pregnancy Terminations

2. (1) No one shall be obliged to participate in a pregnancy termination.

(2) Sub-section 1 shall not be applicable where participation is necessary in order to prevent a danger to the life of the pregnant woman or a risk of severe injury to her health, which cannot be averted by any other means.

Termination of Pregnancy Other Than in an Appropriate Establishment

3. (1) A pregnancy may be terminated only in a hospital or in an establishment in which the necessary medical after-care is assured.

(2) Any person who terminates a pregnancy in violation of the provisions of sub-section 1 shall be considered to have committed an offence. The offence may be punished by a fine of up to 10,000 German marks.

Federal Statistics

4. Federal statistics concerning pregnancy terminations performed under the conditions laid down in Sections 218a and 218b of the Penal Code shall be kept by the Federal Statistical Office. Any person who in his capacity as a physician has performed a pregnancy termination under these conditions must, before the end of the current calendar quarter, report it to the said Office, together with particulars concerning:

1. the reason for the termination of pregnancy;
2. the family status and age of the pregnant woman, and the number of children in her care;
3. the number of previous pregnancies and their outcome;
4. the duration of the pregnancy terminated;
5. the nature of the operation and any complications observed; and
6. the place where the operation was performed and, in the event of the person's being hospitalized, the duration of her hospitalization.

The name of the pregnant woman must not be given.

28. See supra n. 27.
29. 39 BVerfGE 1 (1975).
30. Article 2, Section 2 of the Basic Law states:
    'Everyone shall have the right to life and to the inviolability of his person.' See also supra n. 26 Kommers, p 267.
31. BGB1. I 1213 (1976). The relevant provisions as amended by the Act provide:

Art. 218. Termination of Pregnancy

(1) Whoever terminates a pregnancy shall be punished by imprisonment for a term not exceeding three years or a fine.

(2) In particularly serious cases the punishment shall be imprisonment for a term between six months and five years. As a rule, a case is particularly serious where the perpetrator:
1. acts against the will of the pregnant woman, or
2. frivolously causes the risk of death or of a serious injury to the health of the pregnant woman.

The court may order the supervision of conduct (Art. 68, para. (1), sub-para. 2).

(3) If the act is committed by the pregnant woman herself the penalty shall be imprisonment for a term not exceeding one year or a fine. The pregnant woman is not punishable under the first sentence if the pregnancy is interrupted by a doctor after consultation (Art. 218b) (1), sub-paras. 1, 2) and if not more than twenty-two weeks have elapsed since conception. The court may abstain from punishing the pregnant woman if at the time of the intervention she was in a situation of particular distress.

(4) The attempt shall be punishable. The woman shall not be punished for attempt.

Art. 218a. Indications for Termination of Pregnancy

(1) An abortion performed by a doctor shall not be punishable if:
1. the pregnant woman consents, and
2. in view of her present and future living conditions the termination of the pregnancy is advisable according to medical knowledge in order to avert a danger to her life or the danger of a serious prejudice to her physical or mental health, provided that the danger cannot be averted in any other way she can reasonably be expected to bear.

(2) The prerequisites of para. (1) sub-para. 2 are also considered as fulfilled if, according to medical knowledge:
1. there are strong reasons to suggest that, as a result of a genetic trait or harmful influence prior to birth, the child would suffer from an incurable injury to its health which is so serious that the pregnant woman cannot be required to continue the pregnancy;
2. an unlawful act under Arts 176 to 179 (1) has been committed on the pregnant woman and there are strong reasons to suggest that the pregnancy is a result of that offense; or
3. the termination of the pregnancy is otherwise advisable in order to avert the danger of a distress which
   (a) is so serious that the pregnant woman cannot be required to continue the pregnancy, and
   (b) cannot be averted in any other way she can reasonably be expected to bear;

(3) Provided that, in the cases envisaged in para (2) sub-para 1, not more than twenty-two weeks have elapsed since conception and, in the cases envisaged in para 2 sub-paras 2 and 3, not more than twelve weeks.

Art. 218b. Termination of Pregnancy in the Absence of Advice Being Given to the Pregnant Woman

(1) Whoever terminates a pregnancy although the pregnant woman
1. did not at least three days before the intervention consult a counsellor (para 2), regarding the question of termination of her pregnancy, and was not informed there about the public and private assistance available to pregnant women, mothers and children, in particular about such assistance as facilitates the continuance of pregnancy and the situation of mother and child, and
2. was not advised by a doctor on the medically significant aspects,

shall be punished by imprisonment for a term not exceeding one year or by a fine, unless the act is punishable under Art. 218. The pregnant woman is not punishable under the first sentence.

(2) Counsellor within the meaning of para (1) sub-para 1 is:

1. an advisory board approved by a public authority or by a corporation, institution or foundation under public law;

2. a doctor who does not himself perform the abortion and who

   (a) as a member of an approved advisory board (sub-para 1) is charged to give advice within the meaning of para (1) sub-para (1);

   (b) is approved as a counsellor by a public authority or by a corporation, institution or foundation under public law; or

   (c) has by consulting a member of an approved advisory board (sub-para 1) who is charged with giving advice within the meaning of para (1) sub-para 1, by consulting a social authority or in another appropriate way obtained information about the assistance available in individual cases.

(3) para 1 sub-para 1 does not apply where termination of pregnancy is advisable in order to avert from the pregnant woman a danger to her life or health caused by a physical disease or physical injury.

Art. 219 Termination of Pregnancy Without Medical Certificate

(1) Whoever terminates a pregnancy although no written certificate, by a doctor who does not himself perform the abortion, has been submitted to him on the question whether the conditions of Art. 218a, para (1) sub-para 2, paras (2), (3) are fulfilled, shall be punished by imprisonment for a term not exceeding one year or by a fine, unless the act is punishable under Art. 218. The pregnant woman is not punishable under the first sentence.

(2) A doctor may not give a certificate under para (1) if the competent authority has forbidden him to do so, on the ground that he has been finally convicted of an unlawful act under para (1), or under Arts. 218, 218b, 219a, 219b or 219c, or of another unlawful act which he committed in connection with an interruption of pregnancy. The competent authority may provisionally forbid a doctor to give certificates under para (1) if he has been committed for trial on suspicion of having committed such an unlawful act.

Art. 219a. False Medical Certificate

(1) Whoever as a doctor knowingly gives a false certificate on the conditions of Art. 218a para (1), sub-para 2, paras (2), (3), shall be punished by imprisonment for a term not exceeding two years or by a fine, unless the act is punishable under Art. 218.

(2) The pregnant woman is not punishable under para (1).

Art. 219b. Publicity for Termination of Pregnancy

...

Art. 219c. Dealing With Means for Termination of Pregnancy

...

Art. 219d. Definition

Acts, the effects of which occur before the termination of the implantation of the fertilised egg in the uterus, are deemed not to be interruptions of pregnancy within the meaning of this Code.

32. Article 317. Décr.-L. 29 juill. 1939, Article 82.

Quiconque, par aliments, breuvages, médicaments, manoeuvres, violences ou par tout autre moyen, aura procuré ou tenté de procurer l'avortement d'une femme enceinte ou supposée enceinte, qu'elle y ait consenti ou non, sera puni d'un emprisonnement d'un an à cinq ans, et d'une amende de 1, 800 F à 60,000 F.

33. Loi Number 76–17 du 17 janvier 1975 provides:

18

2. Est suspendue pendant une période de cinq ans à compter de la promulgation de la présente loi, l'application des dispositions des quatre premiers alinéas de l'article 317 du code pénal lorsque l'interruption voluntaire de la grossesse est pratiquée avant la fin de la dixième semaine par un medicin dans un établissement d'hospitalisation privé satisfaisant aux dispositions de l'article L. 176 du code de la santé publique.

34. Décret du 5 octobre 1953.

35. Article 162−1:

La femme enceinte que son état place dans une situation de détresse peut demander à un médicin l'interruption de sa grossesse. Cette interruption ne peut être pratiquée qu'avant la fin de la dixième semaine de grossesse.

36. Décr. Number 70−415 du 8 mai 1970; L. Number 75−17 du 17 janvier 1975.

37. Conseil Constitutionnel, D.S. Jur. 529; A.J.D.A. 134 (1975). See also 'Constitutional Decisions on Abortion', *Comparative Constitutional Law,* (1976), p. 577.

The Conseil Constitutionnel held that the Act on intentional interruption of pregnancy was not incompatible either with the facts to which the Preamble of the Constitution of 4 October 1958 referred or with any provision of the Constitution.

None of the exceptions provided for in the Act were found to be contrary to any of the fundamental principles recognized by the laws of the Republic, nor was there irrespect for the protection of the health of the child as articulated in the Preamble of the Constitution of 27 October 1946. The Act was held not to be in violation of the Constitution.

38. Corte costituzionale, Decision of February 18, 1975, Number 27 (1975) 20 Giur. Const. 117; 43 Rac. uff. corte cost. 201; 98 Foro It. I, 515. See also n. 37, p. 612.

39. Council of Europe, *Newsletter on Legal Activities ,* Number 26 (January-February 1977), pp. 8, 9.

40. Law Number 194, 22 May 1978. See Filicory and Flamigni, 'Legal Abortion in Italy: 1978−1979,' 13 *Fam. Plan. Rersp.* 228 (1981).

41. 'Abortion Laws in Commonwealth Countries' *International Digest of Health Legislation,* Volume 30(3) (1979), p. 457.

Austria

Erhard Mock, Professor of Law, Salzburg University

Introduction

Until the enactment of the Penal Code under Emperor Joseph II on 13 January 1787, abortion was in principle punished by death.[1] The wording of this law in regard to abortion preserved its validity for an astonishingly long period of time. It was by and large adopted by the Penal Code of 3 September 1803 and by its revised version of 27 May 1852. It was only in 1937 that the provisions concerning abortion underwent a change.[2] This mainly consisted of the provision that an abortion should not be punished if it were the only means to prevent an imminent danger to the life of the pregnant woman or at least a lasting damage to her health. However, according to paragraph 144 of the Penal Code, an abortion was still punishable in principle.

The 150 years between Emperor Joseph II's Penal Code and the reform of 1937 did not mean a standstill in the legislation on abortion. After many attempts, a draft of a bill was presented to the House of Lords (*Herrenhaus des Reichsrates*) which adopted it with only a few changes.[3] But before the draft could pass the House of Commons (*Abgeordnetenhaus*), World War I intervened. This draft provided that abortion should no longer be regarded as a serious crime (*Verbrechen*) but only as a minor offence (*Vergehen*). Moreover, it was intended to accept medical indication as legal.[4]

The Austrian Republic did not continue the work begun by the Monarchy. The main goal was, to achieve a unification of the Austrian and the German legal systems. In 1927, nearly identical drafts of a Penal Code were introduced to the German (*Reichstag*) as well as to the Austrian (*Nationalrat*) parliaments. As far as abortion was concerned, a far-reaching liberalization was intended. 'In minor cases' one should even refrain from punishment.[5] However, political developments put an end to this legislation.

Apart from this large-scale attempt, it was the concern of the Social Democratic Party since the establishment of the Republic of Austria in 1918 to repress the punishment of abortion as far as possible. In the first period of legislation of the young Republic of Austria deputy A. Popp brought for-

Comparative Law Yearbook, Volume 7, 1983. ISBN 90-247-2966-1.
© *1984, Martinus Nijhoff Publishers, Dordrecht. Printed in the Netherlands.*

ward such a motion, which she repeated in November 1923. According to it, abortion should only be punishable if it were performed by a third person without the pregnant woman's consent, or if it were committed by the woman herself after the third month of pregnancy.[6]

After the re-establishment of the Republic of Austria after World War II, the idea of a general reform of penal law, and at the same time of the law of abortion, was kept in mind. After the war, the governmental system of a 'Great Coalition' developed, which was formed by the Austrian People's Party (*Österreichische Volkspartei/ÖVP*) and the Austrian Socialist Party (*Sozialistische Partei Österreichs/SPÖ*). The Federal Ministry of Justice thus became a domain of the Socialist Party. From 1954 to 1962, a Commission for the Reform of Penal Law was at work. This Commission recommended a new regulation concerning abortion, which contained in short the following principles:

(1) In order to protect embryonic life, abortion should remain punishable in principle.

(2) An interruption of pregnancy should go without punishment only because of medical reasons (*medical indication*).

(3) 'Health' was defined in a most complex manner. It was to comprise for instance the woman's concern for her psychological constitution, in case she was made pregnant by force.

(4) The maximum punishment for a pregnant woman was to be one year of imprisonment.

(5) In minor cases, one should refrain totally from punishment.[7]

A draft presented by the Federal Ministry of Justice in 1964 was based on the Commission's work. This draft was vehemently criticized by the People's Party and had thus to be changed: the sanction for the pregnant woman was again increased to three years imprisonment and the possibility to abstain from punishment in petty cases was abandoned. But also this revised draft did not meet with approval, especially because the Roman Catholic Church, to whom the majority of Austrians belongs, maintained its point of view, namely that the reform's intentions would lead not only to legal recognition of a medical, but also indirectly to a social, eugenic and ethical indication. Because of the high value of human life, the Church could not permit this to happen.[8] In 1966, the draft was revised to form part of a new Penal Code. It omitted the social indication, a startling omission for a welfare state. Again this draft did not meet with sufficient approval in the political process.[9]

After the parliamentary elections of 1966, which lead to the absolute majority of the People's Party, the socialist Dr. Broda was followed by Dr. Klecatsky as Federal Minister of Justice. In 1968 Dr. Klecatsky successfully introduced the draft of a Penal Code in Parliament. As far as abortion was

concerned, some specifications were made and abortion again was cate-
gorized as a crime.[10]

'Fristenlösung'[11] and Pro-Life Movement ('Aktion Leben')

As a consequence of the parliamentary elections of 1970, the socialist Dr.
Broda became Federal Minister of Justice again. In January 1971, his
Ministry again dispatched a draft for a Penal Code, which was offered to the
Parliament in November of the same year as a Federal Government Bill.[12] In
regard to the problem of abortion, the draft went back to the above-
mentioned proposals made by the Penal Law Commission in 1962, namely
that the interruption of pregnancy should go unpunished if it were based on
medical reasons. The medical indication was conceived in such a manner
that it encompassed socio-medical, eugenic-medical and ethical-medical
reasons. Maximum punishment for pregnant women was suggested to be
one year of imprisonment. And again it was suggested that, in minor cases,
one should refrain from punishment.[13] In June 1971, the Austrian Bishops'
Conference attacked these planned regulations and not only demanded an
effective interdiction of abortion but asked for the exhaustion of all socio-
political possibilities in order to protect and preserve the life of unborn
children.[14] At the same time, Catholic laymen formed a committee to fight
against the proposed regulations on abortion. In a collection of signatures
under the title 'Pro-Life Movement', the recognition and protection of a
right to life for unborn children was demanded. Penal law as well as far-
reaching socio-political measures for increasing the number of children were
asked for to protect unborn life.[15] Up to June 1972, about 820,000 Austrians
signed the petitions of the 'Pro-Life Movement'. The 'Pro-Life Movement'
also formulated an alternative proposal. It provided for an unpunishable
interruption of pregnancy based on medical reasons in a narrow sense. These
reasons would have to be supported by a medical opinion. In all other cases
of conflict, not specifically named by the 'Pro-Life Movement', exemption
from punishment was only provided if the mother-to-be had 'acted in a
generally understandable, extremely unusual distress, which otherwise could
not be averted and if she had tried to gain help from the competent institutions'[16]

With these alternative proposals, the demands for measures in favor of
children and for the institutionalization of advisory boards for pregnant
women were repeated. These advisory boards were meant to point out to
those seeking advice that abortion should be the very last means.[17]

The Federal Government Bill was submitted to the House of Representatives in November 1971 and stirred opposition not only by clerical groups

but also within the Socialist Party itself. In January 1972, an 'Action Committee for the Abolition of paragraph 144' (*Aktionskomitee zur Abschaffung des §144*) was formed, which demanded for every woman the right to have an interruption of pregnancy performed upon herself free of punishment. At least, it was asserted, the interruption of pregnancy should be free of punishment if undertaken before the end of the third month and if performed by a specialist in a clinic. Moreover, the committee held the opinion that an intensive information on the methods of birth control would result in the fact that in the future abortions would be rare exceptional cases. The costs for contra-conceptives and for abortions were to be covered by public health insurance.[18] In the middle of April 1972, the Socialist Federal Conference of Women (*Sozialistische Bundesfrauenkonferenz*) fully adopted the proposals of this committee. From April 17 to April 19, the Socialist Federal Party Conference (*Bundesparteitag der SPÖ*) was held. At that occasion, more than twenty motions and resolutions were presented by member organizations of the Austrian Socialist Party, which demanded a '*Fristenlösung*'.[19] Among these motions were five which asked for a total abolition of abortion regulation in the future Penal Code.[20] Fifteen speakers who addressed the Congress on the problem of abortion came forward with three principle objections. Professor Norbert Leser stressed that the problems of abortion were not to be regarded only under the aspect of the woman's or the involved partners' freedom. The growing life and the right of the community to this life were to be protected as well.[21] Dr. Salcher, at that time chairman of the Tyrolian Socialist Party, drew attention to the fact that the demand for a '*Fristenlösung*' was not generally supported. Especially in the Western provinces of Austria, little understanding could be expected. He appealed to the Congress to reconsider the matter in order to discuss it again after a period of time. And Mr. Strobl, a member of the Study Group for Christianity and Socialism (*Arbeitsgemeinschaft für Christentum und Sozialismus*), objected to the idea of the '*Fristenlösung*' and declared himself in favor of indication together with accompanying measures.[22]

Those who promoted a '*Fristenlösung*' argued, that woman's resp. the involved partners' freedom of decision has to be stressed and that the penal legislature concerning abortion were until now a 'criminal law of social classes of the males'. The latter group succeeded with their arguments. Only ten deputies out of 500 voted against the motion of the Socialist Federal Conference of Women. These five voted against it because no total freedom of abortion was provided, only an interruption of pregnancy during the first three months.[23] Only two days after the Federal Socialist Party Conference, Cardinal König commented on the resolution concerning the '*Fristenlösung*' and stressed that the Catholic Church was not primarily interested in punishment but rather in the protection of life. The '*Fristenlösung*', he said, was not a humane solution.[24]

Parliamentary Procedure Concerning the Penal Code

The resolution of the Socialist governing party raised also another problem at its Party Conference: Since 16 November 1971, the Government Bill for a new Penal Code was with the Parliament. Those parts of the draft concerning aboriton were now endangered.

As already mentioned, the draft contained the proposal of a solution by means of an enlarged indication, which was meant as a compromise and was vehemently criticized. On 8 May 1973, deputies of the Socialist Party entered an amendment to the Judicial Committee (*Justizausschuß*) of the House of Representatives, which was approved and which was based on the following principles:

(1) In principle, at least, human life is to be protected by penal law not only after birth.

(2) An interruption of pregnancy is not punishable if it is performed during the first three months by a doctor after consultation. After the expiration of this period, an interruption of pregnancy is not punishable if a medical or eugenic indication can be established or if the pregnant woman was not yet fourteen years of age at the time of impregnation.

(3) No one can be forced to perform an interruption of pregnancy or to take part in it. Those performing a legal interruption of pregnancy or participating in it should not be subject to any discrimination.[25]

Both opposition parties, the Austrian People's Party and the Austrian Liberal Party, vehemently opposed the realization of the '*Fristenlösung*' and expressed their disapproval on a large scale in the mass media.[26] In addition, these two parties introduced amendments which can best be outlined by means of examination of the debate in the House of Representatives from 27 November to 29 November 1973. The Austrian People's Party in its amendment demanded that only the medical indication on the one hand and 'a generally understandable extremely unusual distress of the pregnant woman, which can not be averted in another way' on the other hand 'should be considered cases of an unpunishable abortion'.[27] The amendment of the Liberal Party is distinguished from the People's Party's amendment mainly as far as the procedural means are concerned. Whereas the People's Party wanted the courts to examine the question of 'distress' in the single case, the Liberal Party wanted the written opinion of two doctors, taking over the responsibility for the abortion.[28]

The Socialist Party argued in favor of its motion to introduce the '*Fristenlösung*' that past experience had shown that even severe punishment could not prevent 30,000 to 100,000 illegal abortions out of a population of about seven millions.[29] The penalization of abortion is, moreover, disadventageous for the poorer classes of population, who are driven into the arms of charlatans,[30] the party said. The '*Fristenlösung*', however, secures for all women equally a free decision. The impunity during the first three months of pregnancy and the commitment to be attended by a doctor prevented women to be forced into the criminal underground and would also avoid grave damages to health. Experiences made in other countries confirm these expectations.[31] The opposition parties, however, made a point of it that the '*Fristenlösung*' means in reality to abandon the protection of life. In the future, illegal abortions would mostly probably not decrease, whereas the legal ones would go up as a consequence of the impunity of abortion.[32] The opposition was mainly concerned to make clear that there does not exist an exclusive right of the woman to decide on the fate of the nasciturus.[33] Socio-political and socio-medical arguments supported the further argumentation of the opposition parties. The community was obliged to advise and assist the pregnant woman. It would not suit a welfare society, the parties said, to permit an abortion by means of the so-called '*Fristenlösung*' because of social or economic reasons. This is also true for the argument that the punishability of abortion makes it the crime of certain social classes. On the other hand, abortions should not be a means of birth control. The danger for life and health of women − mainly if repeatedly abortions were performed − were too great.[34] Above all, the arbitrariness of the '*Fristenlösung*' was criticized: Until the end of the third month of gravidity, destruction of human life is permitted; after this time, the protection of life is expected. This is inhumane, the parties said, because protection of human life is suspended for a certain period of time.[35]

The motion of the Socialist deputies in Parliament was put to the vote and was passed on 29 November 1973, 93 − 88. Thus, the motions of the People's Party and the Liberal Party were in the minority.[36] The representatives of the People's Party proposed a resolution aiming at positive measures for the protection of developing life. This resolution was accepted.[37]

On 6 December 1973, the Upper House (*Bundesrat*), the second chamber of the Austrian Parliament, dealt with the enactment of the House of Representatives for a new Penal Code. The Upper House focused its attention especially on the provisions concerning the interruption of pregnancy. Two motions were presented: The Austrian People's Party wanted to raise objections against the enactment of this law by the House of Representatives, while the Socialist Party wanted to have the enactment accepted.[38] The arguments put forward in this debate were the same as those given in the House of Representatives. It is to be noted that, in the speeches delivered, the aspects of constitutional law and indirectly of international law, which had been more or less neglected in the debates in the first chamber of Parliament, were an important part. One member of the Upper House, Professor Herbert Schambeck, drew attention to the guarantees of Article 3 of the

Universal Declaration of Human Rights of the United Nations of 10 December 1948 and of Article 2 of the European Convention on Human Rights for the protection of human life. Professor Schambeck argued that, whereas the Declaration of the United Nations was a recommendation only, Article 2 of the European Convention on Human Rights, which in Austria undoubtedly has the validity of a constitutional law, guarantees that the state must abstain from any violation of embryonic life. Consequently, the state must protect embryonic life against a violation by private persons.[39] The motion of the *ÖVP* members of the Upper House to raise objections against the enactment of the House of Representatives of 29 November 1973, was accepted, 29 – 28.[40]

On 23 January 1974, the House of Representatives had to deal with the objection of the Upper House. The Judicial Committee, with the votes of its Socialist members, had advised the House of Representatives to insist on its former resolution.[41] In the debate, the pros and cons were repeated.[42] Despite the Upper House objection and the repeated statements of the Catholic and the Protestant Church and their lay organizations, the Socialist Party was firmly determined to put the *'Fristenlösung'* into effect.[43] In the voting, the House of Representatives repeated its former resolution, 92 – 89. In the same meeting, however, a Federal Law for the Promotion of Family Guidance (*Bundesgesetz über die Förderung der Familienberatung*) was enacted.[44] The new Penal Code was published on 23 January 1974 in the *Federal Law Gazette* under Number 60. A motion introduced by the Liberal Party and the People's Party, to submit the provisions on abortion to a referendum, did not obtain the necessary majority in the House of Representatives.[45]

The 'Fristenlösung' before the Constitutional Court

The objections against the *'Fristenlösung'* raised in the parliamentary debates did not diminish but increased because of the ruling Socialist Party's procedure, which brought about principal alterations with a narrow majority and ruled out the possibility of a referendum. Therefore, the opposition sought means offered by constitutional law to fight the new provisions. Thus, the Government of the Province of Salzburg (*Salzburger Landesregierung*), whose majority belonged to the People's Party, on 15 March 1974 furnished an application to the Constitutional Court to abolish the provisions of paragraph 97 (1) number 1 (*Federal Law Gazette*, Number 60, 1974) as unconstitutional.[46] The Salzburg Government considered these provisions to be unconstitutional because of various reasons: they violated the fundamental right of life and the fundamental right of equality before the law. The Salzburg Government stated:[47]

The fundamental right of life is inherent to all other expressly stated fundamental rights and liberties. In addition, it is guaranteed by constitutional provisions, based on international treaties such as Article 2 of the European Convention on Human Rights and Article 63 (1) of the State Treaty of St. Germain.[48] This fundamental right to life is also applicable to the human embryo.[49] The '*Fristenlösung*' seems to be unconstitutional because a simple law permits destruction of human life or at least life equal to it. The embryo is deprived of the fundamental right to life because, in contradiction to valid law, the protection against killing is abolished in this case.[50] The Salzburg Government considered the fundamental right of equality violated in a two-fold manner: on the one hand, as the 'violation of the fundamental right of equality before the law as an essential element of the democratic principle'; on the other hand, as the 'violation of the fundamental right of equality before the law according to constitutional law, not based on international law'.[51] An unequal treatment of embryos of different ages in criminal law lacks any material basis for such a differentiation and therefore violated the right of equality. In addition, it was claimed, the right to respect for one's private and family life (Article 8 of the European Convention on Human Rights) was violated by the unsubstantiated differentiation and, therefore, the right to equality was violated: the child of both parents was exposed to the discretional killing by one of the parents. Thus, the two sexes were treated unequally and the right of the husband to his private family life were violated by a one-sided measure of his wife,[52] it was argued.

The Federal Government commented on the motion of the Salzburg Government in the proceedings before the Constitutional Court as follows: The distinction made in criminal law between the interruption of pregnancy during the first three months, on the one hand, and after this period of time, on the other hand, corresponds to the embryo's development during pregnancy. The Federal Government held the opinion that the embryo during the first three months of pregnancy was far from any extra-utinary life. An equal treatment of the interruption of pregnancy during the whole duration of pregnancy would mean in view of the object an equal treatment of something unequal.[53] Moreover, the period of three months would correspond to the aim to deal with a possible conflict in favor of the pregnant woman, the Federal Government maintained. The protection of the unborn child was only neglected insofar as it seemed necessary to allow for the solution of possible conflicts.[54]

Above all, the Federal Government denied that a fundamental right to life was guaranteed by Austrian constitutional law.[55] Article 2 of the European Convention on Human Rights was interpreted in such a way that the states were obliged only to protect life against violations on the part of the state but not on the part of private persons.[56] In addition, the Federal Government denied the embryo the quality of a human being, which quality can be attributed to it only after birth.[57] Even if considering the states to be bound by Article 2 of the European Convention on Human Rights to protect life against violations on the part of private persons, the 'Fristenlösung' would satisfy to constitutional law.[58] Article 63 (1) of the State Treaty of St. Germain obliges Austria to protect all 'inhabitants' without any discrimination; this means the equal treatment of all born persons in the territory of Austria.[59]

The Federal Government dealt also with the argument of the Salzburg Government that the 'Fristenlösung' caused an intervention into the life of the family insofar as it admits the interruption of pregnancy without the husband's consent. The Federal Government held once more the view that the protection of fundamental rights were an obligation of the state only.

Thus, Article 8 (2) of the European Convention on Human Rights obliges only the states to abstain from interventions into family life. Considering the 'Fristenlösung' under the aspect of family life, one must deal with a case of a balancing of interests between the right of the pregnant woman to make her own decision on the one hand and the husband's interest in progeny on the other hand. These interests were, according to the Federal Government's opinion, well balanced.[60] Finally, the Federal Government stated that, even if one would recognize the embryo's right to life as a fundamental right, this could conflict with the fundamental right of the pregnant woman. The so-called 'Fristenlösung' was a solution of such possible conflicts and did not transgress the constitutional limits by abolishing a punishment for an interruption of pregnancy in the first three months.[61] Because of all these reasons, the Federal Government maintained that the 'Fristenlösung' was not unconstitutional.

In the course of the procedure, the Salzburg Government answered the Federal Government's opinion in a new statement on 9 September 1974. The main points made by the Salzburg Government were the following: the former legal regulations had protected unborn human life as a distinct legal interest but in the same manner as a born child. This was true also in view of the pregnant woman and for each stage of pregnancy. The first constitutional guarantees of fundamental rights and freedoms did not expressly protect unborn life because it was considered self-evident that human life also in its earliest stages was to be protected.[62] According to the provisions of criminal law, it does not depend on the lack of extra-utinery viability, as was the view of the Federal Government. According to the 'Fristenlösung', provisions of criminal law must guarantee the right of life to the embryo after the third month of pregnancy. From the viewpoints of medicine and human genetics, there is no argument in favor of the Federal Government's opinion. Procreation and death represent the beginning and the end of an uninterrupted effectiveness of one and the same genetic information, which in essence remains identical. Therefore, the *'Fristenlösung'* discriminated, because it exempted one period of this uninterrupted effectiveness from legal protection.[63] The Salzburg Government admitted that the conflicts arising between the pregnant woman's interest and that of the embryo might be relevant; despite this, the Salzburg Government held that the *'Fristenlösung'* prefers any other interest, even the mother's mischievousness, to the embryo's right. Such mischief was in no way protected by the constitution.[64] Moreover, it was argued that the state did not violate the fundamental rights and freedoms through active intervention only but also through neglecting to protect them; this latter was the case if the state did not protect life by criminal law provisions, as in the case of the *'Fristenlösung'*.[65]

Even more vehemently than in its original motion, the Salzburg Government drew attention to the fact that, until now, the life of the embryo was protected by the Austrian legal system. It cannot be doubted that the embryo, according to the Austrian legal system, is endowed with legal capacity and, therefore, is to be regarded as a person: The Austrian Civil Code (*Allgemeines Bürgerliches Gesetzbuch/ABGB*), for example, ascribes to 'unborn children' from 'the time of conception' the right 'of legal protection'.[66] It is in no way consistent if the laws protect an unborn child as far as its property interests are concerned and on the other hand if they deny in the right to life during the first three months after conception, it was argued. Article 2 (1) of the European Convention on Human Rights obliges the states, on the contrary, to protect the life of every person. This intention becomes clear when considering the authentic English (*everyone*) and French (*toute personne*) texts. In neither of these texts is the word 'man' (*man, homme*) used as '*Mensch*' in the German translation.[67]

The opinion of the Federal Government that the fundamental rights, especially Article 2 (1) of the European Convention on Human Rights, oblige the states to protect life only against intervention by the state but not against that of private persons was opposed by the Salzburg Government, which urged consideration of Convention's provisions as a whole. Some of the Convention's provisions see their guarantees expressly subjected to the provisions of the 'fundamental rights and freedoms of others'.[68] This means, however, that the states have to counterbalance and to differentiate the status of the single persons against one another. The argument has to be rejected that the fundamental rights and freedoms do not influence the differentiation of the legal spheres of the individuals. In a vast number of cases, the European Commission on Human Rights has decided about the legal status of a private person according to the provisions of the Convention. The guarantees of fundamental rights and freedoms, and especially those guaranteed by the European Convention on Human Rights, are not limited to the relation between the individual and the state.[69] The Consultative Assembly of the European Council has maintained, as well, that the guarantees of the European Convention are universally effective.[70]

Regarding this point, the Salzburg Government had furnished, along with its statement, a reference to the jurisdiction and literature concerning this problem in the Federal Republic of Germany. Here, the applicability of fundamental rights to private parties has been recognized in principle. Only the extent of their effectiveness, whether direct or indirect, is doubted. Considering the same legal situation and the same development of fundamental rights expressed in the European Convention on Human Rights, the Salzburg Government urged, Austria also should acknowledge the application of fundamental rights between private parties.[71]

The Salzburg Government once more repeated the argument that the 'Fristenlösung' intervened the rights of the husband of a wife willing to have an abortion performed, thus violating Article 8 of the European Convention on Human Rights. In addition, the Salzburg Government stated, the one-sided decision of the wife to have an abortion performed violates the husband's right to found a family and is, therefore, a violation of Article 12 of the European Convention on Human Rights.[72]

Concluding its argumentation, the Salzburg Government referred to the fundamental importance of the right to life in the course of history of thought and in the development of fundamental rights, which make clear that it is a natural, indivisible right which may not be exposed to possible mischief.[73]

The desicion of the Constitutional Court concerning the 'Fristenlösung' was made on 12 October 1974.[74]

The Constitutional Court did not comply with the request of the Salzburg Government to abolish the 'Fristenlösung' (paragraph 97 (1), number 1 of the Penal Code of January 1974, Federal Law Gazette Number 60). In its extensive reasoning, one may sum up the Court's arguments as follows:

(1) The fundamental rights guaranteed by the Austrian constitution and not based on international treaties rest upon classical liberal ideas to guarantee the individual protection against the state only. This is true for the Fundamental Law on the Universal Rights of Citizens (Staatsgrundgesetz über die allgemeinen Rechter der Staatsbürger) of 1867. As far as the interruption of pregnancy is concerned, it is not the case of the state's intervention but an intervention on the part of private parties; this intervention is not punishable if it takes place during a certain period of time.[75]

(2) Concerning fundamental rights which are based on international treaties, the Constitutional Court held that no breach of constitutional law

was to be detected. It was the Court's opinion that the notion 'life' did not include unborn life. Should this be the case, Austria at the time of the ratification of the European Convention on Human Rights in 1958 would have had to make a reservation. This was not done, despite the fact that, at that time, an interruption of pregnancy on the grounds of a medical indication was already exempt from penal sanction in Austria.[76] All other guarantees, as for instance Article 63 (1) of the Treaty of St. Germain, protect born man only.[77]

(3) The so-called *'Fristenlösung'* does not mean a violation of the principle of equality. Embryonic life undergoes a development in the uterus, from the natural conditions of a viable fertilized ovum to the extra-utinery viable child. The various stages of development are not necessarily equal in the sense of the constitutionally-guaranteed equality. The legislator of simple laws, therefore, has the possibility – as far as criminal law is concerned – to provide for an interruption of pregnancy depending on the state of the embryo's development without violating the right of equality. Because of medical reasons, an interruption of pregnancy during the first three months is to be tolerated. After this period of time, complications and after-effects increase clearly.[78]

(4) The so-called *'Fristenlösung'* does not infringe the guarantee of privacy and family life granted in Article 8 of the European Convention on Human Rights. This provision does not exclude penal provisions for the protection of family life, but it also does not obligate the legislator to punish the disregard of family life.[79]

(5) The so-called *'Fristenlösung'* does not violate the right to marry and to found a family, granted by Article 12 of the European Convention on Human Rights. These rights are subject to national laws. The German translation says that these rights were granted *'gemäß den einschlägigen nationalen Gesetzen'* (in accordance with the relevant national laws). The two authentic texts, however, refer to the reservation of national laws, using the following wording: '... according to the national laws governing the exercise of this right' respectively ('... *selon les lois nationales régissant l'exercise de ce droit'*).[80]

The reaction to the decision of the Constitutional Court was critical.[81] Mainly, three assumptions of the Constitutional Court were criticized: First the assumption that fundamental rights were directed against the state only; second that embryonic life was not life in the meaning of Article 2 of the European Convention on Human Rights; and third that the embryo's penal protection could vary according to the stages of development.

Concerning the first assumption adopted by the Constitutional Court, the critique argued that an act of legislation could endanger the individual's fundamental rights by exposing certain generally-defined persons to possible mischievous killing, as is the case of the so-called *'Fristenlösung'*.[82] In this context, the Constitutional Court neglected the fact that Austrian jurisprudence speaks of a 'constitutionally founded duty of the state to punish in the interest of constitutionally granted fundamental values'. This is also true for scholars sympathizing with the Socialist Party.[83] The assumption that fundamental rights were directed only against the state was rightly criticized because of the consequences of its generalization: thus, it also would be admissible to abolish the penal protection of property because this also relates to a violation by private persons.[84] The decision of the Constitutional Court rests upon a theory on fundamental rights which neglects totally the functional change of fundamental rights. For more than fifty years the concern in Western democracies has been for more than merely the individual's protection against the state. Fundamental rights are rather regarded as the material basis of the entire legal and social system. Fundamental rights do not exhaust themselves in the function to grant subjective rights against the state. At the same time, they contain objective principles for shaping social life as a whole. It follows from this that the state is obliged to protect fundamental rights in society, even between private parties, and that it has to create such conditions that these rights may be enjoyed.[85] The critique also was directed against the judges of the Constitutional Court, repremanding their sense of duty and criticizing their methods. Concerning the first reproach, one may say that the Austrian Constitutional Court is principally prepared to respect the evalutations of the legislator. This principal attitude is intensified through the methodological predisposition of the majority of judges to Hans Kelsen's 'Pure Theory of Law'. Kelsen held that a norm allows principally for more than one interpretation because it covers more than one solution, all of which solutions are legal. In other words, each case has more than one solution. According to law, various solutions are possible.[86] The German Constitutional Court has decided against the *'Fristenlösung'* despite the fact that the legal situation is basically the same as in Austria.[87]

The second assumption, that developing-life is not life in the meaning of Article 2 of the European Convention on Human Rights, was criticized. It was called into mind that the provisions of the Austrian Civil Code ascribed legal capacity to the embryo, which provision was not sufficiently considered by the Constitutional Court.[88]

The third point of critique considered the *'Fristenlösung'* to be a violation of the right of equality. The development of human life is a continual process which — mainly in the course of pregnancy — does not show any turning points which would allow for any differentiation in respect of the state's protection.[89] Moreover, the period of three months is in reality a fiction because the moment of conception cannot be fixed precisely.[90]

The 'Pro-Life Movements' People's Initiative

During all stages of the legislative procedure which finally led to the so-called *'Fristenlösung'* in Austria, over and over again the question was raised as to whether the population of Austria should be asked to decide this question. The Liberal Party and the People's Party had motioned for a referendum. This motion met with the disapproval of the Parliament's majority.[91] As the opponents of the *'Fristenlösung'* had appealed to the Constitutional Court in vain, the only sensible constitutional means remaining was a people's initiative. According to the legal situation at this time, the Federal Government was obliged to submit every motion proposed by 200,000 voters or by half of the voters in three provinces to the House of Representatives for action in accordance with the rules of procedure.[92] The 'Pro Life Movement' remained inactive in the meantime. In the first days of February 1974, various study groups were formed. A judicial committee drafted an alternative to the *'Fristenlösung'*. The first part of this proposal was to include a constitutional provision which was to protect life beginning with conception. Another committee devoted itself to the way the protection of human life should be emphasized in schools. Still another study group devoted itself to the socio-political problems and their financing.[93] Even before the decision of the Constitutional Court was made, an organizational committee was formed which presented the mentioned draft to be introduced in Parliament and for which support was sought in a press conference.[94] Obviously, it was already taken for granted that the Constitutional Court would decide in favor of the *'Fristenlösung'*. Two days after the decision of the Constitutional Court and at the end of the 'General Meeting of Catholics' (*Katholikentag*) in October 1974, an urgent appeal was issued to support the draft for a 'Federal Law for the Protection of Human Life' (*Bundesgesetz zum Schutz des menschlichen Lebens*). Cardinal König in the presence of Federal President Dr. Kirchschläger, Federal Chancellor Dr. Kreisky, and members of the Federal Government stated that all bishops supported this people's initiative.[95]

The comprehensive draft of a 'Federal Law for the Protection of Human Life', which was presented to the Austrian voters for signature, comprised a large number of legal measures. First, a constitutional provision was formulated: 'Article I: Every man's life is protected from the moment of conception; life is to be promoted and protected through legislation and execution of the laws' (*'Jeder Mensch hat von der Empfängnis an das Recht auf Leben: das Leben ist durch Gesetzgebung und Vollziehung zu fördern und zu schützen'*).[96] Articles II and III sought to have the words 'in order to respect human life in all stages of its existence' inserted in the respective provisions governing Austrian schools. Articles IV to VI suggested detailed measures for the financial support of families and children. These were meant as accompanying measures for the protection of unborn life and to create an atmosphere favorable to families and children. The pressure on women to attend to a job was to be diminished. The first suggestion in this respect was the increase of the children's allowance (*Kinderbeihilfe*) and its differentiation according to the children's age. Also an educational allowance (*Erziehungsbeihilfe*) was suggested, which was meant to acknowledge the role of those mothers who prefer educating their children to working outside of the house. The period of time devoted to the education of children until the youngest child had reached the end of its seventh year was to be considered as qualifying time for old-age insurance (*Pensionsversicherung*).[97] Only Article VII, contained penal provisions. It offered an alternative to the so-called '*Fristenlösung*'. The materials of the people's initiative for a 'Federal Law for the Protection of Human Life' show the following motives for the suggested regulation of the interruption of pregnancy:[98] the main assumption underlying this draft was that an interruption of pregnancy could only be regarded as legal if a danger to the life or serious damage to the health of the pregnant woman were imminent and abortion was the only way to avert it. To prevent a misuse of the medical indication, the opinion of a specialist was to be required and the interruption of pregnancy would be performed only in public hospitals. One could, however think of situations of an unwanted pregnancy in which the woman is without any hope, and the legislator must provide for such tragic situations. It was the aim of the people's initiative to prevent indiscriminate abortions as well in the first three months of pregnancy.

Because of this the plan suggested the admittance of a special defense in all cases in which the pregnant woman 'acted in a generally understandable extremely unusual distress, which she could not avert in another way'. Such a defense should be equal to those provided for in the Penal Code. The suggested solution refrained from enumerating the unpunishable cases exhaustively. Only if various circumstances coincide, which involve the pregnant woman into tragic situations, must one admit the exclusion of guilt. It would be decisive that the pregnant woman had tried hard to find help and counsel, but was left alone.[99] It should be left to the independent courts to examine the circumstances of the case. Impunity should be granted to all persons involved, mainly doctors. Moreover, the draft provided for punishment of men who do not accept responsibility for pregnancies in which they have participated.[100]

This draft of a 'Federal Law for the Protection of Human Life' was supported by 895,665 Austrian citizens, or 17.92 per cent of all voters. The procedure of the people's initiative was closed on 1 December 1975.[101] This initiative, backed by the 'Pro Life Movement', received more support than any previous people's initiative.[102] On 9 March 1976, the Federal Government decided to present this initiative to the House of Representatives. There, a special committee of twenty-one members started its consultations on 1 May 1976.[103] At its meeting of 25 June 1976, three representatives of the 'Pro Life Movement' were given the opportunity to inform the committee about their ideas. The three representatives claimed later that the members of the special committee had no interest in considering the pro-life arguments.[104]

The special committee was in session for about one year. In its meeting of 28 April 1977, the voting on the single sections of the draft took place. None of the sections of the draft met with the necessary majority. The representatives of the People's Party therefore made use of their right to formulate a minority position.[105] The People's Party concluded that the Socialist Party, having turned down the people's initiative, had lost the chance to reconcile the people of Austria with their law.[106]

The meeting of the House of Representatives on 11 May 1977 dealt with the report of the special committee, as well as with the minority votes of the Austrian People's Party. The deputies of this party were concerned mainly with pointing out the damaging consequences of the 'Fristenlösung', which had been in effect for two years.[107] A minority of doctors were performing abortions continuously, partly in their own clinics and at not at all modest costs. The after-effects of such interruptions would increase primary complications, premature deliveries and extra-utinery difficulties in later pregnancies. The speakers of the Party stressed that they also were against abortions but that they had decided in favor of the personal responsibility of the woman, which best was granted by the 'Fristenlösung'.[108] The speakers of the Liberal Party stressed once again their disapproval of the 'Fristenlösung'. In contradiction to the People's Party, they wanted to solve such conflicts without the intervention of courts.[109] By and large, the parliamentary debate did not offer any principal viewpoints, but only a concise summary of the controversies concerning the solution of the problem of abortion. The House of Representatives finally accepted the committee's report, 103 – 75.[110] The people's initiative 'for the protection of human life' had failed.

Conclusion

The constitutional problem concerning the right to life in Austria has not yet been solved, however, through the 'Fristenlösung'. Now, as before, the 'Pro Life Movement' is active, providing information, advice and help.[111] By adopting the 'Fristenlösung', the legislator has withdrawn from the field of

criminal law without taking compensating socio-political measures which
were expected.

Notes

1. Cf. *Hoeger* Geschichte des österreichischen Strafrechts II, Wien 1905, p. 118.
2. BGBl. (Federal Law Gazette), Number 202/1937.
3. 90 der Beilagen zu den stenographischen Protokollen des Herrenhauses (Materials of the House of Lords) XXI. Session 1912.
4. Paragraph 292 of the Draft.
5. Paragraph 253 of the Draft, 1927, in: 49 der Beilagen zu den stenographischen Protokollen des Nationalrates III. Gesetzgebungsperiode, Vorlage der Bundesregierung (Federal Government Bill), p. 27.
6. 71 der Beilagen zu den stenographischen Protokollen des Nationalrates 1920 – 1921. Cf. the motion of the deputies Popp et al., for the alteration of some provisions of the Penal Code, in: Beiblatt zur Staatskorrespondenz, 1923-1924, II. Gesetzgebungsperiode, p. 177, Number 47/A.
7. Sagmeister, 'Die Grundwerte und die Reform der Abtreibungsgesetze in Österreich' (Salzburg, 1981), p. 24.
8. Id., p. 26.
9. Id., pp. 29ff.
10. Id., p. 31.
11. As to my knowledge, there does not exist an English word for this German term, I shall use the latter. It means a legal interruption of pregnancy during the first three months.
12. 30 *der Beilagen zu den stenographischen Protokollen des Nationalrates*, XIII. Gesetz-gebungsperiode. Concerning the development of abortion in the Austrian reform of penal law, I am indebted to Sektionschef Dr. Egmont Foregger from the Federal Ministry of Justice.
13. Sagmeister, supra n. 7, pp. 35ff; 30 *der Beilagen zu den stenographischen Protokollen des Nationalrates*, p. 15.
14. Sagmeister, supra n. 7, p. 37.
15. Kathpress (1 Oktober, 1971), ' 'Aktion Leben' startet in ganz Österreich Unterschriften-aktion'.
16. Kathpress 14 September, 1972, 'Alternativen zur Regierungsvorlage erstellt'.
17. Sagmeister, supra n. 7, p. 42.
18. Id., p. 47.
19. Id., p. 49.
20. Austrian Socialist Party, Protocol of its Federal Party Conference 1972, Wien 1972, pp. 238, 241, 246, 271.
21. Id., p. 160.
22. Sagmeister, supra n. 7, p. 53.
23. Id., p. 54.
24. Cf. Österreichische Bischofskonferenz (ed.), Worte der österreichischen Bischöfe zum Schutz menschlichen Lebens, Wien 1974, p. 12.
25. Cf. 959 der Beilagen zu den stenographischen Protokollen des Nationalrates, XIII. GP, p. 21.
26. Cf. Sagmeister, supra n. 7, p. 59.
27. *Stenographische Protokolle*, 84. Sitzung des Nationalrates der Republik Österreich, XIII. GP, p. 7992: paragraph 84 (1) If this has to be done in order to prevent a serious danger for

the life of the pregnant woman or a grave damage for her health, which could not be averted in another way, then this killing is not to be punished under the condition, that the interruption of pregnancy was based on the opinion of a gynecologist and of the opinion of another specialist of another medical field and if it was performed in a public hospital. Paragraph 82 (2) The pregnant woman is not to be punished if she had acted in a generally understandable, extremely unusual distress, which could not be averted in another way (paragraph 34, numbers 8, 10, 11).

28. Sagmeister, supra n. 7, p. 72.
29. *Stenographische Protokolle*, 84. Sitzung des Nationalrates der Republik Österreich, XIII. GP, pp. 7997, 8157.
30. Id., p. 8105.
31. Sagmeister, supra n. 7, p. 73.
32. Id., p. 74.
33. See the opinion of the Deputy Dr. Karasek, Stenographisches Protokoll, 84. Sitzung des Nationalrates der Republik Österreich, XIII. GP, p. 8047.
34. Cf. Sagmeister, supra n. 7, pp. 76, 83.
35. See the opinion of the Deputy Dr. Broesike, Stenographisches Protokoll der 84. Sitzung des Nationalrates der Republik Österreich, XIII. GP., p. 8086.
36. Id., p. 8183.
37. 961 *der Beilagen zu den stenographischen Protokollen des Nationalrates*, XIII. GP; Stenographisches Protokoll, see above, p. 8184.
38. This procedure is based on Article 42 of the Austrian Federal Constitution:
    '(1) Every enactment of the Nationalrat shall without delay be notified by its President to the Upper House (*Bundesrat*).
    (2) Save as otherwise provided by constitutional law, an enactment can be authenticated and published only if the Upper House has not raised a reasoned objection to this enactment.
39. Article 3 Universal Declaration of Human Rights: 'Everyone has the right to life, liberty and security of person'.
    Article 2 (1) European Convention on Human Rights provides: 'Everyone's right to life shall be protected by law'.
    Cf. *Stenographisches Protokoll*, 326. Sitzung des Bundesrates der Republik Österreich, p. 9818.
40. *Stenographisches Protokoll*, supra n. 35, p. 9839.
41. Article 42 (4) of the Austrian Federal Constitution: 'If the House of Representatives in the presence of at least half its members once more carries its original resolution, this shall be authenticated and published'.
42. Report of the judicial committee: 1011 der Beilagen zu den stenographischen Protokollen des Nationalrates, XIII. GP. cf. Stenographisches Protokoll 98. Sitzung des Nationalrates der Republik Österreich, XIII. GP, p. 9584.
43. Cf. Cardinal König's speech delivered on 31 December, 1973 on Austrian Television, in: Österreichische Bischofskonferenz (ed.), Worte der österreichischen Bischöfe zum Schutz menschlichen Lebens, Wien 1974, p. 72; open letter of Bishop Sakrausky of the Protestant Church in Austria to the Federal Chancellor, in which the '*Fristenlösung*' is compared with the Nuremberg Racial Laws; in: Kathpress-Dokumentation of 28 January, 1974.
44. *Stenographisches Protokoll*, 98. Sitzung des Nationalrates der Republik Österreich, XIII. GP, pp. 9658, 9665.
45. Cf. Article 43 of the Austrian Federal Constitution: 'If the House of Representatives so resolves or if the majority of members of the House of Representatives shall be submitted to a referendum upon conclusion of the procedure pursuant to Article 42 above but before

its authentication by the Federal President'; *Stenographisches Protokoll*, 98. Sitzung des Nationalrates der Republik Österreich, XIII. GP. p. 8184.

46. Paragraph 97 (1), number 1 reads: 'According to paragraph 96 the act is unpunishable 1. if the interruption of pregnancy is performed by a doctor during the first three months of gravidity after previous medical consultation'. Paragraph 96 deals with the punishability of an abortion performed with the pregnant woman's consent or performed by herself. This is to be punished with imprisonment up to one year; in case it is done professionally it is to be punished with imprisonment up to three years. – According to Article 140 of the Austrian Federal Constitution the federation and the federal provinces have the possibility to apply to the Constitutional Court to pronounce a judgment that a federal law resp. a provincial law were unconstitutional. – *Erkenntnisse und Beschlüsse des Verfassungsgerichtshofes* ed. by E. *Melichar*, Volume 39, Wien, 1975, 7400, p. 221; pp. 57 – 70; 1975, pp. 74 – 81.

47. Motion of the Government of the Province of Salzburg of 15 March 1974, reprinted completely in: Waldstein, Das Menschenrecht zum Leben, Berlin 1982, p. 131; the reprint in: Europäische Grundrechte-Zeitschrift is abbreviated.

48. Article 2 (1) first sentence, European Convention on Human Rights: 'Everyone's right to life shall be protected by law', resp. the French text: 'Le droit de toute personne à la vie est protégé par la loi'.; Article 63 (1) of the State Treaty of St. Germain (StGBl. 303/1920) reads in its authentic French version as follows: 'L'Autriche s'engage à accorder à tous les habitants de l'Autriche pleine et entière protection de leur vie et de leur liberté sans distinction de naissance, de nationalité, de language, de race ou de religion'. The English translation reads as follows: 'Austria undertakes to secure to all its inhabitants without distinction as birth, nationality, language, race or religion the full and entire protection of life and liberty'.

49. Motion of the Government of the Province of Salzburg see above, p. 132.

50. Id., p. 133.

51. Id., pp. 143, 145.

52. *Erkenntnisse und Beschlüsse des Verfassungsgerichtshofes*, supra n. 46, p. 222.

53. Statement of the Federal Government of 21 May 1974, reprinted in Waldstein, supra n. 47, p. 151.

54. Id., p. 151.

55. Id., p. 152.

56. Id., p. 154.

57. Id., p. 157.

58. Id., pp. 158, 161.

59. Id., p. 160.

60. Id., p. 162.

61. Id., p. 163.

62. Statement of the Government of the Province of Salzburg in reply to the statement of the Federal Government of 9 September, 1974, reprinted in Waldstein, supra n. 47, p. 164.

63. Id., p. 165.

64. Id., p. 165.

65. Id., p. 166.

66. Paragraph 22 of the Austrian Civil Code (ABGB): 'Even unborn children from the moment of conception are entitled to the protection of the laws. Insofar these rights, and not those of third parties are concerned they are to be regarded as already born. In respect of rights reserved to a child if it were born alive, a dead born child is to be regarded as not conceived'. – Marshall, 'Zum Recht auf Leben und der Schwangerschaftsunterbrechung'', *Juristische Blätter*, Wien 1972, p. 497.

38

67. Id., p. 170.
68. For instance: Article 8 (Private and Family Life), Article 9 (Freedom of thought, conscience and religion), Article 10 (Freedom of Opinion), Article 11 (Right of Assembly and Association).
69. Marschall, supra n. 67, p. 170; Cf. Moser, Die *Europäische Menschenrechtskonvention und das bürgerliche Recht,* (Wien, 1972) pp. 71, 78, to illustrate the effectiveness of fundamental rights between private parties Moser quotes on pages 177 ss. in footnotes 642 – 648 decisions of the European Commission for Human Rights on the rights of parents. Jacobs, in *The European Convention on Human Rights* (Oxford, 1975), pp. 11 and 227, argues that there is some effect on third parties in national law, as well as on the European level.
70. Moser, supra n. 69, pp. 79, 188.
71. Id., p. 171, for the problem of effectiveness on third parties; cf. Maunz, Dürig, Herzog, Grundgesetz, 3. Aufl., München 1968, concerning Article 5 (Freedom of opinion), Rn. 29, 240 and 275.
72. Article 12: European Convention on Human Rights. 'Men and women of marriageable age have the right to marry and to found a family, according to the national laws governing the exercise to this right'.
73. Moser, supra n. 67, p. 173.
74. G 8/74, Slg. 7400 in: Erkenntnisse und Beschlüsse des Verfassungsgerichtshofes, supra n. 46, p. 221.
75. Id., p. 224.
76. Id., p. 230.
77. Id., p. 231.
78. Id., p. 234.
79. Article 8 (1) of the European Convention on Human Rights: 'Everyone has the right to respect for his private and family life, his home and his correspondence'.
80. Erkenntnisse und Beschlüsse des Verfassungsgerichtshofes, supra n. 46, p. 237.
81. I quote here: Pernthaler, *Juristische Blätter* (Wien, 1975), p. 316; Novak, 'Das Fristenlösungserkenntnis des österreichischen Verfassungsgerichtshofes', *Europäische Grundrechte-Zeitschrift* 2, (1975), p. 197; Grimm, 'Die Fristenlösungsurteile in Österreich und Deutschland und die Grundrechtstheorie', *Juristische Blätter* (Wien, 1976), p. 74; Waldstein, 'Zur Rechtsstellung ungeborener Kinder', *Kirche und Staat* (Fritz Eckert zum 65. Geburtstag), hrsg. v. H. Schambeck (Berlin, 1976), p. 477; Waldstein, 'Rechtserkenntnis und Rechtsprechung. Bemerkungen zum Erkenntnis des VfGH über die Fristenlösung', *Juristische Blätter* (Wien, 1976), pp. 505 – 512, 574 – 584; Waldstein, *Das Menschenrecht zum Leben* (Berlin, 1982); Schambeck, 'Die Grundrechte im demokratischen Verfassungsstaat', *Ordnung im sozialen Wandel*, Festschrift für J. Messner zum 85. Geburtstag, hrsg. v. A. Klose u.a. (Berlin, 1976), pp. 445, 482; Groiss, Schantl, Welan, 'Der verfassungsrechtliche Schutz des menschlichen Lebens', *Österreichische Juristen-Zeitung* (1978), p. 1; Schreiner, 'Recht – Macht – Verfassungsgericht', *Festschrift Hans Lechner* (Salzburg, 1978), p. 223; Schreiner, *Die Intersubjektivität von Wertungen* (Berlin, 1980), p. 90.
82. Waldstein, *Das Menschenrecht zum Leben* (Berlin, 1982), p. 50.
83. Cf. Nowakowski, 'Die Grund- und Menschenrechte in Relation zur strafrichterlichen Gewalt', *Österreichische Juristenzeitung* (Wien, 1965), p. 281.
84. Waldstein, supra n. 82, p. 51.
85. Grimm, 'Die Fristenlösungsurteile in Österreich und Deutschland', *Juristische Blätter* (1976), pp. 74, 77.

86. Kelsen, *Reine Rechtslehre*, 2. Aufl. Wien 1960 (1. ed. Wien 1934), p. 348; cf. the critique of this view by Silving, 'The Lasting Value of Kelsenism', *Law, State and International Legal Order, Essays in Honor of H. Kelsen*, ed. by Engel and Métall, (Knoxville, 1964), p. 298.

87. Decision of the German Constitutional Court (Bundesverfassungsgericht) of 25 February, 1975, *Europäische Grundrechte-Zeitschrift* (Strasbourg, 1975), p. 25; *Entscheidungen des Bundesverfassungsgerichts*, (Tübingen, 1975) Volume 39, p. 1, dissenting opinion, p. 68.

88. Waldstein, supra n. 82, p. 52.

89. See Schambeck, 'Die Grundrechte im demokratischen Verfassungsstaat', *Ordnung im sozialen Wandel, Festschrift für J. Messner*, hrsg. v. A. Klose u.a., (Berlin, 1976), p. 484.

90. Waldstein, supra n. 82, p. 55.

91. Stenographisches Protokoll des Nationalrates, XIII. GP, see above (n. 45), p. 8184. According to Article 43 of the Austrian Federal Constitution, every enactment of the House of Representatives previous to its authentication by the Federal President is to be submitted to a referendum, if the House of Representatives so resolves or if this is demanded by the majority of its members.

92. This requirement was eased in 1981. See Article 41 (1) of the Austrian Federal Constitution as amended by BGBl. 1981/350.

93. Sagmeister, supra n. 7, p. 124.

94. Id., p. 125.

95. Id,. p. 132.

96. Id., p. 125.

97. Id., p. 126.

98. Cf. 135 der Beilagen zu den stenographischen Protokollen des Nationalrates, XIV. GP, p. 5.

99. Id., p. 131.

100. Id., p. 132.

101. *Amtsblatt zur Wiener Zeitung*, 24 February, 1976.

102. The people's initiative regarding television and radio in 1964 reached 832,353 (17.27 percent); the people's initiative regarding the thirteenth year of school in 1969, 339,407 (6.7 percent), and the people's initiative regarding an abbreviation of the working time 889,659 (17.4 percent) votes.

103. Sagmeister, supra n. 7, p. 136.

104. Id., p. 217, note 446.

105. 510 der Beilagen zu den stenographischen Protokollen des Nationalrates, XIV. GP, pp. 20, 21.

106. Supra n. 7, p. 146.

107. For the following, cf. Stenographisches Protokoll, 5. Sitzung des Nationalrates der Republik Österreich, XIV, GP, p. 5237, p. 5248, p. 5281, and p. 5287.

108. Id., p. 5268.

109. Sagmeister, supra n. 7, p. 150.

110. Stenographisches Protokoll, supra n. 107, p. 5304.

111. Aktion Leben, 'five Jahre Fristenlösung', *Dokumentation zur Lage* (Wien, 1980).

Federal Republic of Germany

Michael Quaas, Zuck & Quaas, Stuttgart

Introduction

To understand the constitutional development in abortion law and policy in the past few years, all discussion must begin with the decision of West Germany's Federal Constitutional Court of 25 February 1975, invalidating Section 218a of the Abortion Reform Act.[1] This decision in effect drove a wedge into the *Bundestag*'s ongoing efforts to reform German abortion regulation and to bring it into line with modern legislation in other western democracies. After the decision, a new law was passed by the German Parliament. However, the discussion on constitutional ways of punishing and preventing abortion did not cease.

Earlier Abortion Legislation

Prior to the Abortion Reform Act struck down by the Constitutional Court,[2] Germany's abortion legislation dated back to Sections 181 and 182 of the Criminal Code for the Prussian State of 14 April 1851.[3] This formed the basis for the regulation in the Criminal Code for the North German Federation of 31 May 1870,[4] which was taken over word-for-word into the Criminal Code for the German *Reich* of 15 May 1871.[5] The text of that Section 218 read as follows:

> 'A pregnant woman, who intentionally aborts the fetus or kills it in the womb, shall be punished with a term of up to five years in the house of correction.
> 'Should extenuating circumstances be present, punishment shall be for not less than six months.
> 'The same provisions apply to anyone who, with the consent of the pregnant woman, provides the means for abortion or killing; or procures same for her.'

This provision remained unchanged for fifty years until the Law of 18 May

Comparative Law Yearbook, Volume 7, 1983. ISBN 90-247-2966-1.
© *1984, Martinus Nijhoff Publishers, Dordrecht. Printed in the Netherlands.*

1926,[6] which softened the criminal penalties except in the case of abortion by someone other than the pregnant woman. This criminal penalties were sharply increased during the Third Reich by the Regulations for the Protection of Marriage, Family and Motherhood of 18 March 1943.[7] The version which the Abortion Reform Act was designed to modify stemmed from 1969 and read as follows:[8]

'(1)   A woman who destroys her fetus or permits it to be destroyed by another shall be punished by imprisonment, and in especially serious cases by confinement in a penitentiary.
'(2)   The attempt is punishable.
'(3)   Any other person who destroys the fetus of a pregnant woman with a drug or object designed to destroy the fetus, shall be punished by imprisonment, and in especially serious cases by confinement in a penitentiary.'

As can be seen from the above-quoted text, the provision punished all perpetrators alike: the woman herself, the doctor attempting to save her life, or the back-alley abortionist. No allowances were made for extenuating circumstances such as a need to save the mother's life, and punishment was to be the same regardless of the point during pregnancy at which the termination took place. It was this dissatisfaction with just such a blanket ban which led the *Bundestag* to its extensive debate and consideration of the Abortion Reform Act.

Legislative History of the Abortion Reform Act

In February 1972, the Federal Government introduced a draft of the Abortion Reform Act in the *Bundestag*.[9] It recognized certain established 'indications' for abortion[10] and required that the procedure be performed by a physician. In particular the draft allowed an abortion in four situations: to preserve the life and health of the mother ('medical indications'); to avert the birth of a seriously defective child ('eugenic or genetic indications'); to terminate a pregnancy caused by a sexual assault ('ethical or criminological indications'); and to unburden the woman of extremely harmful consequences that would arise in the event of the child's birth ('social indications'). In the last two situations an abortion would have been permissible only in the first trimester of pregnancy, subject to the sole condition that the operation be performed by a licensed physician after the woman had submitted to professional counseling.

At the same time, another draft was introduced by the member of Parliament, Dr. de With, and fifty colleagues of the Federal Parliament. This draft made use of the so-called 'time period regulation' (*Fristenregelung*) treating abortion differently depending on the point during pregnancy at which an abortion was to be performed.[11] This draft removed criminal penalties during the first three months of pregnancy so long as counselling by a doctor was procured first. However, before a vote could be taken, new elections intervened and parliamentary consideration had to be given up. The problem was taken up again by the Seventh German *Bundestag*. This time the Federal Government abstained from proposing its own draft. Instead, four drafts resulted:[12]

(1) 'Heck-Draft'[13] – No penalty was provided if abortion was performed before the implantation of the fertilized egg in the wall of the uterus[14] or if abortion was indicated by medical science and was necessary to protect the pregnant woman's physical or mental health from serious danger or to save her life so long as these dangers could not be alleviated by some other reasonable means. Pregnancy resulting from a criminal act, danger of health impairment of the child, social emergency or other circumstances should not alone remove justification for a criminal penalty, except when in the course of these circumstances there was a corresponding serious threat to the health or life of the mother with respect to the child's right to life. In cases where the medical indications for abortion had not been fulfilled but unusual distress of the pregnant woman was present, it was within the judge's discretion whether or not to use a criminal punishment. The draft further required that the women should receive counseling as well as an examination by an expert authority certifying that the medical indications existed. However, the expert authority's opinion would not have binding effect on the doctor who might proceed with the abortion if he was satisfied that the medical indications were present.

(2) 'CDU/CSU-Draft' – Criminal penalties were provided for abortion after the twelfth week; recognized were only medical and criminological (ethical) indications and when unusual distress existed for the woman which could not be removed by reasonable means. As a rule, if according to medical knowledge a high probability spoke in favor of abortion or if the child would suffer from a hereditary condition or damaging influences before birth, then the abortion was possible.

(3) 'Müller-Emmert Draft'[6] – Recognized medical and ethical indications as well as an indication of a general emergency. The medical indications should not depend solely on the physical and mental health conditions of the mother during pregnancy, but more comprehensive on the condition of the mother's health which could be expected after the

birth. The spectrum of emergency situations was broad, e.g. when the additional burden of pregnancy would be unreasonable upon a woman already handicapped or having herself handicapped children to raise. The ethical indications as well as those of general emergency could only be recognized during the first twelve weeks of pregnancy. It is interesting to note that the draft did not provide for punishment of the pregnant woman herself, regardless of the stage of pregnancy or the undertaking of counseling. This wideranging regulation was designed to remove the pregnant woman's fear of criminal sanctions and encourage her to undertake counseling which the drafters saw as the most effective means for preservation of unborn life as well as the health of the mother. However no examination with regard to the presence of the required indications was foreseen. Rather a professional counselor should advise the doctor, who is to do the procedure, about the indications.

(4) 'SPD/FDP-Draft' ('Time-Period-Regulations-Draft')[17] – Abortion was not punishable before the thirteenth day after conception. It was a criminal act at all times thereafter if not performed by a doctor, i.e. done by the pregnant woman herself or by a lay abortionist. If a physician had caused the abortion during the first twelve weeks there was no punishment so long as the woman had received the statutory counseling regarding aid which would be available during pregnancy and after birth. However, if the doctor undertook the abortion upon a woman who had not received the counseling, he, too, was punishable. After twelve weeks abortion was punishable if not having been then performed by a doctor or in an absence of medical indications up till the twenty-second week. The presence of these indications was to be certified by an expert authority.

Debate on these four drafts and on the issue of abortion went to lengths unprecedented in the history of the *Bundestag*. A special committee was formed, which, among other things, travelled to London, New York and Basel to gather information on the experience of other nations with reform legislation. Hours of hearings were held as well as deliberations stressing the need for replacement of a statute which was viewed as largely ineffective.

None of the before-mentioned drafts received the required majority of the Bundestag. Those two drafts with the highest number of votes were again put for decision in front of Parliament. The proposal of the fraction of the SPD/FDP was approved by the Bundestag on 5 June 1974 by a vote of 260 to 218 with four abstentions. The law was published on 21 June 1974. The text reads as follows:

§218
Abortion

(1) Whosoever aborts a pregnancy following the thirteenth day after conception is punishable by fine or imprisonment of up to three years.

(2) The penalty shall be imprisonment from six months to five years when the perpetrator
1. acts against the will of the pregnant woman, or
2. recklessly brings about a danger of death or serious damage to the health of the pregnant woman.
The court may order probation (§28 (1)(ii)).

(3) If the pregnant woman commits the act, it is punishable by fine or imprisonment up to one year.

(4) Attempt is punishable. The woman shall not be punishable for attempt.

§218a
Punishment of Abortion within the First Twelve Weeks

Whosoever undertakes an abortion by a physician with consent of the pregnant woman is not punishable under §218 if not more than twelve weeks have elapsed since conception.

§218b
Indications for Abortion After Twelve Weeks

Whosoever undertakes an abortion by a physician with consent of the pregnant woman is not punishable under §218 if according to the findings of medical science.

1. abortion is advisable to avert a danger to the pregnant woman's life or the danger of a grave interference in the state of her health, so long as the danger cannot be averted by other means reasonable to her, or

strong reasons argue for the presumption that the child, owing to a hereditary disposition or harmful influences before birth, would suffer from an irremedial injury to its state of health which would be so severe that the continuation of pregnancy could not be demanded of the pregnant woman, and not more than twenty-two weeks have elapsed since conception.

§218c
Abortion Without Instruction or Counseling of The Pregnant Woman

(1) Whosoever aborts a pregnancy without the pregnant woman's
1. first applying to a doctor or an advisory board empowered by this statute on the issue of aborting her pregnancy and there being instructed as to the public and private aid available to pregnant women, mothers and children, especially with regard to such aid as eases the continuation of pregnancy and the circumstances of mother and child, and
2. receiving counseling by a doctor,
shall be punishable by fine or imprisonment of up to one year, if the act is not punishable under §218.

(2) The woman upon whom the operation is undertaken is not punishable under Paragraph 1.

§219
Abortion Without Examination

(1) Whosoever aborts a pregnancy following twelve weeks after conception, without certification by a competent authority that the prerequisites of §218b (1) or (2) exist, is punishable by fine or prisonment of up to one year, if the act is not punishable under §218.

(2) The woman upon whom the operation is undertaken is not punishable under Section 1.

Decision of the Federal Constitutional Court

On 11 July 1974, 193 members of the *Bundestag* filed a claim with the Federal Constitutional Court for review of the new statute, followed shortly by claims from the States of Baden-Württemberg, Bavaria, Rheinland-Palatinate, Saarland and Schleswig-Holstein.[18] Briefs were filed on behalf of the complainants as well as of the government and the Bundestag itself.

At the outset, it should be noted that all parties concerned with the abortion case – the applicants, the Federal Government, all the counsels and even the dissenting Justices – were of the unanimous opinion that life growing in the womb enjoys the constitutional protection of Article 2, Section 2, of the Basic Law which provides: 'Everyone shall have the right to life and to inviolability of his person'.[19]

Invoking Article 2, Section 2 of the Basic Law, the Court held that the right to life embodied in the Basic Law was intended as a reaction against the extermination of 'unworthy' life carried out during the time of National Socialism in West Germany. Looking to the text of the guarantee of a right to 'life', the Court found that in the sense of the historical existence of a human being, life, according to bio-physiological findings, begins in any case no later than the thirteenth day after conception.[20]

The developmental process thereafter is a continuing one which brooks no division. In fact, human development continues long after birth. Therefore, the guarantee of Article 2, Section 2 of the Basic Law extends to everybody who 'lives', thereby construing 'everyone' in the sense of Article 2, Section 2, of the Basic Law as 'everyone' living, meaning 'unborn life' as well as 'born life'.

Thus, in contrast to the United States Supreme Court decisions in *Roe* v. *Wade* and *Doe* v. *Bolton*,[20] the German Federal Constitutional Court disputes the opinion that life of the fetus is divisible into three equal parts (trimesters), signifying a graduation of personhood.[22] The Basic Law's command to respect human life fully extends to the fetus during all time being in the mother's womb.

Once the Court had established that unborn life was included in the conception of 'everyone' within Article 2, Section 2, of the Basic Law, it was necessary to decide just what sort of protection was mandated as a result of the guarantee. Contained within this issue is the question of whether the protection must in the final analysis be insured by criminal sanctions, i.e. whether Article 2, Section 2, embodies not only a duty to enforce this guarantee against the state but also a positive duty on behalf of the state to enforce it with regard to third parties.

Included in these third parties is – according to the Court – the mother herself.[23] The Court recognized the natural tie between the unborn child and the mother as a special relationship for which there is no parallel in other circumstances of life. Pregnancy belongs to a woman's realm of privacy whose protection is constitutionally guaranteed in Article 2, Section 1, in association with Article 1, Section 1, of the Basic Law.[24] Article 2, Section 1, of the Basic Law provides: 'Everyone shall have the right to the free development of his personality insofar as he does not violate the rights of others or offend against the constitutional order or the moral code'. The Court concluded that the woman's right to free development of her personality includes the right to decide against parenthood and the duties growing out of it. However, this right is not unrestricted *vis à vis* to the rights of others, the constitutional order and the moral law. Therefore the Court held that the whole issue must be determined by weighing a number of factors being among them the value of the injured interest and the extent of social harm caused by the injurious act. Against this is to be weighed the traditional legal regulation in this area of life as well as the development of the conception of criminal law in modern society and finally the practical effectiveness of the threat of criminal prosecution and the possibility of replacing it with other legal sanctions.[25]

However, the Court did not hesitate to declare abortion as an act of killing, shown by the fact that criminal penalties were placed in the section of the Criminal Code entitled 'Felonies and Misdemeanors Against Life'.[26] Use of the term 'abortion of pregnancy' could not disguise this fact. A clear legal labeling of the act as a legal wrong (*Unrecht*) could not be dispensed with. Yet, the Court still stated that the decisive factor was whether the entire set of measures, whether criminal or civil, safeguarded the protected interest. So in spite of calling for criminal sanctions the Court saw the issue not as one of an absolute duty to punish, but rather as one of a 'relative' duty to use the threat of punishment when all other means to achieving the goal proved to be insufficient.[27]

The crux of the Court's opinion lies in its view that a weighing or balancing process must take place. Since abortion always results in destruction of the fetus, no balance is possible which allows the pregnant woman an abortion and at the same time guarantees the life of the fetus. The Court solved this problem by declaring that a weighing process must take place in which both constitutional values are seen in their relationship to the dignity of man as the keystone of the constitutional value system being guaranteed by Article 1, Section 1, of the Basic Law. With this orientation then, the decision must be in favor of a preference for protecting the life of the fetus over the womans right of self-determination as embodied in Article 2, Section 1, of the Basic Law. According to the accepted rules of competing constitutionally protected positions, the protection of the fetus' life must be given priority throughout the entire term of pregnancy.[28] Otherwise, this constitutional interest would be destroyed. Therefore, the state must insure that the idea of abortion is clearly labeled as a legal wrong and not an area of decision left up to the individual.[29]

The Court did not overlook the unique situation of the pregnant woman. It did not argue that the right of the unborn child to life must always prevail over the right of the mother to self-determination. The Justices recognized that under the Basic Law the unborn child's right to life may impose a burden upon the mother far in excess of the normal burden linked with pregnancy. These burdens are present if the woman is thrown into either serious mental or physical conflict by fulfilling her duty to carry the pregnancy to term. Thus the Justices concede that penal measures are an inadequate response to situations where pregnancy leads to 'grave hardship'.[30] In particular, the Court states that in order to permit abortion in a special case, circumstances of such considerable weight must exist, that fulfillment of the duty to carry to term would be so unusually difficult that it could not be reasonably expected. By this the Court envisions situations in which abortion is necessary to avert a grave danger to the pregnant woman's life or serious interference with her health. In such case it states the woman cannot be expected to sacrifice her own life for that of the child; rather, her own right to life and inviolability of her person have come into play. Similar extraordinary burdens upon the woman may exist in cases of a severe ethical, social or psychological distress. Under these circumstances, the legislature is not obliged to fulfill its duty by the means of a penal law.[31] In all other cases, however, abortion must remain a punishable offence within the German legal order. In these cases the continuation of pregnancy is 'exactable' (zumutbar) because the burdens of pregnancy do not exeed those normally incurred by a pregnant woman.

One of the most unique aspects of the Abortion Reform Act was the provision regarding counseling within Section 218c. It was the legislature's hope that what could not be achieved through criminal penalties, i.e. convincing the mother to continue with the pregnancy thereby protecting the unborn life, could be brought about through a face-to-face meeting with the woman, advising her of the options available and hopefully convincing her.[32]

In defense of this provision, the Government had argued that this was a central element of the concept of time period regulations. The legislature started from the premise that the decision to abort created a conflict situation weighing heavily on the pregnant woman. The fact that so many pregnant women opted for illegal abortions, despite the threat to life and health − not to mention the criminal penalties involved − made it clear that a situation calling for support and advice existed. Statistics showed that on the whole women were at first ambivalent about whether or not to abort. Therefore, counseling could help to bring them to a positive view of pregnancy. Furthermore, the legislature was convinced that punishment in the first twelve weeks in conjunction with a counseling requirement would not be an effective protection of the unborn. The program was therefore not meant to be a mere formality inevitably proceeding to the desired abortion, but was rather seen as an opportunity for an eyeball to eyeball meeting in which the pregnant woman could be told of what aid was available to her. As well, it was considered important to take into account her entire life situation, and to help her deal with any forces pressuring her to abort.

It was further pointed out that a woman does not suddenly become a mother when she discovers she's pregnant. By counseling the legislature hoped to achieve what criminal penalties had not been able to do, i.e. to take away the time constraints and the fears and thereby encourage the woman to carry out the pregnancy.

The Federal Constitutional Court, however, disagreed. The argument that developing life would be better protected through individual counseling than through a threat of punishment did not convince the Court. The Justices believed the Act lacked sufficient assurances that the woman would be motivated in fact to carry on her pregnancy. Thus, the counseling provisions failed to be truly 'pro-life orientated'.

In particular, the Court worried that the advisory boards would encounter rather materialistic reasons for wanting an abortion, such as adverse living conditions, economic need, inability to support a child while obtaining an education or engaged in employment. The way the counseling provisions were phrased led the Court to interpret it as requiring the advisory board only to inform the woman, without exercising any calculated influence on her motivational process. Such deficiencies in detail meant it lacked effective protection for developing life.

Finally, the Court missed any waiting period between the counseling session and the abortion procedure. For the woman who had already decided on abortion it was only a question of finding a cooperative doctor. Since the very physician consulted by the woman wishing to abort the fetus was entitled under the act to give the required counseling, such a person, the Court surmises, was not likely to act as it is demanded by Article 2, Section 2, of the Basic Law.

To sum up, the Court held Section 218a of the Abortion Reform Act unconstitutional because it failed expressly to embody an official disapproval of abortion during the first twelve weeks of pregnancy and because the counselling plan failed to incorporate a pronounced pro-life orientation.

Two Justices, including the only woman on the high bench, wrote dissenting opinions. In their minds, the majority of the Court had disregarded the accepted rules of judicial self-restraint. They saw the question before the legislature not being one of whether life before birth should be protected, but rather how. For the dissenters, the decision to use criminal or other sanctions is left squarely to the legislature. Nowhere, they argue, does the Basic Law suggest that a particular solution is necessary to meet the social problems of abortion. In effect the two dissenting Justices took their colleagues to task for ignoring the social realities of abortion. They especially cited the high rate of illegal abortions and that criminal penalties had not been effective.[33] The legislature considering this did opt for what it believed to be a better tailored scheme. Furthermore, the two Justices pointed out that the Basic Law did not prohibit the legislature from protecting unborn life in a way which acknowledge the historical fact that unborn and born life have never been governed by the same criminal sanctions.[34]

Abortion Reform Act Revised

As a result of the abortion decision, the Revised Abortion Act of 1976 was passed. It incorporated the 'indications solution' declaring the continuation of pregnancy under certain medical, eugenic, ethical and social or other emergency situations not to be punishable. The most important portions of the new Law are set out as follows:[35]

§218
Abortion

(1) Whosoever aborts a pregnancy shall be punished with fine or imprisonment of up to three years.

(2) In especially serious instances the penalty shall be imprisonment of between six months and five years. As a drule, an especially serious instance is present when the perpetrator
1. acts against the will of the pregnant woman, or
2. recklessly brings about a danger of death or serious damage to the health of the pregnant woman.
The court may order probation (§68 (1)(ii)).

(3) If the pregnant woman commits the act, it is punishable by fine or imprisonment up to one year. The pregnant woman is not punishable according to section (1) if the abortion is performed by a physician after counseling (§218b (1)(i), (ii)) and not more than twenty-two weeks have elapsed since conception. The court may refrain from punishing the pregnant woman under Section (1) if at the time of the act she found herself in particular distress.

(4) Attempt is punishable. The woman shall not be punishable for attempt.

§218a
Indications for Abortion

(1) Abortion of a pregnancy by a physician is not punishable under §218 when,
1. the pregnant woman consents, and
2. the abortion of the pregnancy is according to medical knowledge advisable, considering the current and future living conditions of the pregnant woman, in order to avert a danger to her life or the danger of a grave interference with the physical or

mental condition of her health, and which danger cannot be averted by other means reasonable to her.

(2)   The requirements of Section 1.2 are deemed to have been met, when according to medical knowledge

1. strong reasons argue for the presumption that the child, owing to a hereditary disposition or harmful influences before birth, would suffer from an irremedial injury to its state of health which would be so severe that the continuation of pregnancy could not be demanded of the pregnant woman,

2. an illegal act under §§176 – 179 was perpetrated upon the pregnant woman and strong reasons argue for the presumption that the pregnancy resulted from the act, or

3. abortion of the pregnancy is advisable, in order to avert the danger of a predicament which

(a) would be so severe that the continuation of the pregnancy could not be demanded of the pregnant woman, and

(b) cannot be averted by other means reasonable to the pregnant woman.

(3)   In instances under Section 2.1 not more than twenty-two weeks shall have elapsed since conception, and in the instances under Section 2.2, 3 not more than twelve weeks.

§218b
Abortion Without Counseling of the Pregnant Woman

(1)   Whosoever aborts a pregnancy without the pregnant woman's

1. at least three days before the abortion applying to a counselor with regard to the issue of aborting her pregnancy, and there being instructed as to the public and private aid available to pregnant women, mothers and children, especially with regard to such aid as eases the continuation of pregnancy and the circumstances of mother and child, and

2. being advised by a doctor as to the medically significant aspects,

shall be punishable by fine or imprisonment up to one year, if the act is not punishable under §218. The pregnant woman is not punishable under Section 1.

(2)   A counselor within the meaning of Section 1 is

1. an advisory board of an authority or body, institution or foundation recognized by public law or

2. a doctor who will not himself undertake the abortion of the pregnancy and

(a) as member of a recognized advisory board (number 1) is entrusted with the counseling within the meaning of Section 1 (1),

(b) is recognized by an authority or body, institution or foundation of public law as a counselor or

(c) has informed himself of the aid available in an individual case through counseling by a member of a recognized advisory board (number 1) which is entrusted with counseling within the meaning of Section 1 (1).

(3)   Section 1 (1) is not applicable when abortion is advisable to avert a danger to the pregnant woman's life of health based on physical illness or bodily injury.

§219
Abortion Without Medical Assessment

(1)   Whosoever aborts a pregnancy without the written assessment of a physician stating that the requirements of §218 a (1)(ii), (2), (3) haven been fulfilled shall be punishable by fine or imprisonment up to one year, so long as the act is not punishable under §218. The pregnant woman is not punishable under sentence (1).

(2)   A physician may not make the assessment in section 1 when he lacks competence because

he has been convicted of committing an act under (1) or under §§218, 218b, 219a, 219b or 219c or because of committing another illegal act in connection with an abortion. A physician may be provisionally incompetent to make an assessment under (1) when a proceeding against him has been begun for suspicion of committing an illegal act listed in the previous sentence.

§219a
Erroneous Medical Assessment

(1)   Whosoever as a physician, against his better knowledge, makes an erroneous assessment with regard to the prerequisites of §218a (1)(ii), (2), (3), for submission in accordance with §219a (1) shall be punishable by fine or imprisonment up to two years, so long as the act is not punishable under §218.

(2)   The pregnant woman is not punishable under (1).

As is evident from a comparison of the new statute with that struck down by the Federal Constitutional Court, the concept of time period regulations has been discarded, at least with respect to the first twelve weeks as a free zone of punishment. In the new law there is no mistaking the fact that abortion is viewed as a criminal wrong. The requirement of counseling has been retained but made less ambiguous, showing again the Bundestag's concern that through making the pregnant woman aware of all her options it hopes to convince her to continue with the pregnancy. However, it should be noted that the emphasis on the physical condition of the woman (as in Section 218b) seeks to rule out abortions in cases where the woman's desire for same stems from economic burdens or occupational demands. The emphasis is rather clearly on medical indications.

As can be imagined, all segments of the public were not pleased with this new regulation. A constitutional complaint was filed with the Federal Constitutional Court by two attorneys and members of the Württemberg Synod of the Lutheran Church.[36] The Court, however, refused to hear the case, stating that a constitutional complaint is only admissible when a basic right of the complainant is presently and directly affected by the challenged statute. In this case, the plaintiffs argued against the duties of their health insurance carrier to cover legal abortions under the act. The Court found that the right they were seeking to assert was really an issue of health insurance under public law and that even as members of the insurance plan they themselves were not directly affected.

Court Decisions and Related Issues since 1976

Abortion Expesens

In a recent case, decided on 22 July 1983 by the Higher Administrative Court of Baden-Württemberg (*VGH* Baden-Württemberg), a female civil servant held her employer to be constitutionally-bound to contribute to the costs of an abortion. Being employed by the government, she is generally entitled to reimbursement granted by the state to civil servants for costs of illness, hardships and deaths (so called '*Beihilfe*'). In this case, the request was denied since the abortion had not been indicated on medical but on social reasons.

The Higher Administrative Court agreed.[37] In its opinion, the court held that abortion on occasion of social indications is not a matter of sickness being covered by the governmental repayment-scheme. Sickness being defined as an irregular state of physical or mental constitution does not include such an abortion since the plaintiff physically could have had the child 'in accordance with the regular functions of a woman'.

The abortion decision of the Federal Constitutional Court of 1975 did not prove to be of much help. In particular, the court dismissed the argument that government is compelled to contribute to the costs of abortion on social indications solely because such abortion was declared constitutional. In a striking parallel to the decision of the United States Supreme Court in *Harris v.McRae*,[38] the judges drew a distinction between constitutionally permissible conduct and the duty of government to finance such action. The liberty protected by Article 2, Section 1, of the Basic law does not confer an entitlement to state subsidization as may be necessary to realize such freedom. In addition, the judges dispensed with the contention the public employer would discriminate against these women by withholding money for abortion on social indications. In their minds, it is a question for the legislature to decide on reimbursing the costs, not a matter of a constitutional right. Therefore it is neither constitutionally defective, that the Federal government as opposed to the state legislature had granted such aid to its civil servants.[39] There is no violation of the equal protection clause if the state decides against financial assistance.

Failure to Abort

May a child sue the physician for not having caused an abortion to his mother? The question came to the Federal Court of Justice (*BGH*) in

January 1983.[40] It arose out of a claim by a six-year-old child and his parents against the doctor who had treated the mother throughout her pregnancy.[41]

The child was born with serious defects of his health, including a severe loss of hearing in both ears and an enlarged heart with a hole in one partition. The injuries to its health were due to the fact that the physician negligently had failed to discover that the mother had contracted rubella while pregnant.

It was conceded that the physician did not himself cause the injuries of the child since he had no means preventing them. Rather, plaintiffs argued that the doctor had culpably omitted to hinder the birth of the child in that he had failed to cause the legally justified abortion to the mother.[42]

The Federal Court of Justice, in agreement the majority of German legal scholars,[43] decided against the child. It affirmed a judgement of the Regional Appeal Court in Munich,[44] but on different legal grounds. The court in Munich had pointed out that had a diagnosis of rubella been made and an abortion been performed, the child-plaintiff would not be alive to make its claim for damages. Thus, the plaintiff could not place the claim on an omission which itself was responsible for his life and legal capacity to sue.

The Federal Court of Justice did not follow expressly such logical line of reasoning. It held that in this and similar cases the borders of legal issues and arguments are generally crossed: 'Man has to accept his life as it is given by nature. There is no right to its prevention or destruction by others'.

The Court therefore denied, as a matter of torts, a duty of the physician to prevent the birth of a fetus which probably will be born with serious handicaps. Human life, when according to the Federal Constitutional Court includes the fetus, is of a highest legal value and affords absolute legal protection. No person is entitled to judge the value of human life. The Basic Law guarantees only the right 'to' one's life. It does not recognize a claim of determination 'cover' one's own life or that of a third person. In this context the Court cited an American author who said on the impossibility of weighing life with serious handicaps against non-life: 'Man, who knows nothing of death or nothingness, cannot possibly know, whether that is so'.[45]

In agreement with the lower court, the Federal Court of Justice also refused to find a right to abortion in the child-plaintiff based on the abortion provision of Section 218a as set forth above. It saw this statute as one serving only the interests of the pregnant woman with the decision to abort lying solely with her and something to which no third party could compel her. The lower court foresaw such absurd results as the appointment of a guardian on behalf of the unborn life to force the woman to abort it.[46]

The Federal Court of Justice also considered several claims by the mother. They included one for damages based on the increased financial burden of raising such a handicapped child as well as the claim for pain and suffering attendant to a ceasarian section delivery of the child. In contrast to the decision of the lower court, the Federal Court of Justice recognized principally such damages to be recovered by the mother. Since the mother specifically had asked the physician to examine her as to possible injuries of the fetus the negligent denial of harmfull effects on the health of the child represents in the opinion of the Court a grave violation of the treatment contract.[47]

A Pending Case

An important case concerning the constitutionality of abortion is still pending at the Federal Constitutional Court in Karlsruhe. The Social Court of Dortmund has asked the Constitutional Court to render judgment on the constitutionality of Section 200f of the Social Security Code (*Reichsversicherungsordnung*),[48] which entitles the insured party to health insurance in cases of abortion lawfully ('*rechtmässig*') performed by a physician. In a decision of 29 September, 1981,[49] the Social Court considered this provision of the Social Security Act to violate the constitutionally-protected rights of liberty (Article 2 of the Basic Law), of equality before the law (Article 3 of the Basic Law) and of freedom of faith (Article 4 of the Basic Law). In particular, the court had trouble with the obligation of the health insurance carrier to cover the costs even of those abortions that are solely indicated on social grounds. Since in West Germany only the Federal Constitutional Court is empowered to declare unconstitutional a statute that is passed after the promolgation of the Basic Law in 1949, the court in conformity with Article 100 of the Basic Law[50] stayed its proceeding and asked the Constitutional Court to decide the matter.

The problem with §200f of the Social Security Code is that it only speaks of 'not illegal abortions' being covered by the health insurance. On the other hand, Sections 218 *et seq.* of the Criminal Code do not distinguish between legal and illegal abortions. Rather, the criminal provisions in general regard abortions to be illegal, yet under certain conditions, i.e. in cases of medical, eugenic, ethical and social or other emergency indications the performance of an abortion is not punishable. While it is clear that abortion in such cases is not a punishable wrong, the questions still exists whether the interruption of pregnancy under these 'non-exactable' circumstances is no longer an illegal act at all. Under the old law preceeding the Abortion Reform Act of 1974, only abortion in cases of medical indications were justified. After the implementation of the Revised Abortion Act of 1976, many legal writers were of the opinion that the legislature itself has declared all abortions indicated on grounds specified in the law to be lawful.[51] From this it follows that the health insurance would have to cover all abortions being mentioned in Section 218a, Section 2, of the Criminal Code. The adverse position is now taken by the social court of Dortmund, arguing that the Abortion Act of 1976 only deals with the criminality and not the legality of such conduct. The Federal Constitutional Court is called to decide the dispute on constitutional grounds.

A judgment from the Federal Constitutional Court is not expected before spring 1985. However, it should be noted that the governing coalition of CDU/CSU and FDP under the chancellor Helmut Kohl has paid much attention to the result of this decision. In a 'coalition agreement' ('*Koalitionsvereinbarung*') concluded after the election to the *Bundestag* in March 1983, they decided not to take any steps on reforming abortion legislation before the Federal Constitutional Court has spoken. Yet, there is increasing political pressure on Bonn, especially from conservative forces from Southern Germany, to abolish the social indication solution at all. So far, the government has responded by creating a fund out of which women are being paid in a social emergency situation, thus trying to motivate them not to abort the fetus.[52] The expected decision of the Court is hoped to give a final answer on the constitutionally of abortion indicated merely on social grounds.

Related Issues

There have been no other reported proceedings than the before mentioned in which constitutional questions stemming from the Revised Abortion Act of 1976 were involved.[53]

However, commentators have continued to write on a number of important issues of which the following might soon occupy the courts:

In several parts of West Germany, mostly in Baden-Württemberg and in Bavaria, city and county councils have issued resolutions forbidding hospitals to perform other than medically indicated abortions. The councils were concerned with the increase of abortions on social indications which they thought to be caused mainly on pure economic reasons.[54] The question, however, is, whether such resolutions are compatible with statutory and constitutional law.[55]

In the case of a private hospital, it is recognized that the proprietor is free to decide whether an abortion shall be procured on only medical or also other indications. Physicians and patients are bound by this decision.[56] The same is true in case of a religiously operated hospital. The special constitutional protection accorded to the church in Article 140 of the Basic Law,[57] as well as the guarantee of freedom of conscience in Article 4 of the Basic Law, justifies the hospital in denying the performance of abortions with respect to all legally-recognized indications.[58]

Regarding state and municipal hospitals, the legal situation is different: irrespective of the council's refuse on the subject of abortion, under the governmental system in the Federal Republic of Germany, the hospital has an administrative responsibility to the local community to ensure that hospital care and facilities are available. It is not free to correct the decisions taken by the Bundestag in fulfillment of its constitutional duties. Furthermore, such resolutions impair the right of the hospitals to enter into a contract for the care of patients.[59]

Conclusion

From the foregoing it is evident that many constitutional issues involved in the abortion question were not resolved by the Federal Constitutional Court's opinion in 1975. However, it is also clear that almost any solution of the problem is able to create dissent, whether on constitutional, political or medical grounds. As other nations have found, this is one of the thorniest constitutional problems with which a democracy must deal. While there has been comparatively little debate on this issue in Germany in the past several years, it is not inconceivable that the question will soon come again to the fore.

Notes

The author is grateful to Miss Meril L. Benjamin, attorney-at-law, for her generous assistance in preparing this paper.
  1. See judgment of 25 February 1975, 39 BVerfGE 1-95 (1975); the decisions of the Federal Constitutional Court (Bundesverfassungsgericht) are reported in Entscheidungen des Bundesverfassungsgerichts, hereinafter BVerfGE (1952-date).
  2. The 5. Gesetz zur Reform des Strafrechts (5. StrRG) of 18 June 1974 (BGB1 I at 297 – Federal Law Gazette – Bundesgesetzblatt, hereinafter BGB1); this law is cited hereinafter as 'Abortion Reform Act of 1974'.
  3. Strafgesetzbuch für die preussischen Staaten of 14 April 1851 (Gesetz-Sammlung at 101).
  4. Strafgesetzbuch des Norddeutschen Bundes of 31 May 1870 (Bundesgesetzblatt des Norddeutschen Bundes at 197).
  5. Strafgesetzbuch für das Deutsche Reich of 15 May 1871 (RGB1 – Reichsgesetzblatt at 127).
  6. Gesetz zur Abänderung des Strafgesetzbuches of 18 May 1926 (RGB1 I at 239).
  7. Verordnung zur Durchführung der Verordnung zum Schutz von Ehe, Familie und Mutterschaft of 18 March 1943 (RGB1 I at 1169).
  8. 1. Gesetz zur Reform des Strafrechts (1. StrRG) of 25 June 1969 (BGB1 I at 645); the

English translation is taken from Kommers, 'Abortion and Constitution: United States and West Germany', 25 *Am.J.Comp.L.* 255 (1977).

9. See Entwurf eines 5. Gesetzes zur Reform des Strafrechts – Bundesrats-Drucksache/Federal Council Printed Matter – hereinafter BRDrucks 58/72.

10. The term 'indication' is a literal translation from the German term 'Indikation'. It means a reason for an abortion; thus 'indications solution' means that a pregnancy may be interrupted at any time for reasons being defined by law.

11. The 'time-period-regulation' or 'term-solution' (*Fristenlösung*) means that an abortion is justified on whatever ground within a given state of pregnancy, normally within the first trimester. The main issue in much of the German abortion controversy was whether 'Fristenregelung' or 'Indikationslösung' were appropriate, see also Kommers, supra n. 8, p. 261.

12. According to Article 76 of the Basic Law ('Grundgesetz') bills shall be introduced in the Bundestag either by the Federal government or by the members of the *Bundestag* or by the *Bundesrat*. The term 'Basic Law' is a direct translation of the official German term '*Grundgesetz*'. Germans use the term '*Grundgesetz*' (Basic Law) rather than '*Verfassung*' (constitution) because the '*Grundgesetz*' is thought to be a fundamental statute designed to establish the political order of Germany for a 'transitional period' until the reunification of Germany takes place. For the English text of the Basic Law, see the Basic Law of the Federal Republic of Germany, published by the press and information office of the Federal government, Bonn (1979).

13. See Bundestag-Drucksache 7/561.

14. A distinction is drawn between the time of fertilization of the eggcell and the time when the fertilized egg attaches itself into the wall of the uterus. The latter process will be referred to hereinafter as 'implantation'.

15. CDU = Christian Democratic Union; CSU = Christian Social Union; for the draft see BT-Drucks. 7/554.

16. See BT-Drucks. 7/443.

17. SPD = Social Democratic Party; FDP = Liberal Democratic Party; for the draft see BT-Drucks. 7/375.

18. Under West Germany's constitution, Article 93(1) (ii), the Federal Constitutional Court has jurisdiction to decide '... in case of differences of opinion or doubts on the formal and material compatibility of federal law ... with this Basic Law, at the request of the Federal Government, of a Land government, or of one third of the Bundestag members ...'. This constitutional provision has also been enacted as part of the Gesetz über das Bundesverfassungsgericht (BVerfGG §13(6)). In this case both the opportunity for an application by state governments and also by a section of the Bundestag was employed.

19. See Benda, 'New Tendencies in the Development of Fundamental Rights in the Federal Republic of Germany', 1977 *John Marshall Journal of Practice and Procedure*, pp. 1, 10; the full text in German of Article 2, Section 2, reads 'Jeder hat das Recht auf Leben und körperliche Unversehrtheit. Die Freiheit der Person ist unverletzlich. In diese Rechte darf nur aufgrund eines Gesetzes eingegriffen werden'.

20. 39 BVerfGE at 37.

21. See 410 U.S. 113 (1973) and 410 U.S. 179 (1973).

22. 39 BVerfGE at 37.

23. Id., pp. 42, 48.

24. Article 2, Section 1, of the Basic Law provides: 'The dignity of man shall be inviolable. To respect and protect it shall be the duty of all state authority'.

25. 39 BVerfGE at 45.

26. 'Verbrechen und Vergehen wider das Leben'.

27. 39 K BVerfGE at 46.
28. Attention is given here especially to the 'principle of proportionality' ('Verhältnismässig-keitsgrundsatz'); see 29 BVerfGE 312, 316; 35 BVerfGE 185, 190; 39 BVerfGE 1, 47; the principle of proportionality is one of the basic tenets of constitutional law under the German system. It simply requires that the means selected to meet a legislative goal must be suitable, as well as necessary to meet that goal. The bounds of reasonableness must be kept in mind; see also Quaas, in: *Business Transactions in Germany* (B. Rüster ed.), 'Constitutional, Administrative and Public Business Law' (1983), at §7.02.
29. 39 BVerfGE at 50.
30. Id., p. 49.
31. Id., p. 48.
32. See Ehmke, in: Arndt/Erhardt/Funcke (ed.), Der §218 StGB vor dem Bundesverfassungs-gericht, Dokumentation zum Normenkontrollverfahren wegen verfassungsrechtlicher Prüfung des 5. Strafrechtsreformgesetzes (Fristenregelung), 1979, hereinafter cited as 'Arndt', p. 208.
33. In the early 1970s the rate of abortion in West Germany was estimated to amount up to forty percent of the living births; for statistics see Arndt, supra n. 32, pp. 100, 143, 174 *et seq.*
34. 39 BVerfGE at 80.
35. 15th Law to amand the Criminal Code, 1976 (BGB1 I at 1213).
36. See decision of the Federal Constitutional Court of 1 November 1976 – 1 BVR 357/76 – in 1976 EuGRZ (Europäische Grundrechte-Zeitschrift) at 410.
37. See judgment of 22 July 1983, – 4 S 1035/83 – so far unpublished; the decision of the lower court (administrative court of Freiburg), being affirmed, is printed in 1983 MedR (*Journal of Medicine Law*), p. 159.
38. 100 S.Ct. 2671 (1980).
39. Federal officers as opposed to civil servants being employed by the Länder are those who are engaged directly by the Federal administration (e.g. Foreign Service, Federal Finance Administration, the Federal Railroads, Federal Postal Service etc.) – see Article 83 *et seq.* of the Basic Law.
40. Decision of 18 January 1983 in 1983 *NJW* (*Neue Jurische Wochenschrift*), p. 1371.
41. The legal issues involved here, i.e. the problem of a 'wrongful life' are not new to English and United States courts. Claims of such a child were recently denied by the London Court of Appeals in the case McKay v. Essex Health Authority and Another, see 1982 *The Weekly Law Reports*, p. 890; the opposite position was taken by the Court of Appeal in California in Curlender v. Bio-Science (1980), see Stephenson, 1982 *The Weekly Law Reports*, pp. 890, 904. As to further references see BGH, 1983 MedR, pp. 101, 102, 103.
42. See Section 218a, Section 1, of the Criminal Code.
43. As to references see BGH, in: 1983 *MedR*, at 101, 102; Fischer, 1981 *NJW* at 1991; Emmerich, in: 1983 *JuS* (*Juristische Schulung*), p. 632.
44. Decision of 2 February 1981, in: 1981 NJW at 2012.
45. See Stephenson, 1982 *The weekly Law Reports*, p. 90.
46. 1981 *NJW*, pp. 2012, 2013.
47. BGH, 1983 *MedR*, p. 103.
48. The full text of Section 200f Social Security Code reads 'Versicherte haben Anspruch auf Leistungen bei einer nicht rechtswidrigen Sterilisation und bei einem nicht rechtswidrigen Abbruch der Schwangerschaft durch einen Artzt. Es werden ärztliche Beratungen über die Erhaltung und den Abbruch der Schwangerschaft, ärztliche Untersuchungen und Begut-achtung zur Feststellung der Voraussetzungen für eine nicht rechtswidrige Sterilisation oder für einen nicht rechtswidrigen Schwangerschaftsabbruch, ärztliche Behandlung,

Versorgung mit Arznei-, Verband- und Heilmitteln sowie Krankenhauspflege gewährt. Anspruch auf Krankengeld besteht, wenn Versicherte wegen einer nicht rechtswidrigen Sterilisation oder wegen eines nicht rechtswidrigen Abbruchs der Schwangerschaft durch einen Artz arbeitsunfähig werden, es sei denn, es besteht Anspruch nach Section 182 Abs. 1 Nr. 2.'

49. See 1983 *NJW*, p. 360.
50. Article 100 of the Basic Law reads as follows:

    (1) If a court considers a law unconstitutional the validity of which is relevant to its decision, the proceedings shall be stayed, and a decision shall be obtained from the Land court competent for constitutional disputes if the constitution of a Land is held to be violated, or from the Federal Constitutional Court if this Basic Law is held to be violated by Land law or if a Land law is held to be incompatible with a federal law.

    (2) If, in the course of litigation, doubt exists whether a rule of public international law is an integral part of federal law and whether such rule directly creates rights and duties for the individual (Article 25), the court shall obtain a decision from the Federal Constitutional Court.

    (3) If the constitutional court of a Land, in interpreting this Basic Law, intends to deviate from a decision of the Federal Constitutional Court or of the constitutional court of another land, it must obtain a decision from the Federal Constitutional Court.
51. See Esser, 'Die Rechtswidrigkeit des Aborts', in: 1983 *Med*R, p. 57, with further references.
52. See *Stuttgarter Zeitung* (19 November 1983), p. 2.
53. As to the discussion in parliament, see 1980 *ZRP* (*Zeitschrift für Rechtspolitik*), p. 307; in particular the CDU/CSU is opposing the indication on social grounds – see 'CDU/CSU: Karlsruher Erklärung zur Rechtspolitik', in: 1980 *ZRP*, pp. 154, 155.
54. Narr, *Ärztliches Berufsrecht* (1982), p. 497 (N 815).
55. See Maier, 1974 *NJW*, p. 1404; Grupp, 1977 *NJW*, p. 329; Narr, supra n 54, p. 497.
56. See Maier, 1974 NJW at 1407; Narr, supra n 54 at 497.
57. As to the constitutional protection accorded to the church in West Germany – and in comparison to the legal situation in the United States – see Quaas, 'Neuere Entwicklungen im amerikanischen Recht zum Verhältnis von Staat und Kirche', 1981 *Europäische Grundrechte-Zeitschrift* (*EuGRZ*), p. 321.
58. See BVerfGE 24, pp. 236, 247; Maier, 1974 *NJW*, p. 1407; Narr, supra n 54, p. 498.
59. See Grupp, 1977 *NJW*, p. 329; Maier, 1974 *NJW*, p. 1407; Narr, supra n 54, p. 498.

United States

Charles D. Kelso and *R. Randall Kelso**

Introduction

Constitutional limits on state power to prohibit or regulate abortion became a hotly debated topic in the United States during the 1970s, following the decision by the Supreme Court of the United States in *Roe* v. *Wade*, 410 U.S. 113 (1973). As explained below, two things seem clear ten years later: First, the debate probably will continue through the 1980s. Second, it is likely that abortion will continue to be legally available in the United States, as a constitutional right, subject to increasingly close state regulation.

Supreme Court Decisions on Abortion

In the 19th century, many states in the United States enacted anti-abortion statutes. Their purpose was to protect prenatal life and restrain what was then a hazardous medical procedure. The statutes occasionally were enforced by criminal prosecutions as recently as the early 1970s.

In 1973, the Supreme Court held in *Roe* v. *Wade* that a pregnant woman, in consultation with her physician, has a constitutionally protected freedom − a fundamental liberty within the Fourteenth Amendment (see generally p. 72) − to decide to have an abortion. No state may unreasonably infringe on that aspect of the right of privacy (see p. 67), said the Court, and a restrictive regulation is invalid unless it reasonably serves a compelling state interest in the health of the mother or the life of a viable fetus.

A state's interest in material health, said Justice Blackmun, writing for a six-to-three majority in *Roe* v. *Wade*, does not become compelling until after the first trimester. Until then, he explained, a women faces less risk from abortion than from childbirth. A state's interest in the life of a fetus does not become compelling until the fetus is viable. When a fetus is viable,

*Charles D. Kelso is Professor of Law at the University of the Pacific McGeorge School of Law. R. Randall Kelso is Assistant Professor of Law at South Texas College of Law.

Comparative Law Yearbook, Volume 7, 1983. ISBN 90-247-2966-1.

however, a state may proscribe abortion except when necessary to preserve the life or health of the mother.

According to the Supreme Court, a fetus is viable when it is capable of 'meaningful' life apart from the mother by natural or artificial life support systems. *Planned Parenthood of Central Missouri* v. *Danforth*, 428 U.S. 52 (1976). The viability of a fetus, under that test, is a matter for medical judgment. It is not for legislative definition in terms of weeks of gestation, fetal weight, or any other single factor. The point of viability is thus left 'flexible for anticipated advancements in medical skill'. *Colautti* v. *Franklin*, 439 U.S. 379 (1979). In 1973, viability before twenty-eight weeks was considered unusual. Recent studies have demonstrated fetal viability at increasingly early times. For example, one study showed that infants born alive with a gestational age of less than twenty-five weeks and a weight between 500 and 1,249 grams have a twenty percent chance of survival. *City of Akron* v. *Akron Center for Reproductive Health*, 103 S. Ct. 2481, 2507 (1983) (dissenting opinion).

The Supreme Court has held that certain state regulations are not an unreasonable interference with the protected freedom to have an abortion because they have *no significant impact* on a woman's exercise of her right to decide to have an abortion. The state interest to which such regulations must be reasonably related need not be compelling. It is enough that the interest be legitimate and important, such as an interest in maternal health or fostering childbirth. Only rarely will a statute be invalidated when the Court thus defers to legislative judgment. Accordingly, the Court has held that a state may:

(1)   Bar abortions by anyone other than a licensed physician. *Connecticut* v. *Menillo*, 423 U.S. 9 (1975).

(2)   Require written, informed consent by the mother, even during the first 12 weeks. *Planned Parenthood of Central Missouri* v. *Danforth*, 428 U.S. 52 (1976)

(3)   Require that routine medical records include data on abortions. *Planned Parenthood, supra*.

(4)   Refuse to permit abortions in a city hospital even though childbirth procedures are provided. *Poelker* v. *Doe*, 432 U.S. 519 (1977).

(5)   Provide that all surgically removed tissue, including fetal tissue, be submitted to a pathologist. *Planned Parenthood Association of Kansas City* v. *Ashcroft*, 103 S. Ct. 2517 (1983).

The doctrinal approach by which these decisions were justified can be seen in the case of *Maher* v. *Roe*, 432 U.S. 464 (1977). In *Maher*, the Court held 6/3 that a state may withhold funding for nontherapeutic abortions (abortions where the health of the mother is not at stake) even though the costs of other medical procedures are funded by the state. Replying to constitutional challenges, Mr. Justice Powell said that the Court would review the statutory classification under the usual 'rational basis' standard rather than the 'strict scrutiny' standard applicable to classifications involving a 'suspect class' or a 'fundamental right'. He explained that an indigent woman who desires an abortion does not come within the limited category of disadvantaged classes recognized as 'suspect' and given special protection by the Court via the 'strict scrutiny' standard of review. That standard requires compelling reasons or a compelling state interest for differences in classification and treatment.

As to whether the *Roe*-based fundamental right was implicated by the statutory classification, Mr. Justice Powell explained that the 'fundamental right' recognized in *Roe* and its progeny protect a freedom from burdensome interference with the freedom to decide whether to terminate a pregnancy. However, 'It implies no limitation on the authority of a State to make a value judgment favoring childbirth over abortion, and to implement that judgment by the allocation of public funds'. Such a state policy, said Justice Powell, does not place obstacles in the path of a pregnant woman's decision on whether to have an abortion. Thus, Connecticut's regulation did not impinge on the fundamental right recognized in *Roe* and there was no basis for heightened scrutiny.

In the view of Justice Brennan, dissenting with Justices Marshall and Blackmun, a disparity in state funding, which supports childbirth but not abortion, operates to coerce indigent pregnant women to bear children they would not otherwise choose to have. Thus, it unconstitutionally infringes on the fundamental right of pregnant women to be free to decide whether to have an abortion. Justice Marshall added that the regulations were in reality intended to impose a moral viewpoint that no State may constitutionally enforce.

Maher v. *Roe* was accompanied by *Beal* v. *Doe*, 432 U.S. 438 (1977), in which a similarly divided 6/3 Court (Justice Brennan, Marshall, and Blackman dissenting) held that the federal Social Security Act does not require a state to fund nontherapeutic abortions as a condition of participation in the joint federal-state medical assistance program. The majority said that nothing in the federal act suggests it is unreasonable for a participating state to encourage normal childbirth. *Maher* and *Beal* foreshadowed *Harris* v. *McRae*, 448 U.S. 297 (1980), in which a 5/4 Court held that the federal government can refuse in its Medicaid program to reimburse expenses for some medically necessary abortions even though childbirth expenses are reimbursed. Justice Stevens joined Justices Brennan, Marshall and Blackmun in dissent, insisting that *Harris* was fundamentally different from *Maher* because medically necessary abortions were involved. Justice Stewart, for the majority, replied that it was not irrational for Congress to refuse reimbursement for certain medically necessary abortions even though it authorized federal reimbursement for other medically necessary services. He explained that abortion, which involves the purposeful termination of a potential life, is inherently different from other medical procedures. Another case in this series was *Williams* v. *Zbaraz*, 448 U.S. 358 (1980) (state governments need not fund abortions excluded from the federal Medicaid program).

Even where infringement on the fundamental right to have an abortion has been involved, some state regulations that substantially interfere with the freedom to choose an abortion have been upheld under the Court's strict test of reasonably supporting a *compelling* state interest in maternal health. Thus,

(1) A state may require that all abortions after the first trimester be performed in a hospital, where hospital is defined to include outpatient surgical hospitals as well as full-service, acute care hospitals. *Simopoulos* v. *Virginia*, 103 S. Ct. 2532 (1983).

(2) A state may require that a second physician attend the abortion of a viable fetus and take all reasonable steps in keeping with good medical practice to preserve the life and health of the viable unborn child whenever that does not pose an increased risk to the life or health of the mother. *Planned Parenthood Association of Kansas City* v. *Ashcroft*, 103 S. Ct. 2517 (1983).

Nevertheless, the Supreme Court has invalidated a number of state abortion regulations as substantial interferences with a pregnant woman's constitutional right of choice because those regulations were not reasonably related to a compelling state interest in fetal life or the health of pregnant women. Thus, a state may not:

(1) Require that all abortions during the first three months be performed in a licensed hospital. *Doe* v. *Bolton*, 410 U.S. 179 (1973).

(2) Require approval of the abortion by a hospital committee or the concurrence of another physician. *Doe* v. *Bolton* 410 U.S. 179 (1973).

(3) Require that the attending physician must use the same care to preserve the life of a fetus as if a live birth were intended. *Planned Parenthood* v. *Danforth, supra*.

(4) Bar the use of saline amniocentesis (the most commonly used method of abortion after the first 12 weeks of pregnancy, and safer than most other methods). *Planned Parenthood* v. *Danforth, supra*.

(5) Require written consent by the parents or spouse of a woman seeking an abortion in the first 12 weeks of pregnancy (unless the life of the mother is in danger). *Planned Parenthood* v. *Danforth, supra*.

(6) Require that all abortions after the first trimester be performed in a

full-service hospital. *City of Akron* v. *Akron Center for Reproductive Health, Inc.*, 103 S. Ct. 2481 (1983).

(7)   Require that a woman be 'truly informed' by the attending physician of the risks of abortion where much of the required information is designed to persuade the woman to withhold consent and where by insisting upon the recitation of a lengthy and inflexible list of information, the state imposes unreasonable obstacles in the path of the doctor/patient relationship. *City of Akron* v. *Akron Center for Reproductive Health, Inc.*, *supra*.

(8)   Require a 24 hour delay after signing a written consent form. *City of Akron* v. *Akron Center for Reproductive Health, Inc.*, *supra*.

Physicians who perform abortions are protected by several Supreme Court decisions from criminal liability for violating a state regulation where the prohibition is unclear or the doctor does not intend to do the prohibited act. Thus, the Court has declared void for vagueness a statute which required an attending physician to attempt to preserve the life of an aborted fetus if there is a 'sufficient reason to believe that the fetus may be viable'. *Colautti* v. *Franklin*, 439 U.S. 379 (1979). The Court explained that it was unclear whether the doctor was to use his best judgment or refer to objective facts that other physicians might think relevant. The Court has also invalidated for vagueness a criminal statute which required physicians to dispose of fetal remains in a 'humane and sanitary manner'. *City of Akron* v. *Akron Center for Reproductive Health*, *supra*. The Court explained that the phrase suggested a possible intent to mandate 'some sort' of burial. But the Due Process Clause does not permit this level of uncertainty, said the Court, where criminal liability is imposed. Again, attending physicians are protected not only by holdings on vagueness but also by the Court's clear indication that a physician can be held criminally liable for aborting a viable fetus only if the physician knows that the fetus is viable or the physician 'in bad faith' ignores facts pertaining to viability. *Colautti* v. *Franklin*, 439 U.S. 379, 396 (1979).

The Court has extended the principle of *Roe* v. *Wade* to minors. *Bellotti* v. *Baird*, 428 U.S. 132 (1976). However, it has also recognized that states have a significant interest in protecting minors. Accommodating these competing interests, the court in *Planned Parenthood Association of Kansas City* v. *Ashcroft*, *supra*, approved a carefully drafted statute which allows abortions to be performed on minors only if (1) the minor and one parent or guardian consent, or (2) the minor is emancipated, or (3) by court order the minor is granted the right to consent, or (4) a court orders the abortion after finding no emancipation, that the minor was not mature enough to make an informed decision, and that an abortion is in the minor's best interests. The

Court has made clear that a parental consent requirement with respect to minor females is unconstitutional unless, as in *Kansas City*, the law assures a prompt judicial proceeding for obtaining a decree that the minor is mature enough to make the decision herself or that it is not in the minor's interest to require parental consent. *Belotti* v. *Baird*, 443 U.S. 622 (1979), *Planned Parenthood of Kansas City* v. *Ashcroft*, 103 S. Ct. 2517, 2525 (1983).

Some states have enacted statutes which require that the parents of a minor female be notified before an abortion is performed. The Court approved the application of a parental notice statute in a situation where the minor was living with and dependent upon her parents, and there was no showing of maturity or the details of her relationship with her parents. *H.L.* v. *Matheson*, 450 U.S. 398 (1981). However, the Court has not approved the application of a parental notice statute in any case where the minor was emancipated or was prepared to show in court that notification was detrimental to her best interests. It is highly likely that the Court will apply to parental notice requirements the same tests it has applied to parental consent statutes, as Justice Powell said he would do. *H.L.* v. *Matheson*, 450 U.S. 398, 413 (1981) (concurring opinion). Thus, a notice statute would have to provide for a judicial procedure which frees mature minors from notice or which permits a court to dispense with notice upon finding that the minor's best interest would not be served by notice.

The Continuing Debate: Holmesians v. Instrumentalists

Since the Court has reaffirmed the basic holding of *Roe* on a number of occasions, and six Justices expressly did so again in the Court's most recent term, *City of Akron* v. *Akron Center for Reproductive Health, Inc.*, *supra*, why should there be a continuing debate about *Roe* and its progeny? One reason is that some scholars as well as the dissenting Justices in *Roe* and *Akron* think that the technique of decisionmaking used by the Court in *Roe* was an improper exercise of judicial power. *See* e.g., Ely, *The Wages of Crying Wolf: A Comment on Roe* v. *Wade*, 82 Yale L.J. 920 (1973). Professor Ely pointed out that the Constitution says nothing about abortion, includes no reference to a right of privacy, and does not draw a distinction between economic regulations (now reviewed only by a rational basis test) and non-economic regulations (some of which, as in *Roe*, are given 'strict scrutiny' and invalidated if not adequately justified by a compelling state interest). Ely questioned whether the Court has been able to identify any value other than the democratic process which the Justices are able adequately to define or protect.

Scholarly criticisms of *Roe* were anticipated by Justice White, whose dissent in *Roe* v. *Wade* asserted that the Court was engaged in the 'exercise of raw judicial power'. Justice Rehnquist, also dissenting, said that the Court's use of substantive due process arguments in *Roe* to review a non-economic regulation was similar to the use of substantive due process for strictly reviewing economic legislation, as in *Lochner* v. *New York*, 198 U.S. 45 (1905) – a position the Court has formally repudiated in a number of cases. *See*, e.g., *West Coast Hotel Co.* v. *Parrish*, 300 U.S. 379 (1937) (over-ruling *Lochner*), and *United States* v. *Carolene Products Co.*, 304 U.S. 297 (1938).

Defenders of *Roe* argue that a woman's freedom of choice is a value properly protected from majoritarian lawmaking by the Supreme Court, which can impartially define who should have what decisionmaking role in the matter of abortion. See Tribe, 'Toward of Model of Roles in the Due Process of Life and Law', 87 *Harv. L. Rev.* 1 (1973). Further, the doctrine of precedent can be invoked in support of *Roe* by pointing out that concept of privacy, on which *Roe* was based, had been given a broad scope in *Griswold* v. *Connecticut*, 381 U.S. 479 (1965) (invalidating a state bar on the use of birth control devices by married persons) and *Eisenstadt* v. *Baird*, 405 U.S. 438 (1972) ('If the right of privacy means anything, it is the right of the individual, married or single, to be free from unwarranted governmental intrusion into matters so fundamentally affecting a person as the decision whether to bear or beget a child'). See Nowak, Rotunda & Young, *Constitutional Law*, 2d. Ed., 744 (1983) ('Virtually all of the justices who have sat on the Court have realized that they must protect values which are only implied by the Constitution or its amendments').

The debate over techniques of decisionmaking that one finds in discussions of *Roe* is replicated today in many other areas of Constitutional Law. Indeed, the same debate occurs over decisionmaking style in cases that involve common law or the interpretation of legislation. Essentially, the question is whether courts should follow the judicial philosophy of Justice Holmes; whether courts should follow the lead of Justice Cardozo, as most courts have done since the mid 1930s; or whether a new approach should emerge.

Full exploration of the situation will require that we back away, temporarily, from the specifics of the abortion decisions and consider constitutional law within a larger framework. The following chart summarizes the main dimensions:

Decision-Making Styles in American Law

	Law is separable from morals and should be guided and tested by its own 'internal' standards	Law and morals blend in that law should be guided and tested by an external, normative, standard
Law is a System of Rationally Related Rules	*Formalism* (1850 – 1920)	*Natural Law* (1776 – 1870)
Law Functions as a Means to an End	*Holmesian* (1900 – 1950)	*Instrumentalism* (1930 – Today)

This chart depicts the shift from pre-civil war Natural Law jurisprudence to late 1800s Formalism followed in the early to mid 1900s by Holmesian decisionmaking and by the current style, Instrumentalism. The time periods overlap by twenty years to emphasize that the chart depicts tendencies and trends rather than sudden changes.

In the Natural Law era, judges acknowledged that they needed to make law. They resorted to natural law (or rights) as an external source of rational principles. Despite its apparent invitation to make law, however, the Natural Law approach did not lead to judicial activism with respect to interpretations of the Constitution. The reason is that the goal of interpretation, according to the natural law approach, was to carry out legislative purpose, and legislative purpose was to be found in legislative text and structure and in the mischief that the legislation was designed to remedy.

Starting around 1850, there was a gradual transformation to Formalism – a style of deciding which retained the assumption that law is composed of a system of rationally related rules, but which played down external standards of justice. It emphasized, instead, that a judge's task is to apply the rules logically, accordingly to their implicit premises, in order to achieve certainty and predictability. In this view, judges should not inquire into the particular consequences of applying a rule in the case before them. Thus, the study of law by a formalist such as Langdell, the inventor of the case method, is a kind of science, a science of categorization and deduction.

When interpreting legislation (both statutes and the Constitution), formalists give language its plain meaning and then apply the legislation logically to facts characterized in terms of that meaning. Only the legislative language is to be considered as a source of meaning, unless the words are ambiguous on their face, or unless the legislation would produce absurd results if applied according to its literal meaning.

The difference between the formalist and natural law styles of decisionmaking does not require courts to reach different results. A formalist could reach either liberal or conservative results, depending on whether the relevant precedents and rules reflected liberal or conservative values. In practice, however, each of the styles has been associated with particular substantive rules.

In the formative era of natural law (the late 1700s and early 1800s), both personal and economic rights were thought to deserve protection against majoritarian calculations. With respect to personal rights this was reflected by Jefferson in the opening paragraph of the Declaration of Independence (the unalienable rights to 'Life, Liberty, and the pursuit of Happiness'), the Constitution's Bill of Rights, and works such as Thomas Paine's *The Rights of Man* (1792). Economic rights were also given careful protection. This was the era of John Locke's labor theory of property and Adam Smith's *An Inquiry in the Nature and Causes of the Wealth of Nations* (1776). A number of decisions protecting individual property and contract rights were handed down by the Supreme Court, among the most famous being *Fletcher* v. *Peck*, 6 Cranch 87 (1810) and *Dartmouth College* v. *Woodward*, 4 Wheat. 518 (1819). Richard Faulker remarked in *The Jurisprudence of John Marshall* 17 (1968) that in *Fletcher* v. *Peck* and in other cases Marshall 'called the property right 'sacred'. Marshall considered it to be unequivocally a natural right, thus following such liberal republicans as Locke and Adam Smith.'

In the age of formalism (1850 – 1920), the economic theory of *laissez-faire* dominated both common law and constitutional decisionmaking. Under formalism, the individual's natural right to economic freedom and liberty of contract became a shield to bar any efforts at economic reform. However, the Court did not create a similar shield against laws that intruded upon personal rights. Following the *Slaughter-House Cases*, 16 Wall. 36 (1873), and *The Civil Rights Cases*, 109 U.S. 3 (1883), the protection of civil rights under the 14th Amendment was almost eliminated as a branch of constitutional law and a subject for the exercise of Congressional authority. It was left for more than a half century to whatever the legislature of the respective states decided to pass.

Formalist courts never connected economic rights and personal rights as did enlightened natural law judges. When economic power becomes concentrated in the hands of a few, this can cause others to lose both economic and non-economic personal and civil liberties. Natural law judges were concerned about protecting both groups; judges in the American era of formalist decisionmaking protected only the businessman's freedom of contract.

This situation could not last forever, and it did not. Legislatures began to react. In the area of torts, for example, legislatures passed workers' compensation statutes to ameliorate the harsh effects of the pro-employer common law. In the economic area, Congress passed the Sherman Anti-Trust Act. Legislatures passed minimum wage laws, maximum hours laws, health and safety laws, and child labor laws. Many were held unconstitutional by the Supreme Court as violating the Due Process or Commerce Clauses. These decisions were typically justified by a formalist use of phrases such as 'liberty of contract' or 'interstate commerce'.

Even so, the legislative action reflected the fact that the views of most people on the needs of society tended to differ from the views of the Court. In such a climate, it was natural for Holmesian jurisprudence, which leaves protection of both economic and personal rights up to the political process, to come into vogue. It fit the economic reform needs of society to adopt a jurisprudence that took concerns for the contract and property rights from the Surpeme Court and handed them over to the legislatures.

Justice Holmes, who had a powerful influence on American law during the early years of this century, agreed with formalists that law is separate from morals. Since Holmes thought that an important aspect of law was the certainty and predictability toward which it always tended, he agreed with formalists that law can be studied as a science. However, Holmes did not agree with formalists that legal rules were universally true because he thought that (1) the content of English and American law at any time pretty much corresponds with what the majority thinks is convenient and (2) the dominant group in society often changes. Therefore, the life of the law has not been the logic emphasized by formalists but, rather, experience – as the 'felt necessities of the times' are translated into law. Certainty and prediction were desirable goals but they could never be attained because the law will and should change as community feelings change. Said Holmes:

> The truth is that law is always approaching and never reaching consistency. It is forever adopting new principles from one end, and it always retains old ones from history at the other, which have not yet been absorbed or sloughed off. It will become entirely consistent only when it ceases to grow. Holmes, *The Common Law* 36,37 (1881).

Holmes' recognition of change in the common law was not a call for judicial activism, however, because Holmes emphasized deferring to the dominant political group in society. He said that:

> 'The first requirement of a sound body of law is that it should correspond with the actual feelings and demands of the community, whether right or wrong'. Holmes, *The Common Law* 36 (1881).

Applied to constitutional law, this approach permits greater flexibility for legislatures to experiment with different statutory schemes.

This difference between formalism and Holmesian decisionmaking is most easily seen in the famous case of *Lochner* v. *New York*, 198 U.S. 45 (1905). In that case a majority of the Court held that a maximum hours statute (no more than 60 hours a week) unconstitutionally interfered with the 'liberty of contract' of a master and servant to deal with one another. The phrase 'liberty of contract' was formalistically applied. Holmes' classic dissent, in language now known to every American lawyer, set out a theory on the limits of judicial review that was at odds with formalism. He wrote:

> The liberty of the citizen to do as he likes so long as he does not inter-fere with the liberty of others to do the same, which has been a shib-boleth for some well-known writers, is interfered with by school laws, by the Postoffice, by every state or municipal institution which takes his money for purposes thought desirable, whether he like it or not. The 14th Amendment does not enact Mr. Herbert Spencer's Social Statics .... /A/ constitution is not intended to embody a particular economic theory, whether of paternalism or the organic relation of the citizen to the state or of *laissez faire*. It is made for people of fundamentally differing views, and the accident of our finding certain opinions natural and familiar, or novel, and even shocking, ought not to conclude our judgment upon the question whether statutes embodying them conflict with the Constitution of the United States.

On the theory of judicial review generally, Holmes wrote:

> General propositions do not decide concrete cases. The decision will depend on a judgment or intuition more subtle than any articulate major premise. But I think that the proposition just stated, if it is accepted, will carry us far toward the end. Every opinion tends to become a law. I think that the word 'liberty', in the 14th Amendment, is perverted when it is held to prevent the natural outcome of a domi-nant opinion, unless it can be said that a rational and fair man neces-sarily would admit that the statute proposed would infringe funda-mental principles as they have been understood by the traditions of our people and our law. It does not need research to show that no such sweeping condemnation can be passed on the statute before us. A reasonable man might think it a proper measure on the score of health. Id. at 75 – 76.

Holmes' theory of judicial review was finally adopted by the Court in the 1930s. In *Nebbia* v. *New York*, 291 U.S. 502 (1934), for example, the Court held that so far as Due Process is concerned, a state is free to adopt whatever economic policy may reasonably be deemed to promote public welfare, and it may enforce that policy by legislation adapted to its purpose. Overruling a 1927 decision which found minimum wage legislation unconstitutional as an interference with liberty of contract, the Court said in *West Coast Hotel Co.* v. *Parrish*, 300 U.S. 379 (1937) (a 5 – 4 decision), that,

> /T/he liberty safeguarded /by the 14th Amendment/ is liberty in a social organization which requires the protection of law against the evils which menace the health, safety, morals and welfare of the people. Liberty under the Constitution is thus necessarily subject to the restraints of due process, and regulation which is reasonable in relation to its subject and is adopted in the interests of the community is due process. Id. at 391.

Thus, the Supreme Court in the late 1930s and early 1940s turned away Due Process and Commerce Clause challenges to economic regulation. Since then its approach in that area has been 'hands off', and it has allowed an almost free reign to the legislative process under the Holmesian rational relation test. Not so, however, with regard to legislation that infringes on non-economic liberties. If a law interferes with an individual right which is specifically mentioned in the Constitution or which is considered so fundamental as to be a 'liberty' protected by the Due Process Clause of the Fifth or Fourteenth Amendment, the law will be declared unconstitutional unless it passes a strict scrutiny test. To pass that test the law must be precisely tailored and necessary for a compelling governmental interest. This difference in the standards of review for economic and non-economic rights could occur because the basic perspective of the Court moved from a Holmesian perspective to modern instrumentalism. Justice Cardozo was the primary originator of instrumentalism and thus of the movement away from Holmes. In Cardozo's enormously influential book, *The Nature of the Judicial Process* (1921), he conceded, with Holmes, that precedent was the place to begin a judicial analysis. Cardozo went on to say, however, that greater weight should be given in judicial decisionmaking to what he called the method of sociology – an inquiry into how the law, in its actual functioning, will relate as a means to the welfare of society. Said Cardozo,

> We must keep within those interstitial limits which precedent and custom and the long and silent and almost indefinable practice of other judges through the centuries of the common law have set to judge-made innovations. But within the limits thus set, within the range over which choice moves, the final principle of selection for judges as for legislators, is one of fitness to an end.

Later instrumentalists, such as Chief Justices Stone and Warren, and Justices Brennan and Douglas, gave less emphasis to 'interstitial limits' and greater emphasis to making legislative-like choices on what rules best fit social interests that seem fundamental. Under this theory, a court should also strive to interpret statutes and the Constitution in such a way as to reach a fair and sensible result in terms of dealing with the developing legal and social context, community expectations, and the situation of the parties and others similarly situated.

During the instrumentalist era of our law (the last fifty years), there has been increased protection for personal and civil rights amid growing governmental regulation of economic enterprises and extreme judicial deference to legislative judgments on governmental regulation of economic enterprise. In short, the Surpreme Court has retained a Holmesian 'hands-off' policy with respect economic regulatory legislation. However, it has not given similar deference to legislative judgments in the area of individual non-economic civil rights. Instead, the Court has identified a number of rights as 'fundamental', and has given strict scrutiny to legislation which impinges upon them. The list of protected rights includes interstate travel, *Shapiro* v. *Thompson*, 394 U.S. 618 (1969), the right to vote, *Harper* v. *Virginia State Board of Elections*, 383 U.S. 663 (1966), and certain important personal or family choices (e.g., to bear a child or to have an abortion). This development has created the same tension that existed during the formalist era: how can the Court justify giving special protection to one kind of right (at that time economic rights) without giving similar protection to the other kind of right?

In addition, instrumentalism seems to leave it up to judicial conscience to determine what rights are to be protected − a slender reed and one in tension with the concept of a representative democracy. A clash between Holmesian and instrumentalist judges exists on many courts in the United States today. In the Supreme Court, the main battle ground is over the extent to which, if at all, it can plausibly be maintained with respect to certain alleged rights that they are 'fundamental' or of such special significance that they can properly be regarded as implicitly protected by one or more clauses of the Constitution. Holmesians (such as Justices Rehnquist, Burger, and O'Connor) prefer to test the constitutionality of legislation by applying Holmesian rational basis scrutiny (i.e., asking whether legislators could rationally find that a statute advances legitimate governmental interests). They think it improper to find that a right has greater constitutional protection simply because a majority of the Court thinks it should be regarded as 'fundamental' or of especial significance. See, e.g., Chief Justice Burger's dissent in *Plyler* v. *Doe*, 102 S. Ct. 2382. In contrast, today's instrumentalists (e.g., Justices Brennan and Marshall), when seriously troubled about the predictable consequences of a law for their favored social values, are very likely to find that (1) the law should be interpreted so as not to affect those values or, if that conclusion cannot be avoided, that (2) the law should be declared unconstitutional unless it satisfies 'strict scrutiny' (i.e., is necessary for a compelling governmental interest) or satisfies 'mid-level scrutiny' (i.e., the law is substantially related to a substantial governmental interest). Justices Blackmun and Stevens increasingly side with Justices Brennan and Marshall. Justice White frequently joins Justices Rehnquist, Burger, and O'Connor. That leaves Justice Powell, a moderate, frequently the swing vote on crucial issues.

Moving from individual Justices to critical issues, the Holmesian/Instrumentalist debate boils down in constitutional cases to whether judges will give greatest weight in decision-making to their notions of what is sound social policy, or whether they will give greater weight to values such as certainty, predictability, and the will of the people as manifested in democratically elected legislatures and the text of the Constitution. Instrumentalists on the Supreme Court are more willing to find the constitution flexible – adjustable to the times – and are willing to import into it twentieth century values, as the Justices perceive those values. The Holmesians tend to stick closer to constitutional text and are more apt to defer to the legislature, seeing their function as applying express and clearly implicit constitutional limitations on legislative power and imposing Congressional will upon the States rather than the Supreme Court's will on the country.

The Latest Round on Abortion in the Supreme Court

The analytic framework developed in Part II may help to clarify the present abortion controversy in the United States. In the initial period of natural law and formalism, the emphasis in constitutional interpretation on the purpose of various Constitutional provisions and on a literal reading of the Constitution meant that the existence of an implied constitutional right to have an abortion could not become an issue. Similarly, Holmesian deference to the political process meant that no implied right to an abortion would be found. However, the instrumental period's emphasis on reaching sound social policy results (seen first with respect to decisions affecting reproduction in *Griswold* v. *Connecticut*, supra, and *Eisenstat* v. *Baird* supra), ushered in the new Supreme Court approach and foreshadowed the Court's decision in *Roe* v. *Wade*.

As the Supreme Court is currently constituted, it appears that three classic Holmesian Justices on the Supreme Court (Rehnquist, White, and O'Connor) would be willing to reconsider and possibly overrule *Roe* v. *Wade* if they could obtain two additional votes. In the meantime, via Justice O'Connor's dissent in *Arkon*, supra, they have questioned the trimester approach of *Roe* v. *Wade* and contend that the strict scrutiny standard used in *Roe* should be invoked by the Court only if state law imposes a significant burden on the protected right – a level of burden that they would not easily find. At the same time, it appears that the three most instrumental Justices (Brennan, Marshall, and Stevens) remain firmly committed to the view that *Roe* was correctly decided. That leaves Chief Justice Burger, Justice Blackmun, and Justice Powell as the swing votes. For reasons discussed below, Chief Justice Burger and Justice Blackmun are likely to disagree on the tough cases in this context, leaving Justice Powell as the lone swing vote.

Justice Blackmun's decisions generally reflect a moderate instrumentalist/natural law position. This is particularly clear in Justice Blackmun's opinion for the Court in *Roe*, an opinion neatly poised between instrumental and natural law concerns. Natural law concern with individual liberty supports the aspect of *Roe* which focuses on a women's right to choose to have an abortion, (absent a determination that the fetus is a life with liberty claims of its own). An instrumental concern with social consequences is reflected in that aspect of *Roe* which focuses on the consequences of permitting the State to deny the woman a right to choose an abortion. Said Blackmun:

> The detriment that the State would impose upon the pregnant woman by denying this choice altogether is apperent .... Maternity, or additional offspring, may force upon the woman a distressful life and future. Psychological harm may be imminent. Mental and physical health may be taxed by child care. There is also the distress, for all concerned, associated with the unwanted child, and there is the problem of bringing a child into a family already unable, psychologically or otherwise, to care for it. In other cases, as in this one, the individual difficulties and continuing stigma of unwed motherhood may be involved. 410 U.S. at 153.

It is apparent that Blackmun's opinion blended instrumental concerns over social consequences with arguments not based on such considerations. Both kinds of concern, however, support a woman's right of choice with respect to the issue of abortion and, thus, it is not surprising that Justice Blackmun typically joins with the three instrumental judges to provide a solid fourth vote supporting a woman's right of choice.

Chief Justice Burger is somewhat more difficult to characterize. As Chief Justice, he has the right, when he votes with the majority, to assign the writing of a majority opinion to whichever Justice in the majority he chooses. When five Justices have already formed a majority to resolve a specific case, the Chief Justice sometimes appears to go along with that majority, whatever his actual views, in order to exercise the right to assign the opinion. This right has some value because lower courts and later Supreme Court opinions are influenced in subtle but quite real ways depending on how broad or narrow the opinion for the Court has been written. Thus, it is only when the Court is otherwise split four-to-four that one can be sure that Chief Justice Burger's vote reflects his true sentiments. From this discussion, Chief Justice Burger is best characterized as a Holmesian, perhaps with traces of formalism.

In the area of abortion, Chief Justice Burger's voting pattern is enigmatic because of his concurrence in *Roe* v. *Wade*. Joining the already formed majority in *Roe*, the Chief Justice concurred, as one might predict a Holmesian would, on much narrower grounds than those stated by Justice Blackmun. Burger focused primarily on the right to have an abortion in the case of nonconsensual pregnancies, such as rape or incest, as well as the right to an abortion when the mother's life or health would be seriously compromised by childbirth. He stated that the Court's opinion could not be read to suggest that the Constitution guarantees the right to abortion on demand. Of course, the impact of *Roe* has been to constitutionalize just that principle, at least before the fetus becomes viable. Faced again with abortion issues in the recent term, the Chief Justice again went along with an already formed majority to join in an opinion which emphasized, in part, the importance of adhering to *Roe* v. *Wade* on the grounds of *stare decisis*. The concern with certainty and predictability which underlies the doctrine of *stare decisis* obviously would appeal to a judge who typically votes in a Holmesian or partly formalist style.

Given this line-up, the tension existing on the Court can perhaps best be understood by examining the reasoning of Justice Powell in two recent abortion cases, *Akron* and *Kansas City*. Justice Powell provided the swing vote in each of the cases and wrote the decisive opinion in each case.

In *City of Akron* v. *Akron Center for Reproductive Health*, 103 S. Ct. 2481 (1983), one of the main questions presented was whether a state could require that all abortions after the first trimester be performed in a full-service hospital. The main question in *Planned Parenthood Association of Kansas City* v. *Ashcroft*, 103 S. Ct. 2517 (1983) was whether a state may require the presence of a second physician at all abortions. Deciding that restricting abortions to full-service hospitals was unconstitutional, Powell joined with Brennan, Marshall, Stevens, and Blackmun to settle that aspect of the *Akron* case 5/4. To the contrary, however, he decided in *Kansas City* that a state could require two physicians at all abortions. In upholding the two physicians law involved in *Kansas City*, Justice Powell was joined by Justices Rehnquist, White, and O'Connor, all of whom had dissented in *Akron*, and by Chief Justice Burger. Justice Burger, without opinion, had gone along with the already-formed majority in *Akron*, to invalidate the hospital requirement. However, as noted above, where it made a difference, in the *Kansas City* case, he sided with the Holmesians, as he usually does, to form a different majority upholding the second physician requirement.

Justice Powell, as noted, wrote opinions for both majorities. Each opinion reflected Justice Powell's moderate, common-sense, natural law approach. Thus, in natural law fashion, he focused exclusively on the liberty interests involved in each case and not on the instrumental concerns that also appeared in Blackmun's *Roe* v. *Wade* opinion.

In *Akron*, Justice Powell began by citing *Griswold* and *Roe* for the proposition that central among the liberties protected by the Due Process Clause is an individual's freedom of personal choice in matters of marriage and family life. Thus, state regulation of abortion must be supported by a compelling state interest rather than merely a legitimate interest. The right is not unqualified, he admitted, but restrictive state regulation of the right to choose an abortion must be supported by a compelling state interest, such as an interest in the life of a viable fetus. Also, the state's interest in maternal health becomes compelling only at approximately the end of the first tri-mester (for until then abortions are safer than childbirth). A state may regulate the abortion procedure whenever that reasonably relates to protect-ing maternal health.

Applying those general principles, Powell concluded that the hospital requirement places a significant obstacle in the path of a woman who desires an abortion. He cited testimony in the case which indicated that a second-trimester abortion costs more than twice as much in a hospital as in a clinic. There was also impressive evidence at trial that the most common method of abortion may be performed as safely in an outpatient clinic as at a full-service hospital. By preventing the performance of such abortions in an appropriate nonhospital setting, *Akron* had imposed a heavy and unneces-sary burden on women's access to a relatively inexpensive, otherwise accessible, and safe abortion procedure. On the other hand, said Powell, a second physician may be of assistance to the woman's physician in preserving the health and life of a fetus which survives the abortion procedure. That reasonably furthers the State's compelling interest in protecting the life of a viable fetus and therefore is constitutional.

Justice O'Connor, for the Holmesians, and Justice Blackmun, for himself and the instrumentalists, disagreed with different parts of Justice Powell's reasoning. In support of her conclusion that both statutes were constitu-tional, Justice O'Connor, for the Holmesians, said that before the strict scrutiny standard of 'a compelling state interest' is applied, it should first be necessary to find that a state law imposed a significant burden on the protected right. If a particular regulation does not unduly burden the right, then the Court's evaluation of the regulation should be limited to determining whether the regulation rationally relates to a legitimate state purpose. To support her theory, Justice O'Connor quoted language from several recent cases, e.g., *Bellotti* v. *Baird*, 428 U.S. 132, 147 (1976), *Maher* v. *Roe*, 432 U.S. 464, 473 (1977), and *Harris* v. *McRae*, 448 U.S. 314 (1980), which said that *Roe* protected women from unduly burdensome interference. Justice O'Connor said this indicated that a regulation imposed on a lawful abortion is not unconstitutional unless it unduly burdens the right to seek an abortion. *Roe* v. *Wade*, she said, did not declare an unqualified constitutional right to an abortion. Rather, it was only intended to protect against state action that drastically limited the availability and safety of the desired service.

Among an array of statements from previous cases that she analyzed in support of her interpretation of *Roe*, Justice O'Connor included a statement by Justice Powell that,

> 'In my view, /*Roe* and *Griswold*/ make clear that the /compelling state interest/ standard has been invoked only when the state regulation entirely frustrates or heavily burdens the exercise of constitutional rights in this area'. *Carey* v. *Population Services International*, 431 U.S. 678, 705 (1977).

Questioning the trimester framework of *Roe*, Justice O'Connor said that the 'unduly burdensome' test standard should be applied to challenged regulations throughout the entire pregnancy without reference to the particular stage of pregnancy involved because of the limited nature of the fundamental right that has been recognized and because the trimester framework is unworkable. With respect to workability of the trimester framework she explained that as the medical risks of various abortion procedures decrease, the point at which the State may regulate for reasons of maternal health is moved further forward toward actual childbirth. However, as medical science becomes better able to provide for the separate existence of the fetus, the point of viability is moved further back towards conception. She added,

> /I/t is clear that the trimester approach violates the fundamental aspiration of judicial decision making through the application of neutral principles 'sufficiently absolute to give them roots throughout the community and continuity over significant periods of time ...'. A. Cox, The Role of the Supreme Court in American Government 114 (1976).

Justice O'Connor was thus concerned that the trimester approach would not yield certain and predictable rules, rules 'sufficiently absolute to give them roots' – a basic concern for Holmesians.

Applying the above analysis, Justice O'Connor said that a hospitalization requirement is not unduly burdensome. The Court's concern about increased costs was misplaced, she added, because almost any state regulation increases costs. A health regulation, she said, simply does not rise to the level of official interference with the abortion decision. The second physician requirement is constitutional because the state possesses a compelling interest extant throughout pregnancy in protecting and preserving fetal life.

In reply, Justice Powell said that Justice O'Connor's analysis was wholly incompatible with the existence of the fundamental right recognized in *Roe*. The cost and limited availability of general hospitals is such, he said, that the dissenters' views would drive the performance of many abortions back underground free of effective regulation and often without the attendance of a physician. Further, he added, the dissent would uphold virtually any abortion-inhibiting regulation because of the State's interest is preserving potential life. Justice Powell thus questioned the rationality behind Justice O'Connor's assertion that the cost of requiring performance of abortions in a hospital was insignificant (recall that concern with rationality is an important aspect of natural law decision-making). Justice Powell also questioned the extreme Holmesian deference in Justice O'Connor's opinion to decisions of the political process.

Justice Blackmun's dissenting opinion on the second physician issue pointed out that the most commonly used method of second-trimester abortion entails no chance of fetal survival. Accordingly, he said, the second physician requirement is irrational and overbroad in that it imposes burdens on women in some cases where the burden is not justified. Also, the statute's failure to provide a clear exception for emergency situations renders it unconstitutional. Thus, reflecting his moderately natural law views, Justice Blackmun disagreed with Justice Powell over the rationality of the second doctor provision. If no chance of fetal survival exists, it is not rational for a state to require the presence of a second doctor to help ensure that survival.

The Future

What is suggested about the future by the above and by other current events? Several proposals have been introduced in Congress to overrule *Roe v. Wade* by amending the Constitution. On 19 April 1983, the full Senate Judiciary Committee, after deadlocking 9–9, sent without recommendation to the floor of the Senate a proposed constitutional amendment which stated that, 'A right to abortion is not secured by the Constitution'. The Senate rejected the amendment in a 50–49 vote on 28 June 1983, and thus it fell eighteen votes short. (Under Article V of the Constitution, Congress can propose an

Amendment by a two thirds vote of both the Senate and the House of Representatives). Proposed amendments to create constitutional rights in the unborn have been introduced and referred to the House and Senate Judicial Committees. President Reagan has said that he prefers to leave abortion to the states and would support a constitutional amendment to that effect. In view of the Senate vote, however, it does not seem likely that any abortion amendment will be passed by Congress in the near future.

If President Reagan is elected to a second term, it is probable that he will have several opportunities to appoint new Justices since five members of the present Court are age seventy-five or older. It does not seem likely that any specific legal issue would be used by the President as a litmus test for the selection of new Justices. Nevertheless, given President Reagan's propensity to appoint Holmesian conservatives, it is likely that his future Supreme Court appointments will bring to the Court, as did Justice O'Connor, something other than strong pro-abortion perspectives.

Public opinion polls in the United States consistently report that more than sixty percent of the people favor allowing a woman to have an abortion if she so desires. Further, it has been estimated that about half of all pregnancies are now being terminated by abortions. The public will in the United States gets served by its government – if not promptly, then eventually. Thus, the Supreme Court's current pattern of decisions, a compromise resolution of the problems, is likely to be retained – although given the Supreme Court's current and probable future personnel, the states probably will be allowed more and more room to regulate, particularly if President Reagan is re-elected. If a Democratic President is elected in 1984, any new Justices would likely be Instrumentalists. This would solidify *Roe* v. *Wade*.

Over the long-run (twenty-five years or so), the possibility should be mentioned that the present unstructured natural law perspectives of Justices Powell and Blackmun will become more explicitly defined. Though no new Holmes or Cardozo has emerged, a number of scholarly writings have laid a foundation for the emergence of a new natural law perspective on decision-making.

If a natural law approach to decision-making emerges, what is likely to be its impact on abortion cases? What would be thought on this topic by rational persons thinking rationally?

Several things are clear. If a pregnant woman is not allowed to carry out her decision to have an abortion, there will be an unwanted child. There will be a number of adverse consequences for the mother and the child and, possibly, for other family members, as Justice Blackmun pointed out in *Roe* v. *Wade*.

From a natural law perspective, such considerations are not decisive. The relevant question is the liberty interest of the mother and the liberty interest of the fetus if it is determined that the fetus is a human life. If a unique, individual soul is denied life by an abortion, then abortion would violate the standard of protecting natural life; if not, not. From this perspective, the abortion issue is particularly intractible because of the lack of agreed-upon empirical tests to resolve the problem. According to one natural law approach, perhaps styled religious natural law, and based on some concept of faith, a unique living soul arises in a fetus at the moment of conception. From another perspective, perhaps styled natural rights, and based on western science, a life does not exist until a fetus is capable of independent life – that is, until it is viable. Until then, it is merely potential life, with a probability of eventual life, much as an egg or sperm cell has a probability of potential life, but not more.

In *Roe* v. *Wade*, the Court avoided choosing between these two views. Justice Blackmun said that the Court did not have to decide when life began because the constitutional question was to identify who are 'persons' within the meaning of the Fourteenth Amendment. After examining traditional and current state law on the rights of the unborn, Justice Blackmun concluded that the 'persons' protected by the Fourteenth Amendment do not include the unborn. Thus, the unborn have no constitutional rights to be weighed in the balance.

From a pure natural law perspective, however, the issue will have to be faced on its own terms. Since the basic points of view involve religious beliefs, and strong organizations hold opposing views, it seems likely that the matter will continue to be felt as a problem that cannot be accommodated by a single, clear solution. As long as the evidence remains unclear, it is likely that the fundamental natural law concern with liberty and autonomy will continue to lead the Court to conclude that the people, through their legislature, should not be able to impose majoritarian views on when life begins. For most people, however, the situation will continue to include an unresolvable doubt unless a strongly held religious view creates a faith-based certainty.

In conclusion, it appears that if indeed a natural law perspective begins to influence Supreme Court decisions on other matters by giving greater weight to individual autonomy interests which do not cause injury to other persons, that perspective would not resolve definitively the underlying issue involved in the abortion controversy. It would, however, support a redefinition of the issue away from the social consequences of unwanted pregnancies or the value of deferring to political processes. The Court would be guided by a natural law perspective towards more direct consideration of the life and liberty interests of the parties concerned. Since two versions of natural law currently exist (religious natural law and natural rights), and they lead toward opposite conclusions, the abortion issue would probably remain controversial in the absence of startling new discoveries or insights not now foreseeable.

In the meantime, pending any new discoveries or insights, all participants can agree on the positive benefits to be obtained from working toward changing the underlying social situation to help insure that unwanted pregnancies do not occur. Given that result, the issue of abortion would disappear from the national scene because few woman who became pregnant would wish to seek an abortion. Judges and citizens of all persuasions can certaintly agree that making the abortion issue moot should be the ultimate goal of all our efforts in this area.

Italy

Giovanni Bognetti, Professor of Law, University of Milan

Introduction

Since the advent of Christianity, through the Middle Ages and modern times, voluntary abortion was considered a serious crime by the law in force in the various regions of Italy. As is well known, the old English Common Law seems to have regarded the abortion procured or consented to by the woman as a crime only after the 'quickening' of the fetus and, even with respect to that, the law was not clear, so that voluntary abortion was practically made with certainty a punishable offense only by legislation enacted in England and in the United States during the nineteenth century. On the European continent, and in any case in Italy, the law always had been clear. The law would punish abortion performed both after and before 'quickening' (although with different penalties; after the '*animatio*' of the fetus, abortion was equated to homicide and punished by death). The law would punish both the consenting woman and all who participated in procuring the abortion. It did not contemplate any justifying circumstances.[1]

The traditional severity of the law in matters of abortion was approved and continued (death penalty apart) by the new Italian state born out of unification in 1861. The Italian Penal Code of 1889 held abortion a crime punishable by imprisonment: the woman was to be imprisoned from one to four years (Article 381); all other persons who had participated or aided, from thirty months to five years. Forty years later, the fascist Penal Code of 1930 made the penalties heavier; it inflicted imprisonment from two to five years on persons procuring the abortion of a consenting woman as well as on the woman herself (Article 546). It maintained the penalty of imprisonment from one to four years only for the woman who had acted alone (Article 547). Neither the Code of 1889 nor the Code of 1930 distinguished between abortions in the early and in the later stages of pregnancy: all were, in principle, punished alike. No specific justification was admitted. Court decisions, however, would excuse the woman (and those who helped her) if the abortion was committed to save the woman's life, and this on the ground of the general exculpating principle of 'action taken in a state of necessity'

Comparative Law Yearbook, Volume 7, 1983. ISBN 90-247-2966-1.
© *1984, Martinus Nijhoff Publishers, Dordrecht. Printed in the Netherlands.*

(Article 54 of the 1930 Code). The principle of 'necessity', on the other hand, was given here a very narrow scope of application. Abortion was justified only if the life of the woman was in immediate danger and if there was absolutely no other means than pregnancy interruption to prevent the death of the woman. (It was accordingly ruled, for instance, that the serious danger of a woman committing suicide as a consequence of the continuation of pregnancy would not meet the requirements of the principle, inasmuch as suicide could be prevented, in the abstract, otherwise than through abortion).[2]

The law of the Penal Code continued to be applied whenever abortions were discovered and recognized as unmistakably voluntary, even after World War II. The soundness of the law was not contested until 1970. Catholic jurists sometimes objected to the fact that incriminating norms were included in the Code under the title dedicated to the protection of 'the integrity and the health of the race' (a way of envisaging the problem of abortions that aptly fitted the fascist table of values). They claimed that voluntary abortions were instead a crime against the person of the fetus. But the criticism was mainly of a doctrinal and abstract nature; it did not call into question the appropriateness or the excessive severity of the law. For all practical purposes, public opinion acquiesced in the law for more than two decades after the end of the war. When opinion started moving against it, it took two different lines of action: that of contesting the constitutionality of the law with the Constitutional Court and that of fostering statutory reform.

The 1975 Decision of the Constitutional Court

In Italy, courts did not have the power to declare statutes unconstitutional under the regime of liberal monarchy (nor obviously did they have it under fascism). The republican Constitution of 1948 introduced judicial review but in the form of a new institution invented and first tried in Europe by the Austrian Constitution of 1920: a special court, endowed with the special power of review and composed of justices appointed for a twelve – (later nine) – year term, part by Parliament, part by the President of the Republic, part by the Judiciary. The new court had a difficult beginning. It was fully organized and began functioning only in 1956, because of delays due to fears in the political class that it could disturb the delicate balance of the Italian political system. Democracy rested in Italy upon thin foundations. Among other things, a large fraction of the electorate (approximately twenty-five percent) voted for the Communist Party which in many respects was considered – and was – an 'anti-system' party. A court wielding the tremendous power to declare statutes unconstitutional was a potential risk for the stability and the image of the Government: hence, the hesitation in setting it up. When it was finally allowed to work, the Court's own perception of the facts that had retarded its coming into being reflected upon the quality of its work. Not that the Court chose to efface itself as a policy-making organ of the state. Instead, it showed from the beginning a tendency to act as a serious defender of human rights, making use of all the relevant clauses of the Constitution. But its role was marked from the beginning – and it has always been so marked even later – by a cautious attitude. The United States Supreme Court and the Constitutional Court of Federal Germany have at times boldly challanged the Government and public opinion, forcing upon the legal system solutions that popular majorities highly disliked. This has never been done by the Italian Court. For reasons that have to do with the political, cultural and social background of a weak democracy, the Italian Court has displayed an almost structural repugnance against bold 'activism'. Its permanent attitude through the years has been one of moderate self-restraint.[3]

The behavior of the Court with respect to the constitutional problems of abortion fully corresponds to this assessment of its performance in general and it can be pointed out as one of the most emblematic expressions of the Court's ingrained vocation to avoid decisive commitments. A brief comment on its decision of 1975 will supply evidence for this.

In the early 1970s, several 'progressive' groups began questioning the constitutionality of the existing law of abortion on various grounds. Some contended that the law did not allow for causes of justification that were implicitly sanctioned by the constitutionally-protected right of the woman to health (Constitution, Article 32). Others – among whom were representatives of the 'Partito radicale' – suggested that freedom of abortion was one of those rights of the woman that the Constitution tacitly protects through its general clause on the 'inviolable rights of the person' (Article 2). The example of the United States decision Roe v. Wade (1973) was invoked. These arguments did not remain without an answer. On the opposite side, conservative Catholics maintained that any substantial liberalization of the law of abortion not only was not required by the Constitution but it would run directly against it. In fact, the very clause of Article 2 that was adduced by the radicals as ground for an alleged right of the woman to free abortion was held by them to give constitutional dimensions to the right of the embryo to life. As the life of the unborn was constitutionally protected, it had to be defended through criminal sanctions and it could be sacrified, if at all, only and strictly to save the life of the mother. Up to a certain point, this was the line of reasoning that the German Constitutional Court would adopt shortly thereafter in its decision of February 1975 when it struck down the liberalizing reform of Article 218 of the German Penal Code.

The Italian Constitutional Court was seized with the question of the constitutionality of Article 456 of the 1930 Penal Code in 1972 by an ordinary
judge called upon to apply the law to a woman who had had an abortion
without her life being in danger. The judge raised the question with reference
to the possible violation of Article 32 of the Constitution. The Court post-
poned deciding until 1975; when it rendered its decision, it took an almost
salomonic position.

On the one hand, the Court pleased the Catholic supporters of the 'right
to life' by stating that the unborn had indeed a constitutional right under
Article 2 of the Constitution. On the other hand, that right was declared to
be not absolute. It had to be balanced against the rights of the pregnant
woman. Among the woman's rights was not only her own right to life but
also a right to health. Thus, the Court was able to please also the votaries of
liberalization. It held that the principle of 'necessity' did not provide
sufficient protection to the woman's constitutional rights and that Article
456 of the Penal Code was unconstitutional to the extent that it did not allow
for an abortion in cases where the continuation of pregnancy would
seriously endanger the physical health or the psychic equilibrium of the
woman (Decision Number 27 of 1975).[4]

The decision, with respect to the existing law, enlarged the area of justified
abortions. But it did so very cautiously, without acknowledging any right of
the woman to 'privacy' in the sense of *Roe* v. *Wade*,[5] without giving any hint
that the Court would go farther than its present ruling in the future, and
leaving in addition the impression that a possible abrogation by statute of
criminal sanctions against abortion not justified by situations of danger for
the life or the health of the mother might be held by the Court to be against
the Constitution. To be sure, the Court did not state the latter principle in so
many words. It did not openly tie together the protection of the life of the
unborn and the infliction of penalties upon unjustified abortionists (the way
the German Court was doing in its almost contemporary decision). But it
laid such a stress on the need that there be adequate checking of the existence
of the alleged danger for the woman in order for the abortion to be 'lawful'
in the eyes of criminal law that an inference in that sense was almost suggested. The decision was highly equivocal. It spoke of an 'inviolable' right of
the unborn as a human being while denying him the quality of a 'person' in
the full sense of the word. It declared the right to life of the unborn less
worthy than the psychic welfare of the mother while insisting on the duty of
the state to provide serious protection of that 'inviolable' right. It did not
acknowledge – but neither did it exclude expressly – a constitutionally-
protected 'right to privacy' of the woman. The equivocal nature of the
decision was probably the effect of the Court's choice not to take upon itself
the burden to solve a thorny, highly controversial political issue that

threatened to dangerously divide the country. The issue of divorce had torn the country apart only a few years before.[6] The Court did not wish to be the umpire in the new struggle that was being engaged between the Catholics and their adversaries. It issued a decision which could be read in different ways. Somehow, it called itself out of the game.

The Statutory Reform of 1978

The forces that wanted a serious reform of the law quickly realized that little was to be expected at this point from the Constitutional Court. They turned to Parliament to get a convenient liberalization through statute.[7]

In Parliament, the Christian Democratic Party and the '*Movimento sociale*' (Neofascist Party) immediately objected to all projects aimed at seriously liberalizing the law beyond what the decision of the Constitutional Court had already done. They cited that very decision in support of the contention that the Constitution required voluntary abortion to be regarded as a crime except in extraordinary cases. However, all the other parties – Liberals, Republicans, Social-Democrats, Socialists, and Communists – formed a majority, and they were able to pass a law whose principles are even more 'liberal' than those of the French law of 1975 and almost as 'liberal' as the Austrian law of 1974. The majority pointed out that the Court's decision could, after all, bear also a different reading from that suggested by the Christian Democrats and the Neo-Fascists and that the mass of clandestine illegal abortions performed in Italy was enormous,[8] so that it was proved that the existing law (or any law along similar lines) could not constitute a real barrier against the sad phenomenon. Under such circumstances, it was better to make a new law that would at least induce women on one hand to avoid clandestine practice and on the other hand, as far as possible, to accept voluntarily to continue and complete unwelcome pregnancies.

The statute carrying new rules 'on social protection of maternity and on voluntary termination of pregnancy' was promulgated on 22 May 1978 (*Legge* number 194 of 1978).[9] Its main principles can be summarized as follows:

(a) Article 1 of the statute lays down the solemn principle that the state 'guarantees the right to responsible procreation, recognizes the social value of maternity and protects human life from its very beginning'. It also says that 'the voluntary termination of pregnancy, as defined in the present statute, is not a means to achieve birth control' and that the state, the regions and other local authorities are held to promote the creation of adequate socio-sanitary services that will facilitate avoiding the use of abortion as a way to contain births. In view of what subsequent statutory rules provide, Ariticle 1 seems to have mainly rhetorical or, at best, hortatory value. The principle that 'the state ... protects human life from its beginning' is practically rendered nugatory — as we shall see — by the rules of Articles 4, 5 and 8. It has, therefore, been included in the law only to pay lip-service to the *dicta* of the 1975 Constitutional Court decision and in order to sooth and propitiate the conservative side of public opinion.

(b) Article 4 provides that 'within ninety days from the beginning of pregnancy the woman who believes that the continuation of pregnancy, or delivery, or maternity, would constitute a serious danger to her life or physical or psychic health — either on account of her state of health or of her economic or social or family conditions, or of the circumstances of conception, or of fears of malformation or abnormalities in the fetus — can address herself to a family advisory bureau or to an authorized socio-sanitary unit or to a physician of her choice' and ask to be allowed to abort.[10] According to Article 5, the advisory bureau, the socio-sanitary unit and the physician have a duty to make all the appropriate medical inquiries and to examine with the woman the possible ways of removing the causes that are inducing her to have an abortion. They must apprise her of the rights she enjoys to social benefits and to social aid under the existing laws and of all other relevant legal and non-legal opportunities she as a mother (or the child) might have. When they find out that 'conditions exist that make the abortion urgent', they issue a certificate to that effect. If they do not so find, and the woman insists on having the abortion alleging the circumstances mentioned in Article 4, they issue a document, which the woman must sign, attesting the request of the woman and inviting her to abstain from action for seven days. Upon presentation to the medical centers authorized by law to terminate pregnancies of the certificate of 'urgency' or, after seven days, of the document just mentioned, the woman has a right to obtain the abortion. The termination of pregnancy must take place (Article 8) either in a public general hospital (which is held to perform the operation, if duly requested) or in a public special hospital, in a hospital run by a recognized ecclesiastical institution, in an authorized private clinic (provided they have decided to perform abortions: they are free not to effect that kind of operation and must ask for a permit in order to be allowed to). From the combined dispositions of Articles 4, 5 and 8, it appears clearly that the law somehow intends to subject early voluntary abortions to some sort of public control, but that in the end it makes the final decision rest exclusively with the woman. Indeed, no authority has the power to stop the woman, even if it is certain that 'the grave danger to her health', upon which Article 4 seems to make the lawfulness of abortion dependent, does not exist at all. After a seven-day delay from the consultation with the advisory bureau, the socio-sanitary unit, or the physician, the woman is in any case entitled to obtain the abortion; and, once the abortion is performed, she cannot be brought in any way to answer for a possible violation of Article 4 (in case of actual lack of the alleged 'danger'). The law does not even try seriously to have her exposed to pressures meant to dissuade her from a hasty decision. In fact, the woman is allowed to avoid the possibly unpleasant contact with public agencies (the family advisory bureau, the socio-sanitary unit) by choosing an easier consultation with a physician she trusts. She can also choose to have the operation performed in a private clinic. In addition, the identity of the woman who gets an abortion must remain strictly secret: a secret protected by serious penal sanctions against all who divulge her name or facts that may lead to her name (Article 21). There is little doubt that the regulation of voluntary abortion within ninety days from conception provided by Articles 4, 5 and 8 does not meet the requirement laid down by the 1975 decision of the Constitutional Court that the law protect the life of the unborn by establishing a system of serious checks upon the alleged 'danger' to the health of the mother. The statute of 1978 not only does not punish first tri-mester abortions that have been decided without the justification of a real 'danger' for the woman. It does not even care to compel the woman to go through a process of strict screening of her allegations; nor does it provide non-penal sanctions in case the choice she makes to abort has no other ground than her caprice. The protection the statute accords to the life of the unborn is therefore, to speak frankly, so weak as to be practically illusory. If the above rules of the Italian statute cannot be considered in harmony with the *dicta* of the Constitutional Court decision of 1975, they are, however, in line with the trend of reforms brought about by other European legal systems during the 1960s and 1970s with regard to the law concerning voluntary abortions in the early stages of pregnancy.

(c) After the first trimester, pregnancy can be terminated only if its continuation seriously threatens the life of the woman or when 'pathological processes' — among which in particular those relative to important malformations or abnormalities of the fetus — create a serious danger to the physical or psychic health of the woman (Article 6). The existence of such threat to life and of such 'pathological processes' must be certified by a physician of the hospital or authorized clinic where the operation will take place (Article 7).

(d) If a voluntary abortion is performed during the first trimester of pregnancy without compliance with the procedures contemplated in Articles 5 and 8, it is a crime. The woman is fined up to 100,000 *lire* (less than 100 United States dollars). Other people who aided or abetted are punished by imprisonment up to three years (Article 19). If a voluntary abortion is performed after the first trimester, in the absence of the circumstances described in Article 6, or if the procedure of Article 7 is not followed, it is a crime. The woman is punished by imprisonment up to six months; other participants, by imprisonment from one to four years (Article 19). The procedures contemplated in Articles 5, 7 and 8 are, of course, not obligatory when an immediate intervention is necessary to save the life of the woman. But the health officer in the province must then be informed (Article 7).

(e) To request to be allowed to abort is a personal decision of the woman. The father of the unborn can be admitted to the consultations that article 5 prescribes only if the woman consents (Article 5). If the woman requesting the abortion is less than eighteen years old, she must have, in principle, the consent of those persons exercising parental power. However, that consent is not necessary in case of abortions performed after the first trimester according to the rules of Articles 6 and 7. In first trimester abortions, the advisory bureau, the socio-sanitary unit or the physician, may for special reasons decide not to inform the persons exercising parental power at all, or disregard their refusal to consent. In such cases, the abortion must be authorized by a judge. No consent or authorization is required if a physician certifies that it is urgent to intervene to protect the health (the health: not the life only) of the minor (Article 12).

(f) Physicians, nurses and other personnel are not held to take part in the procedures of Articles 5 and 7 as well as in the operations to terminate pregnancies, if they raise conscientious objection through a previous, general declaration to that effect. The objection cannot be invoked to justify abstaining from cooperating in abortions necessary to save the life of the woman. The right to abstain is forfeited if the physician or the nurse participates in any procedure or intervention aiming at bringing about an abortion. If the participation by the conscientious objector concerns an abortion that is punished as a crime, the penalties are aggravated (Article 9).

(g) All expenses arising out of the consultations and medical examinations of Articles 5 and 7 and of the interventions performed in the hospitals and clinics indicated in Article 8 are to be born by the social security system or by the regions – presently they are all taken care of by the national health system (Article 10).

Subsequent Developments

Statute Number 194 of 1978 has not been amended in subsequent years and is, therefore, the law presently in force in Italy with respect to voluntary abortions. Some events, however, took place after 1978 which are worth a brief mention because they cast interesting light on the present attitude of the Italian people toward abortions, on some practical problems raised by the application of Statute Number 194, and, finally, on the evolution of the Constitutional Court jurisprudence on the subject.

The enactment of Statute Number 194 aroused the impassioned reaction of many Catholics because they thought the law negated, in fact, the inviolable rights of the unborn. In Italy, it is possible to abrogate statutory norms through popular referendum.[11] In 1980, a group of citizens requested, in due form, that a referendum be held on a proposition to abrogate several dispositions of Statute Number 194 so that only voluntary abortions truly performed to save the life or health of the woman would be exempted from punishment. Another group, composed of Catholic extremists, asked in turn for another referendum on a harsher proposition, aiming at making all abortion, without *any* exception, a crime.

Statute Number 194 did not satisfy the radicals of '*Partito radicale*' either. They claimed that the freedom of the woman to decide about herself and her body was still unjustly encroached upon by a law that did not make all voluntary abortions entirely free. They also pointed out several practical defects in the law. There, were, for instance, serious difficulties in some parts of the country for a woman to obtain an abortion according to the procedures described by the statute because of lack of adequate staff in hospital and clinics, owing to the great number of physicians and nurses who had exercised the right conferred by the law to raise conscientious objection. For reasons of principle and for practical reasons, radicals proposed, therefore, to put to the people the question of the abrogation of all the statutory rules in force limiting in any way the freedom of the woman, regardless whether the abortion took place in the first trimester or after.

For a question to be submitted to the judgment of the people in referendum, a previous decision of admissibility by the Constitutional Court is necessary under Italian law. The Court must check, among other things, whether the proposed abrogation would bring about a situation in the legal system in conflict with the Constitution. If so, admissibility must be denied.

The Constitutional Court (Decision Number 26 of 1981) ruled that the 'radical' referendum as well as the first 'Catholic' referendum, intended to limit, but not to eliminate entirely the lawfulness of voluntary abortions, were admissible. The Court instead declared inadmissible the second 'Catholic' referendum, because the effect of a favorable popular vote on it would be to deny the woman the right to get an abortion even when her life or health are seriously at stake, which would be tentamount to depriving her of constitutionally protected rights.[12]

On the surface, Decision Number 26 of 1981 seems to reaffirm, through the ruling on the second 'Catholic' proposal, the principles the Court had laid down in its decision of 1975. In reality, the Court silently takes a great step beyond that decision. By admitting the 'radical' referendum, the Court implicitly ruled that an unlimited freedom of the woman to perform or have performed upon herself an abortion, at whatever stage of her pregnancy, is a legal situation not conflicting, *per se*, with the Constitution. Such a doctrine, however, is clearly irreconcilable with the *dicta* of the 1975 decision that held the Constitution to require a serious protection of the 'inviolable' right of the unborn.

Decision Number 26 of 1981 must be regarded as a careful adjustment of the Court's jurisprudence to the developments that had meanwhile occurred in the legal system and, above all, in public opinion. After decision Number 27 of 1975, Parliament had voted the reform statute of 1978: a sign that there was in the country a majority favorable to a liberal treatment of voluntary abortions. Polls seemed to confirm that trend in public opinion. Consequently, the Court, in 1981, decided to drop, without saying it, the *dicta* of 1975 on the rights of the unborn. It did not suggest that there is a constitutional right of the woman to free abortion (indeed, that is practically excluded by the ruling admitting the first 'Catholic' referendum). But a choice of the people (or of the Legislator) to totally liberalize the law of abortion would not encounter the Court's blames. In sum, Decision Number 26 of 1981 is another expression of that attitude of self-restraint and adaptation to the country's prevailing trends which had already permeated the decision of 1975. Of course, something had changed since then in the country and in the law: and the Court had to adjust somehow, if it wanted to keep out of the struggle, in a sort of neutral position, its posture.

The Court's choice to avoid friction with the will of the majority while at the same time shunning a neat commitment in favor of liberal principle is confirmed by another decision of the same year (Number 108 of 1981).[13] Article 22 of *Legge* Number 194 of 1978 exempts from punishment all voluntary abortions performed before 1978 under the abrogated rule of Article 456 of the Penal Code, provided the judge finds that the exculpatory circumstances defined in Articles 4 and 6 of the statute were existing. Called upon to try cases of abortions occurred before 1978, some judges referred to the Constitutional Court the question whether the application of the exculpatory circumstances of Articles 4 and 6, prescribed by the law, would not offend the Constitution, inasmuch as it would deprive the unborn of that 'serious protection' of its constitutional rights that the Court itself had vouched in 1975. The Constitutional Court refused to enter the merit of the question on the ground that to declare unconstitutional Articles 4 and 6 would be tentamount for the Court, in the cases under judgment, to creating a new figure of crime, which would be contrary to the constitutional principle of legality (crimes can be legally defined only by statute). As the ground adduced by the Court seems to be of very dubious value (and is probably erroneous altogether), Decision Number 108 stands only for the stern determination of the Court not to let itself be dragged to pass judgment on the constitutionality of the liberalization brought about by the statute of 1978. The Court now considers that liberalization constitutional. But it does not want to hurt Catholic feelings by saying it openly, and so it has chosen to validate the reform statute indirectly, through a refusal to judge.[14] After Decision Number 108 of 1981, it is unlikely that the constitutional question of the insufficient protection of the unborn under Statute Number 194 will ever again reach the Constitutional Court or that the Court will anyway rule anew on it. For all practical purposes, that question is now settled in Italian law.

In May 1981, the Italian people, voting in the *referenda* the Court had amitted, rejected both the 'radical' and the 'Catholic' proposition by overwhelming majorities (the vote was, respectively, eighty percent and seventy percent against). Statute Number 194, after the implicit *nihil obstat* by the Court, thus received an indirect and yet significant endorsement by the public.

Notes

1. See Pertile, b*toria del diritto italiano*, 9 Volumes, Volume 5 (Torino: Utet, 1892), pp. 588 ff.; Marongiu, 'Aborto (Storia)', *Enciclopedia del diritto* (Milano: Giuffrè, 1958), Volume 1, p. 126. In the pre-Christian classical world, voluntary abortion was not considered a crime. See Nardi, *Procurato aborto nel mondo greco-romano* (Milano: Giuffrè, 1971).
2. See Tribunale Milano, *ordinanza* of 2 October 1972, in *Giurisprudenza Costituzionale* (1973), pp. 125 ff.; Bognetti, 'Esperienze straniere: la libertà di abortire, diritto della donna costituzionalmente garantito', *Rivista Italiana di Diritto e Procedura penale* (1974), Volume 17, pp. 8, 44.
3. Bognetti, 'The Political Role of the Italian Constitutional Court', *Notre Dame Lawyer* (1974), Volume 49, p. 981.
4. *Giurisprudenza Costituzionale* (1975), Volume 20, I, p. 117. See also *L'aborto nelle sentenze delle Corti Costituzionali. U.S.A., Austria, Francia, Republica Federale Tedesca, Italia* (Milano: Giuffrè, 1976), p. 327.
5. It must be kept in mind, however, that the Court was not held, strictly speaking, to address itself to that problem, inasmuch as the question of constitutionality had been raised only with reference to Article 32, and not to Article 2, of the Constitution. But the Court could, of course, have alluded to the woman's right to 'privacy' in *dictum*.
6. Divorce had been introduced for the first time into the Italian legal system in 1970 (*Legge*, Number 898, 1 December 1970).
7. Actually, they first tried to get it through the presentation in 1975 of a referendum proposition. The referendum was in the end not held because meanwhile Parliament had approved in 1978 Statute Number 194. See *Giurisprudenza Costituzionale* (1980), Volume 25, I, p. 218.
8. It ranged apparently in the numbers of more than one million a year. *Atti parlamentari*, VI L., Number 3435, p. 3.
9. A commentary on Statute Number 194 is provided by Galli, Italia, Realmonte, Spina,

Traverso, *L'interruzione volontaria della gravidanza* (Milano: Giuffrè, 1978).

10. Family advisory bureaus (*consultori familiari*) have been organized under Law Number 405 of 29 July 1975 as agencies meant to advise couples and singles in matters concerning sex, generation, and health. They are composed of physicians, psychologists, social workers. Socio-sanitary units (*strutture socio-sanitarie*) are agencies which, under the control of the regions, are meant to provide social assistance and first medical aid.

11. Constitution, Article 75. It must be remarked that the people by referendum can only abrogate existing norms; they cannot vote on a proposition introducing a new disposition into the legal system. Hence the special difficulties, existing in Italy, in shaping referendum questions that suit the final objectives of the initiators. But these have acquired great skill in phrasing propositions that, by cutting down the existing norms in the right measure, will bring about, if accepted by the people, the results desired by them.

12. *Giurisprudenza Costituzionale* (1981), Volume 26, I, pp. 134 ff.

13. Id., p. 908.

14. Instead, a direct validation has been granted by the Court to the special rules concerning minors (Article 12 of Statute Number 194) in Decision Number 109 of 1981. *Giurisprudenza costituzionale* (1981), Volume 26, I, p. 948. Those rules do not offend, in themselves, against the principle of equality or the constitutional principles concerning parental power.

Part II

Significant Developments
in Private International Law

SIGNIFICANT DEVELOPMENTS IN PRIVATE INTERNATIONAL LAW

The following survey and analysis of significant and recent developments in the sector of private international law has been prepared by and is published in cooperation with the Pacific International Law Society, a member of the Association of Student International Law Societies with offices at the University of the Pacific, McGeorge School of Law, 3200 Fifth Avenue, Sacramento, CA 95817, U.S.A. Special appreciation is expressed to Professor Stephen McCaffrey of McGeorge School of Law and Professor Jack J. Coe Jr., Assistant Director, McGeorge International Programs, for their assistance in this project.

Editor-in-Chief

Patrick T. Markham

Editors

Emma L. Childers	Jean S. Heselden
Thomas Keith Fraser	Andrea C. Thompson

Writers

Kevin Briggs	*Commercial Law*
	(1) Arbitration
	(2) Banking
Ulrich W. Smith	(3) Multilateral Trade
	(4) Transportation
Thomas Keith Fraser	(5) Admiralty
Dana M. Beernink	(6) Contracts
Steve Benton	(7) Taxation
Kathleen Ann Iriguchi	*Intellectual Property Rights*
Thomas Keith Fraser	*Antitrust*
Sally F. Cunningham	*Procedure*
John D. Robinson	*Domestic Relations*
	Treatment of Aliens
Sussana Reyes	(1) Asylum
Sussana Reyes, Kathleen Ann Iriguchi	(2) Corporate Nationality

COMMERCIAL LAW

(1) Arbitration

United Kingdom

Recent British cases have dealt principally with the autonomy of arbitrators and the limits of judicial review of their decisions.

In *Paal Wilson and Co.* v. *Partenreederei Hannah Blumethal*[1] the court had to decide whether long delay in bringing a matter to arbitration frustrates the agreement to arbitrate. The lower English courts (both the High Court and the Court of Appeal) sought to distinguish this case from the unpopular decision in *Bremer Vulkan* v. *South India Shipping Corp,*[2] which held that arbitrations could not be abandoned even after an unduly long delay. The House of Lords, however, unanimously reaffirmed that decision stating that an agreement to arbitrate is not frustrated by delay though such delay may make a fair trial impossible. Instead, both parties have a duty to approach the arbitrator for directions to end the delay.[3]

In *Moran* v. *Lloyd's,*[4] an underwriter employed by Lloyd's insurance syndicate was found guilty of 'discreditable conduct', and was suspended under the terms of an arbitration award. The suspended underwriter challenged the award in court alleging arbitrator 'misconduct' consisting of a finding based on a premise not put forth by Lloyd's in the arbitration hearing. The Court of Appeal decision stressed the fact that inconsistency in an arbitrator's reasoning might constitute error of fact or law in a judicial setting but would not amount to misconduct in the arbitration setting.[5] Since the English Arbitration Act of 1979, the English Appellate Courts have given more weight to the need for finality in arbitration awards.[6] Commentators view such cases as indicators of a shift in the balance between the need for finality in arbitration and the need for judicial review.[7]

Hong Kong

The Hong Kong Arbitration Amendment Ordinance of 1982 came into effect 1 June 1982.[8] The Ordinance is patterned after the English Arbitration Act of 1979 but differs from it in several important details.

First, the English Arbitration Act of 1979 allows pre-dispute agreements which bar judicial review and intervention in 'non-domestic' arbitrations, with the exeption that 'special category' arbitrations, i.e. those dealing with maritime, insurance or commodity disputes, are prohibited from contracting out of judicial review. The Hong Kong Ordinance adopts the contracting out

Comparative Law Yearbook, Volume 7, 1983. ISBN 90-247-2966-1.
© *1984, Martinus Nijhoff Publishers, Dordrecht. Printed in the Netherlands.*

provisions but allows the 'special category' disputes (maritime, insurance and commodity) to be dealt with in the same manner as other non-domestic arbitration agreements.[9] Thus, the Hong Kong Ordinance goes one step beyond the English Act of 1979 in providing flexibility to the contracting parties.

Second, the Hong Kong Ordinance gives courts power to grant sanctions if there is undue delay in instituting a claim pursuant to an arbitration agreement. The High Court may confer power to proceed with arbitration in default of appearance and may also strike out a claim in arbitration proceedings on grounds of delay where it is the interest of justice.[10] This position is in contrast with the position taken by the English Courts as exemplified by the case of *Bremer Vulkan* v. *South India Shipping Corp.* and its progeny.[11]

Switzerland

The Swiss Federal Council sent to the Federal Parliament a proposed new code relating to international arbitration in recognition of the fact that Switzerland must update its arbitration system if it is not to lose its place in the international field.

The new bill lays down the criteria for international commercial arbitration in very broad terms in an effort to ensure the widest possible freedom for the parties, at the same time maintaining the minimum legal requirements necessary to ensure enforcement of arbitral awards.[12]

The following are highlights of several important articles in the proposed bill:

Article 169
I. Scope of Application
1. The provisions of this chapter apply to any arbitration from the time when the seat of the arbitral tribunal occurs in Switzerland and where at least one of the parties at the time of the conclusion of the arbitration agreement was not domiciled or permanently resided in Switzerland.

Article 170
II. Arbitrability
1. The subject matter of an arbitration may be any claim in connection with the rights of property.
2. A State or any enterprise dominated by a State or organization controlled by a State party to an arbitration agreement may not involve its national law to contest the arbitrability of any dispute covered by the arbitration agreement.

Article 175
VII. Awards *ex aequo et bono*
The parties may authorize the arbitral tribunal to decide ex aequo et bono.

Article 176
VIII. Challenge to the jurisdiction
1. When a party intends to dispute the jurisdiction of the arbitral tribunal, the plea to the jurisdiction must be raised prior to any defense on the merits.

Article 177
IX. Method of Appeal 1. Principle
1. The decision as to jurisdiction may be the subject of appeal to the Swiss court for the place of the seat of the arbitral tribunal.
2. Any arbitral award as to the merits may be the object of an appeal on the grounds of denial of justice or pour arbitraire to the Swiss court for the place of the seat of the arbitral tribunal.

Article 180
XI. Foreign Arbitral Awards
The recognition and enforcement of foreign arbitral awards are governed by the Convention of New York of 10 June 1958 for the Recognition and Enforcement of foreign arbitral awards.[13]

Italy

Law 28 of 9 February 1983 amends the Italian law of arbitration procedure in a small but significant way. Italian arbitration procedure no longer requires that arbitrators be Italian. The law also provides that the award becomes final upon the signing of the last member of the panel.[14] Members need not be present for the signing in order for the award to be binding.

United States

The following cases deal with the maintenance of arbitrator's awards, and the jurisdictional question regarding foreign sovereigns in United States courts.

Sperry International Trade, Inc., v. *Government of Israel.*[15] In July 1978, Sperry International Trade, Inc. (Sperry) and Israel entered into a contract for a communications system for the Israeli Air Force. As part of the contract Sperry caused Citibank to open an irrevocable letter of credit for $15-million. Under the terms of the contract Israel could draw on the credit, to the extent of its payments to Sperry, upon presentation of a sight draft and Israel's own certification that it was entitled to such draft by reason of a 'clear and substantial breach' of contract by Sperry. All disputes that could not be resolved by negotiations were to be submitted to arbitration in accordance with the rules of the American Arbitration Association.

In August of 1981, Sperry instituted arbitration on the basis of breach of contract. Israel counterclaimed alleging non-performance by Sperry. In September 1981, Sperry instituted suit in New York State Court to compel arbitration and to enjoin Israel from drawing on the letter of credit pending a decision by the arbitrators. The district court enjoined Israel from drawing on the letter of credit, but the appellate court reversed on the grounds that Sperry had made no showing it would be irreparably harmed in the absence of such an injuction. On 27 January 1981, Israel attempted to draw on the letter of credit. Sperry obtained an ex parte order to attachment. Israel then removed to federal court and moved to vacate the order.

While this action was pending in the judicial courts, the arbitrators ordered that the proceeds of the letter of credit be placed in a joint escrow account in the names of Sperry and Israel. Israel moved to vacate the arbitrator's award as inconsistent with the lower court ruling.

The United States of Appeals for the Second Circuit pointed out that under 9 U.C.S. Section 10 (1947), a court may vacate an arbitral award only under specific conditions:[16]

(1) the award was procured by fraud, corruption, or undue means (10(a));
(2) there was evident partiality or corruption on the part of the arbitrators (10(b));
(3) the arbitrators were guilty of misconduct by which the parties rights were prejudiced (10(c));
(4) the arbitrators exceeded their powers or failed to make a mutual final and definite award (10(d)); and
(5) a non-statutory ground of manifest disregard of the law.

The Court rejected Israel's claim that arbitrators exceeded their powers and manifestly disregarded the law stating that, though under the custom of the American Arbitration Association no explanation was given, and though there was no precedent cited for the action, New York Law gives arbitrators substantial power to fashion remedies that they believe will do justice between parties. Citing *Sprinzen* v. *Nomberg*, 46 NY2d 623, 629 (1979) the court stated:

> An arbitrator's paramount responsibility is to reach an equitable result, and the courts will not assume the role of overseers to mold the award to conform to their sense of justice. Thus, the arbitrators award will not be vacated for errors of law and fact committed by the arbitrator ...[17]

The court therefore affirmed the arbitrator's award.

Maritime International Nominees Establishment v. *Republic of Guinea*[18]

By provision of contract entered into by Maritime International Nominees

Establishment (MINE), a Liechtenstein Corporation, and the Republic of Guinea in August 1971, the settlement of disputes was to be by arbitration by a panel of arbitrators chosen by the President of the International Center for Settlement of Investment Disputes (ICSID) located in Washington D.C.

Under ICSID procedures when parties choose to submit a dispute to ICSID, that course is deemed to be their sole remedy unless otherwise specified. Further, after initial consent, one party may invoke the ICSID arbitration process even if the other party refuses to participate.

Communication between the parties broke down and MINE filed in federal court to compel arbitration under the Federal Arbitration Act (FAA) 9 U.S.C. Section 4 (1976) 28 U.S.C. Section 1602 *et seq.* (1976) and the Federal Sovereign Immunity Act (FSIA) in January 1978. MINE's order was granted, and an award was granted by the American Arbitration Association for $25-million in compensatory damages, after which MINE returned to federal court to enforce the award on 2 August 1980. On 9 December 1980, Guinea entered the proceedings for the first time filing a motion to dismiss for lack of jurisdiction. Guinea's motion was denied by the district court, but that decision was overturned by the appellate court.

The court stated that for purposes of the FSIA a sovereign may be subjected to jurisdiction by implicitly waiving immunity (FSIA 1605(a)(1))[19] or by engaging in commercial activity (FSIA 1605 (a)(2)).[20] The court reasoned that a sovereign's agreement to submit to arbitration under the procedures of the ICSID does not amount to waiver since the arbitration need not take place in the United States even though the ICSID is centered in Washington D.C. The court also concluded that Guinea had not purposefully availed itself of the benefits of conducting business in the United States and thus had not engaged in commercial activity.[21] FSIA requires substantial contacts as opposed to the minimum contacts requirements employed in extending personal jurisdiction.[22]

In a similar development, the International Centre for Settlement of Investment Disputes sponsored by the World Bank was established as a result of the Convention on the Settlement of Investment Disputes convening on 14 October 1966. The ICSID has, however, been slow in gaining international recognition.[23] According to one recent survey only 15.8 percent of major United States multinational corporations were familiar with the work of the ICSID. This is partially due, according to one commentator, to the lack of publicitly for the ICSID's work.[24] The problem is fed by the ICSID's own policy of confidentiality of awards. During the past year, International Legal Materials with the permission of the participants published several arbitral awards.[25] It is hoped that such publicity will help to increase investors awareness of the ICSID's work.[26]

(2) Banking

El Salvador

As of 15 March 1982, branches of foreign banks no longer may accept deposits from the Salvadoran public.[27]

Qatar

Establishment of new foreign banks has been forbidden. Two new national banks have been established; one is an Islamic Bank with a majority state holding, the other is a normal commercial bank in which the State owns fifty percent.[28]

Portugal

On 19 July 1982, Portugal and the European Economic Community (EEC) reached an agreement that a seven-year transitional period will follow Portugal's accession to the EEC before EEC banks will have freedom of establishment in Portugal.[29] There was no agreement regarding what proportion of their resources EEC banks will be able to raise in Portugal.

Norway

On 14 December 1982, a report of the Royal Commission of the future structure of the banking industry was completed. The report recommended that foreign banks be allowed in Norway, conditioned on the fact that they be established as Norwegian companies, and not as branches of the foreign institutions.[30]

European Court of Justice

The European Court of Justice found Italy and Belgium guilty of failing to implement the first EEC Banking Directive. The court rejected the defense that the directive was *de facto* implemented because the necessary legislation had not been passed.[31]

Switzerland

On 31 August 1982, the United States and Switzerland entered into a Memorandum of Understanding[32] which, in certain cases, will give the American Securities and Exchange Commission (SEC) access to information in Swiss bank records regarding accounts used to cover securities exchanges which violate SEC regulations prohibiting inside trading.

The memorandum is an improvement and extension of the 1977 treaty between the United States and the Swiss Confederation on Mutual Assistance in Criminal Matters. Prior to these agreements, the SEC had been unable to gain access to bank records.[33] The Memorandum is made up of two principle provisions. First, under Swiss Penal Code Article 148,[34] inside trading may constitute fraud, unfaithful management, or disclosure of business secrets in which case rendering assistance to the SEC would be mandatory under the 1977 agreement. Second, the Memorandum describes a private agreement with the Swiss Banker's Association which was signed 20 November 1982.[35] This agreement is limited in that it is binding only on signatory banks. It provides for the creation of a Commission of Inquiry to assist the SEC when reasonable grounds exist for requesting assistance. Reasonable grounds may include a showing by the SEC of fluctuations in the price and volume of a security during a given period prior to the public announcement of an acquisition or a business merger. The Commission will review the information to determine if there is a basis for rendering assistance.[36]

While it is noted that the memorandum is an improvement over past cooperation between the SEC and Swiss banks, its strength is questioned; enforcement provisions are weak, and scope is limited to insider trading involving business acquisitions or mergers. The agreement's effect may also be diluted by the existence of other states with stricter bank secrecy laws, i.e., the Bahamas, West Germany, Curacao, Hong Kong, and Bermuda. Commentators feel, however, that Switzerland's history of political and economic stability will continue to attract foreign investors to Swiss banks.[37]

United States

On 30 September 1982, a Senate and House Committee approved legislation which allows savings and loan institutions to offer interest rates competitive to those offered by commercial banks. The legislation was designed to boost the floundering savings and loan industry and abolishes the interest rate differential between the two types of institutions.[38]

The Federal Reserve Board has issued guidelines for how United States

Banks may invest in banks in other states.[39] The Board specified that banks may buy non-voting stock in out-of-state banks provided this does not give the buying bank control of the target bank. This is viewed as a slight relaxation of rules promulgated under the Bank Holding Company Act of 1956, as amended, which forbids a bank in one state to buy more than five percent of the voting stock in a bank located in another state.[40]

Some commentators maintain that the United States already has de facto interstate banking in the form of loan production offices, Edge corporations, failing savings and loan associations, discount brokerage services, and other banking related subsidiaries.[41] It has been suggested that the current trend toward deregulation may result in allowing interstate banking deals. At present an investment in controlling interest in an out-of-state bank is only permitted in the emergency purchase of a failing bank. Some institutions are already gearing up for the arrival of interstate banking by purchasing non-voting shares convertible into voting shares when the interstate ban is lifted.[42] Such relaxation of interstate banking regulation is dependent on the continuation of current trends toward deregulation.

On 3 March 1983 the Securities and Exchange Commission changed the method by which banks report their earnings. In the future, banks may not report their earnings as a separate after-tax figure. Banks are now to report income and losses included in estimates of pre-tax income.[43]

(3) Multilateral Trade Negotiations

Termination of Countervailing Duty and Antidumping Investigations

On 21 October 1982, the United States Department of Commerce announced that it had successfully negotiated withdrawal of the American steel industry's countervailing duty and antidumping suits against forty European companies.[44] Withdrawal followed the conclusion of an Arrangement that imposed limitations on European carbon steel to the United States, effective from 1 November 1982 through 31 December 1985.[45]

The action was initiated on 11 January 1982 when several United States' producers of carbon steel products filed the first petitions with the United States Department of Commerce (DOC) and the United States International Trade Administration. The petitions were filed on behalf of the United States steel industry against certain members of the European Community and a number of other countries.[46] The petitions sought the imposition of antidumping and countervailing duties on most carbon steel products imported by the respondents. The petitions filed through 3 September 1982 were found to have sufficient grounds, according to the DOC, to intitiate investigations.[47] Final determinations of the DOC were that the governments of certain member states of the European Economic Community (EEC) were providing certain manufacturers, producers and exporters of the subject products with benefits that constituted subsidies. Further, the DOC found that certain carbon steel products were being sold, or would likely be sold, in the United States at less than fair market value.[48]

The Arrangement reached by the DOC is intended to create a period of trade stability with reference to certain carbon steel products as a result of giving the parties time for restructuring.[49] The effect of the agreement compels the European Coal and Steel Community (ECSC) to exercise restraint in exporting the subject products to the United States. The quantitative limitations are based on the type of product and percentages of United States domestic apparent consumption.[50] Termination of the agreement by the ECSC will be considered if petitions for relief are filed within the prescribed duration of the Arrangement.[51]

Brazil

The DOC suspended the countervailing duty investigation involving carbon steel wire imported from Brazil. The basis of the suspension was an agreement by the government of Brazil to offset, by means of export tax, all benefits found to be subsidies on the export of the subject product to the United States. This measure is effective 27 September 1982.[52]

Argentina

The DOC suspended the countervailing duty investigation that involved carbon steel wire rod from Argentina. The basis of the suspension was an agreement by the Government of Argentina to eliminate all benefits which were found to be bounties or grants on exports of the subject product to the United States. This agreement is effective 27 September 1982.[53]

Venezuela

The DOC suspended the antidumping investigation that involved carbon steel wire rod exported from Venezuela to the United States. The basis for the suspension was an agreement between the only known producer/exporter of the subject product in Venezuela and the DOC. The agreement requires the cessation of exports of the subject product to the United States from Venezuela. This agreement is effective 7 October 1982.[54]

Conclusion

On 21 October 1982, representatives of the United States government and the EEC concluded agreements with respect to imports into the United States of certain steel products from the EEC. This is indicative that both parties sought an end to the then pending suits. The agreement provided the United States steel industry with a needed boost in employment, and both parties benefited from the removal of the most severe trade friction between the United States and the European Community.[55]

National Harbor Improvement and Maintenance Act of 1983

On 5 April 1983, the Senate and House of Representatives of the United States enacted the National Harbor Improvement and Maintenance Act (NHIMA), effective date 1 October 1983.[56]

The purpose of the act is to provide maintenance of deep-draft channels and harbors of the United States to the depths and widths authorized by law.[57] This particular piece of dredging legislation was considered and approved in conformity with the General Agreement on Tariffs and Trade (GATT).

In reference to GATT, concerning the basis for a user fee that would be most defensible under the Agreement, it was recommended that a port-specific fee based on the gross tonnage or draw of the vessels using the port where the dredging is done, would comport with GATT, in particular with Articles III and VIII thereof.[58] Article III applies to the non-discriminatory application of taxes and other regulations which relate to matters generally applicable to both imported and domestic products.[59] Article VIII limits charges affecting foreign trade, other than duties and taxes covered by Article III, to the cost of services rendered to such trade by the bodies applying the charges.[60] Any of these Articles would be relevant to fees relating to imports. It is not clear whether certain types of fees would be treated under GATT as a tax under Article III or as a user fee under Article VIII.

The least defensible fee under these articles would be any fee based solely on imported cargo. Other issues likely to raise GATT problems would be fees applied to all cargo on an ad valorem basis or on a specific basis but at different rates for different products.[61] From the perspective of GATT, fees should not place a greater burden on the imports than on like or competitive products.[62]

Section 102 of Title 1 of the Act also specifies the imposition of a uniform cargo tonnage fee on vessels having a maximum draft of more than twelve feet and engaged in commercial waterway transportation.[63]

GATT Ministrial Meeting And Declaration

The Ministers responsible for the trade policies of the eighty-eight GATT member countries met in Geneva at a Session of the Contracting Parties from 22 to 30 November 1982.[64] The participation of seventy members resulted in a declaration that the ministers would make determined efforts to resist protectionist measures and refrain from taking or maintaining any measures inconsistent with GATT. The meeting, however, failed to produce any firm agreement or statement of commitment to open trade.[65]

Gamani Corea, the Secretary-General of the United Nations Conference on Trade and Development (UNCTAD), voiced a few of the primary concerns that motivated the calling of the meeting. Mr. Corea emphasized the worsening of the world economy and urged against the current protectionist trends of developing countries.[66] Noting the growing concern about the functioning of the international trade system, he suggested that successful action in the field of trade was 'crucially dependent on parallel actions to stimulate recovery and growth in national economies'.[67] With reference to the 'devasting impact' which the world economic crisis is having on the developing countries, the Secretary-General pointed out that those countries might be the key to world recovery due to their high rate of imports.[68]

Paragraphs 1 – 4 of the declaration constitute an agreement as to the diagnosis of the problems facing the world trade system.[69] Paragraph 5 affirms a basic commitment against protectionism and a consensus in support of the GATT system. Paragraph 6 sets forth the following decisions: to abide by GATT obligations and to support and improve the GATT trading system, to preserve the system's unity and consistency, and to ensure that GATT provides a continuing forum for negotiation and consultation.[70] The final paragraph sets out the undertakings on which the contracting parties have agreed in drawing up their work program and priorities for the 1980s.

The practical consequences of these political commitments for GATT's future work are set out in separate decisions which constitute the bulk of the declaration. Measures agreed to include: extension of conciliation procedures for the settlement of disputes within the GATT; commitment to avoidance of obstructing a settlement agreed upon by the consensus; establishment of a framework for negotiations at the official level when a nation might seek to officially curb imports; and establishment of a new agricultural committee to examine farm export subsidies and financial supports for national farming industries over the next two years.[71]

(4) Transportation

Warsaw Convention: Montreal Protocol Number 4

On 10 February 1983, the United States Senate Committee on Foreign Relations submitted to the Senate for its advice and consent to ratification thereof, a favorable report[72] regarding the Montreal Protocol Number 4, done at Montreal on 26 September 1975,[73] to amend the Convention for the Unification of Certain Rules Relating to International Carriage by Air, signed at Warsaw on 12 October 1929[74] (Warsaw Convention), as amended by the Protocol done at the Hague on 28 September 1955.

The Montreal Protocol Number 4 is an amendment to the original Warsaw Convention of 1929 and designed to modernize the rules applicable to the international carriage of passengers, baggage and cargo. The Warsaw Convention was initially drafted as a means of protecting the fledgling aviation industry in the late 1920s. The protection was aimed at the alternatives of ruinous damage suits or exhorbitant insurance premiums and was also intended to insure a degree of uniformity in what was expected to be an industry of international character.[75]

At present, 117 countries are parties to the Convention,[76] including the United States.[77] Until 1972, negotiations and changes focused on the liability of air carriers for passengers and baggage. Negotiations with respect to the cargo provisions were held at an International Civil Aviation Organization (ICAO) Legal Subcommittee meeting in Montreal in September 1972.[78] and an ICAO Legal Subcommittee meeting in Montreal in April 1975.[79] The draft cargo provisions prepared by the 1974 ICAO Legal Subcommittee[80] formed the basis for the Diplomatic Conference held in Montreal from 3 September through 25 September 1975.[81]

The Montreal Protocol Number 4 will represent significant changes from the current version of the Warsaw convention in three principle areas:

(1)   Airlines will be held strictly liable for lost or damaged cargo, subject only to four defenses.[82]

(2)   Documentation will be required to expedite cargo handling procedures.[83]

(3)   Gold will be replaced with the far more stable Special Drawing Rights (SDR) as the monetary unit for quantifying treaty liability for loss, damage, or delay of cargo shipments.[84]

If the Montreal Protocol Number 4 is adopted by the United States, it will represent the most recent rules with respect to cargo documentation and liability limits in cargo cases. This Protocol would also attempt to clear up the problem of liability limits under the Warsaw Convention, a problem that has plagued the United Stated Federal Courts.[85] The latter point is illustrated in the Federal Court decisions in *Franklin Mint Corporation* v. *Trans World Airlines, Inc.*[86] and *Maschinenfabrik Kern, A.G.* v. *Northwest Airlines, Inc.*[87] These cases reflect the need for the adaptation expressed by protocol Number 4.

Article 22 of the Warsaw Convention limited a carrier's liability for damaged goods to 250 French gold francs per kilogram. That sum was to be converted 'into any national currency in round figures'.[88] At the time the Convention was entered into, this posed no difficulties but after the gold standard was abandoned by the United States, other countries and the International Monetary Fund (IMF),[89] it became evident that a problem existed in ascertaining what standard to utilize to limit liability.

In *Franklin Mint* that parties had suggested four possible standards:

(1) the last official price of gold in the United States;
(2) the free market price of gold;
(3) the Special Drawing Right (SDR), a unit of account established by the IMF;[90] or
(4) the exchange value of the current French franc.[91]

All of these alternatives were rejected. Among the reasons were: a lack of international consensus on the proper unit of conversion; congressional repeal of the last official price of gold ($42.22); creation of SDR's by the IMF without basis in the Warsaw Convention; subjection of the French franc to unilateral change; and the highly volatile condition of the free market price of gold.[92]

Deferring to the executive branch of the government, the court concluded that it had no authority to set policy as to a new unit of conversion in an international matter.[93] The Court further held that the limitation provision of the Convention was prospectively unenforceable by courts of the United States, and that there will be no liability limit.[94]

In *Kern v. Northwest*, the Court was faced with virtually the identical issues. Referring to *Franklin Mint* the Court concurred that it had no authority to select an alternative basis for limiting liability absent congressional direction, but the Court was unwilling to dispose of liability limits:[95]

'... Northwest's liability should not be unlimited, since the clear intention of the Warsaw Convention in Article 22 was to limit the liability of air carriers on international runs. To conclude as the

Second Circuit did in *Franklin Mint* that the action of Congress in eliminating an official price of gold should operate to eliminate all limitations of liability found in the Warsaw Convention reads too much into an unrelated act of Congress'.[96]

With this background, the Senate will consider the Montreal Protocol Number 4.

United States: Shipping Act of 1983

On 1 March 1983, the United Stated Senate passed S 47, also known as the Shipping Act of 1983, with amendments, to improve the international ocean commerce transportation system of the United States.[97] Supporters contend that the legislation would help increase competition by putting U.S. flag liners on an equal regulatory footing with foreign ships in an international industry in which price-fixing and other joint practices are normal.[98] Extensive debate centered on the provisions providing for antitrust immunity, and a compromise was reached in a 'right of independent provision' limiting the antitrust immunity of carrier conferences.[99] Backing S 47 were the Reagan administration, United States and foreign carriers, maritime labor, ports and the American Farm Bureau Federation.[100]

Similarly, the House of Representatives approved HR 1878 on 23 March 1983, which would ensure that ship liners, both American and Foreign, in cartels serving U.S. trade, could fix rates, set levels of service and take other actions free from the antitrust laws that were designed to prevent joint activity.[101]

United Kingdom

The requirement for the wearing of seat belts in front seats of cars and vans in the United Kingdom will come into force on 31 January 1983, subject to certain exemptions and exceptions: Motor Vehicle Regulations 1982, S.I. 1203.[102]

European Communities

The European Communities Council of Ministers has approved the decision concluding the Agreement on the International Carriage of Passengers by Road by means of Occasional Coach and Bus services (ASOR).[103]

The European Communities Commission plans to relax the requirements governing the installation of tachographs in commercial vehicles on the grounds that the present regulations, which apply to virtually all vehicles over 3.5 gross tons, are too extensive and are not being properly enforced in such countries as France, Italy and Greece.[104]

The European Community Council of Ministers has adopted a directive laying down the technical requirements for vessels operating on inland waterways. It includes the list inland waterways for which the requirements are applicable, the requirements themselves, and the specimen 'Community Certificate' for vessels. Member states must comply with the directive's requirements by 1 January 1983 at latest.[105]

(5) Admiralty

The Queens Bench Division held in *Polish Steam Ship Co.* v. *Atlantic Maritime and others,*[106] that the interest earned on funds deposited with the court after the bringing of a successful limitation action was the rightful property of the injured party.[107] The issue arose following a collision in 1969 between the Zaglebie Debrowskie, the plaintiff's vessel, and the Garden City, the defendant's vessel, which sank along with most of her cargo. The defendants' vessel along with her cargo was a total loss. After the determination of liability through litigation, the plaintiffs brought a limitation action before the Admiralty judge. The day after the limitation action was brought, the plaintiffs deposited with the Court a sum equal to the limitation figure plus the interest on the damages determined from the date of the collision to the date of deposit with the Court at the rate of 8.25 percent. The interest rate was the mean of the interest rates awarded by the Court during the period in question.[108]

On 2 March 1982, four years after the limitation action was brought and thirteen years after the collision, the plaintiff successfully established their right to limit, and the Court fixed their liability for the incident to the value paid into the Court which included the interest on the damages to 30 April 1978.[109] The subsequent problem was who would be entitled to the interest on the fund on deposit with the Court. The Court held that the purpose of a limitation action was to limit the liability of the plaintiff including the accruing of further interest. The defendant should be entitled to the interest earned when the Court holds the funds since the defendants are being deprived of the use and benefit of the funds while on deposit. Justice dictates that the interest earned be considered part of the limitation fund and therefore accrue to the benefit of the defendant.[110]

The issue of when the time of breach resulting from non-payment of the hire occurs was decided by the House of Lords in *Afovos Shipping Co., S.A., Appellants and Romano Pagnan and Pietro Pagnan (Trading as R. Pagnan & F. lli), Respondents.*[111] Under a contract for the charter of Appellants' vessel Afovos, payment of the hire was to be made to a London Bank in United States currency. The failure to make punctual and regular payments of the hire gave rise in the Appellants the right to withdraw the vessel from the service of the charterers.[112] The rights created by Clause 5 of the charter contract were amplified by the 'anti-technicality' Clause 31 which required the owners to give 48 hours notice when exercising the option to withdraw the vessel, but leaving the charterers the right to pay the hire any time during this 48 hour period which removed the right of withdrawal from the owners.[113]

Because of an error in the entry of telexes, the payment scheduled for arrival at a London Bank on 14 June 1979 did not arrive. At 16:40 hours on 14 June 1979, the owners' agent notified the charters that the owners would exercise their option to withdraw the ship. On Monday, 18 June 1979, at 19:20 hours the owners gave notice that the vessel would be withdrawn because of failure to make the scheduled payment. The credit error was discovered and corrected on 19 June 1979.[114]

The House of Lords in dismissing the appeal upheld the Appeals Court, which held that the last possible moment for the charterers to fail to make a punctual payment was at midnight on 14/15 June 1979 regardless of banking practices. The concise rule of law presented by the case is that when a day for performance is specified without other limitations, the whole of the day is acceptable for performance.[115] Since the 48 hours for notice could only begin to run after midnight on 14/15 June the notice given by the owners in this case was faulty when given at 16:20 hours on 14 June prior to the actual breach.

The House of Lords considered the problem of course of performance to determine the rights of parties and whether some rights lapsed when not always enforced in *Scandinavian Trading Tanker Co. A.B.* v. *Flota Petrolera Ecutoriana.*[116] Under a time charterparty, the disponents let the Scaptrade to the charterers under an agreement which required the payment of the hire monthly in advance.[117] Payments under the agreement for two years were made with varying degrees of regularity in relation to the date required for payment with some payments up to three days late.[118] When the payment due on 8 July 1979 was not made, the owners sent notice on 12 July that the vessel would be withdrawn.[119] The owners then sought a declaration from the Commercial Court that they were entitled to the ship which the Commercial Court granted. The charterers contended that the owners were estopped from exercising their right to withdrawal because late payments were accepted in the past without protest.[120]

The United States Court of Appeals, in dismissing the appeal, agreed with the Commercial Court that there had not been an unequivocal representation by the owners that they would not enforce their contractual right of withdrawal if payments were not punctually made. The Court held that because the charterers were not affected by the past conduct of the owners when payments were accepted late, the charterers could not claim that the owners were estopped from asserting their right of withdrawal.[121]

In a second holding, the United States Court of Appeals held that the need for certainty in commercial transactions would prevent the exercise of equitable jurisdiction through a grant of relief against forfeiture to a time charterparty. The charterers therefore can not look to the power of equity for relief from the effects of the withdrawal.[122]

The House of Lords refused to enforce the choice of forum clause in a shipping contract because the effect of the choice of forum would be contrary to The Carriage of Goods by Sea Act 1971. This act incorporates the Hague-Visby Rules as amended. The case being considered on appeal by the House of Lords was *The Hollandia*.[123] This case involved a contract for the shipping of goods from Scotland to the Dutch West Indies on a Dutch ship.[124] The contract for shipping contained standard contract terms for the carrier making the contract a contract of adhesion. One of these standard clauses contained a section which stated that all claims would be heard in the Court in Amsterdam.[125]

The Hague-Visby Rules provide that any contract clause in a contract of carriage which either lessens or relieves the carrier of liability for loss or damage resulting from negligence, fault, or failure in the performance of the duties and obligations other than as provided in these rules would be null and void and of no effect.[126] Holland has never accepted the Hague-Visby Rules into Dutch law, but continued to recognize the Hague Rules when the bill of lading was issued. Under the Hague Rules, the carrier's liability could be limited by the terms of the contract.[127]

The Court of Appeals, as later affirmed by the House of Lords, held that the shippers were to be allowed to continue with their action which was contrary to the stay as granted by the Admiralty Court. The choice of forum clause was held ineffective, and since there was no other ground upon which a stay could be sustained against the shippers, the shippers were allowed to proceed.[128]

The Carriage of Goods Act established that the time when a choice of forum clause was to be interpreted was at the time when the condition subsequent to the formation of the contract takes place and the carrier seeks to bring the clause into operation and to rely upon it. Since the clause would not operate until a legal controversy arose regarding the rights of the respective parties. The Carriage of Goods Act clearly seeks to defeat choice of forum selection clauses which have the effect of limiting liability.[129]

The action was originally brought before the Admiralty Court as an action in rem against the sister of the carrier ship.[130]

United States

The case presented to the District Court for the Southern District of Texas was a consolidated action resulting from the collision of the M/V Amoco Cremona and the S/S Mason Lykes on 2 April 1980. The case was the *Amoco Transport Co.* v. *S/S Mason Lykes.*[131] All of the claims and couterclaims had been settled prior to the commencement of the trial leaving only the claims of the holders of an interest in the cargo of the Mason Lykes.[132]

The Mason Lykes was significantly damaged after a collision with the M/V Amoco Cremona; thereafter, the operator of the Mason Lykes opted to abandon the voyage and claim the freight under a bill of lading. The holders of a cargo interest in the Mason Lykes claimed that the carrier had not earned the freight since the abandonment was improper.[133]

The Court determined that the Amoco Cremona was 90 percent at fault since she was proceeding at an excessive speed along with other negligent acts. The Mason Lykes was held to be 10 percent negligent because of piecemeal course changes and for failure to post a bow lookout.[134]

The Carriage of Goods by Sea Act would not make the carrier liable for a collision caused by navigational negligence. The actions following the collision were reasonable, and therefore, the freight had been earned by the carrier since the expected delay caused by the damages to the ship justified the abandonment of the voyage. The bill of lading which provided for payment even if the voyage was abandoned required that the abandonment be forced and not due to a fault for which the carrier is responsible under the Carriage of Goods by Sea Act if the Court so concludes. In an attempt to recover the loss of the freight from the negligent ship, in this case the Amoco Cremona, the holders of cargo interests are barred from recovery by the rule established by the United States Supreme Court in *Robins Dry Dock* v. *Flint.*[135] Robins stood for the proposition that 'a tort to the person or property of one man does not make the tortfeasor liable to another merely because the injured person was under contract with the other, unknown to the doer of the wrong'.[136]

In a split decision, the United States Supreme Court considered the constitutionality of an admiralty action in rem against a State of the United States. In *Florida Department of State* v. *Treasure Salvors, Inc.,*[137] both parties entered into a contract which allowed the Respondent to salvage the artifacts of the Nuestra Senora de Atocha, a seventeenth century Spanish galleon. The first contract was agreed to under threat of arrest of the president of Treasure Salvors and similar contracts were executed for each of the next three years. The State of Florida claimed the right to the treasure trove and artifacts abandoned on state owned property or state owned sovereignty submerged lands through a Florida statute which vested the title to such property in the State.[138] Under the contract, the property was deemed to belong to the State subject to a subsequent distribution.[139]

In litigation separate from the salvage operation litigation, a Special Master determined that the seaward boundary of submerged lands was landward of the wreck of the Atocha. Subsequent to the filing of the Special Master's report, the Treasure Salvors filed an admiralty action in rem naming the Atocha as defendant. The United States intervened in the action claiming title to the artifacts, but the Court held that 'possession and title are rightfully conferred upon the finder of the res derelictae'. On appeal, the United States Court of Appeals modified the rule of the decision of the lower Court to limit the holding to the res located in the jurisdiction of the district. In this special case, the title could be determined as to property outside of the district because the United States stipulated to the Court's admiralty jurisdiction and intervened in the action. The Government waived the usual requirement that the res be located within the district.[140]

The State of Florida asserted the Eleventh Amendment to the United States Constitution as a defense to the in rem admiralty action. The District Court, as upheld by the Court of Appeals and the United States Supreme Court, held that the Eleventh Amendment does not prevent the in rem arrest of the res by the Marshal. The Fifth Circuit Court of Appeals did not exceed its power when it attempted to adjudicate the ownership of the property.[141]

The United States Supreme Court upheld the lower Courts as to the propriety of the execution of the warrant, but reversed as to the adjudication of the State's property rights in the artifacts.[142]

On remand to the Fifth Circuit Court of Appeals,[143] the Court held that the artifacts became the property of the salvors since the issue of the State's ownership was never brought before the Court, and therefore, was never a controversy for the Court to resolve.[144]

(6) Contracts

United States: Choice of Law/Choice of Forum

Conflict of laws issues have pervaded recent American litigation in the contracts area. In *Fojo* v. *American Express Company,*[145] a group of Puerto Rican residents brought suit for injuries suffered in an automobile collision that occurred in Hong Kong while riding as tourist passengers on defendants' tour bus.[146] Defendant tour organizers, American Express Company and American Express, S.A., were Delaware and Mexican corporations respectively. The issue presented was whether the law of Puerto Rico where the pre-packaged tour was arranged, advertised and agreed upon, or the law of Hong Kong, the situs of the accident, would be applied by the United States District Court for the District of Puerto Rico. The Court held that 'the dominant and most significant contacts in this cause of action lie in Puerto Rico', and, therefore, applied the substantive law of the forum to adjudicate the merits of the case.[147]

The collision was allegedly caused by the negligence of defendant's employee, the driver of the tour bus. The court, therefore, identified two possible theories of recovery in order to determine the characterization of the cause of action and the applicable conflicts rules. Those theories were: (1) an agency theory whereby defendants would be liable for the negligent acts of the driver, (2) a breach of contract theory based on defendant's failure to provide the tour services represented to plaintiffs.[148] The Court noted that the law of Puerto Rico required that contracts be executed without negligence.[149] The Supreme Court of Puerto Rico, however, had indicated that the 'mere fact that a wrongful act takes place as a consequence of a breach of contract does not alter the nature of the action'.[150] Thus, the conflict of laws principles in Puerto Rico allowed the Court to characterize a breach such as in *Fojo* as a tort; however, the Court is not precluded from characterizing such an occurrence as a contract action. The former characterization would require the application of the law of the situs; the latter characterization would 'hinge on the determination of which forum has the most significant contacts in relation to the matter in controversy'.[152] The court characterized the action as a breach of contract, and held that under a contacts analysis the most significant contacts were in Puerto Rico. The court further held that policy considerations favored the application of Puerto Rican law, therefore, the law of Puerto Rico was applied to adjudicate the matter.

By comparison, *Day and Zimmerman* v. *Exportadora, Etc.,*[153] decided by the United States District Court for the Eastern District of Pennsylvania, held that in a breach of contract suit the conflict of laws principles of

Pennsylvania combine both the grouping of contacts and an interest analysis.[154] The disputed contract was entered into by plaintiff engineering firm to provide design, engineering, procurement and construction services for defendant's cocoa bean processing plant in Guayaquil, Ecuador. Defendant claimed that performance of the contract resulted in the construction of a substandard plant in Ecuador. Defendant sought application of Ecuadorian law and moved for dismissal based on forum non conveniens. The latter motion was a result of defendant's contention that the court must have access to the cocoa bean plant in Ecuador as a matter of evidence.

The conflict of laws issue required an analysis of the relevant contacts which included the place of negotiation, contracting and performance, location of the subject matter of the contract, and citizenship of the parties.[155] The interest analysis required consideration of both the private and public interests. The court held that under either a contacts or interest analysis the law of the forum was applicable.[156]

Defendant's motion to dismiss for forum non conveniens on the grounds that trial in Pennsylvania would preclude the Ecuadorian defendant from presenting crucial evidence was denied.[157] The court determined that plaintiff's role in the project was chiefly limited to design and procurement. The evidence presented therefore, would be limited chiefly to the books and records located in Pennsylvania. The defendants, furthermore, would not be precluded from introducing video tapes and photographic evidence regarding the condition of the plant.[158] The court noted that 'plaintiff's choice of forum should be disturbed only where the balance of convenience strongly favors the defendant'.[159]

Gulf Trading and Transport Co. v. *M/V Tento*[160] involved a time charter providing that American law would be applied to resolve certain disputes. Supplies obtained in Italy and Egypt became the subject of the litigation. Normally, the source of such supplies would have controlled the choice of law, but the United States Circuit Court of Appeals for the Ninth Circuit agreed with the Second Circuit's rejection of the source of supply rule in *Rainbow Line, Inc.* v. *M/V Tequila*.[161] The court, utilizing a multiple contacts analysis, held in *Gulf Trading* that American law was applicable because the vessel involved had done a significant amount of trade in United States ports, the charter stipulated that American law would be applied in the event of a dispute under the charter, and the injured parties were companies of the United States. These facts were utilized by the court for its holding under the rule that choice of law questions involving maritime liens would be resolved by weighing and evaluating points of contact between the transaction and sovereign legal systems touched and affected by it.[162] (This view does not have universal acceptance in the United States.[163])

United Kingdom

In England, the House of Lords has upheld the general rule that in contracts that do not contain an express choice of law provision for disputes arising under the contract, the law of the country with the closest relation to the subject matter will be applied. The House of Lords affirmed the lower court in the case of *Amin Rasheed Corporation* v. *Kuwait Insurance Co. CA*.[164] The case involved a standard Lloyds policy for insurance of a vessel. The plaintiff sought jurisdiction in the English courts after the vessel was seized and the crew imprisoned. The House of Lords upheld the Court of Appeals by concluding that English law was appropriate under the circumstances. Of greater importance was the question addressed by the House of Lords regarding the service of a writ abroad. They reached the conclusion that this was not a proper case for such service.[165]

The law Commission has taken action to make recommendations concerning the law that governs contracts for the supply of services. In particular, the Law Commission will focus on the terms to be implied into such contracts, the consequences for breach of those terms, and the possibility of excluding liability for breach.[166]

Bankers in Great Britain have become concerned over the recent rescheduling by Yugoslavia of its foreign debt. The bankers concern has arisen primarily due to the illegality clauses that were frequently excluded from its syndicated loan agreement documentation. Illegality clauses were designed to protect bank lenders: they provided a suitable procedure for resolving cases where through the imposition of a law or similar instrument it became illegal for a bank to make all or part of its participation available under a loan agreement and/or to continue its participation in that loan. Under English law, when a situation such as this arises, the performance of those obligations is excused due to the fact that the basis of the contract was frustrated. The result could be that the mechanics of the agreement become unacceptable to the borrower and the affected bank. The law relating to frustrated contracts was not created with cases on syndicated loans as a consideration; therefore, bankers need provisions setting out what should happen in the event of illegality.[167]

The London International Financial Futures Exchange (LIFFE) is a newly created means of guaranteeing futures contracts. The guarantee is accomplished by LIFFE substituting itself as the seller for each buyer on the market, and as buyer for each seller. The exchange is then in a position to offset the sales against purchases as long as members of the market perform their obligations. In addition, LIFFE requires members to pay an initial margin when a contract is registered with the International Commodities Clearing House (ICCH). LIFFE debits members with a variation margin where losses on contracts transacted by them justify it. It may also meet emergencies by requiring payment of additional margins.

The object of LIFFE is to provide facilities for members and their clients to hedge against the risk of future fluctuations in interest rates and foreign currency rates of exchange. The rules of LIFFE provide that members shall be deemed to act as principals in all contracts made with one another and with non-clearing members.[168]

The Netherlands

Compagnie Europeenne Des Petroles S.A. v. Sensor Nederland B.V.[169] was a case involving a choice of law question. The parties had made no choice of law upon entering the contract. The court applied the general rule that in the event of a failure of the parties to make such a choice, an international contract is governed by the law of the country to which it is most closely connected.

China

A new law on economic contracts within China has been adopted. It applies to agreements between legal persons seeking to achieve a certain economic purpose and for defining each party's rights and obligations. The law was specially formulated to protect the legal rights and interests of the parties concerned in economic contacts, to safeguard social and economic order, to improve economic benefit for the contracting parties, to guarantee implementation of state plans, and to promote the development of the socialist modernization program. The law sets out general provisions for contract formation and performance. For the resolution of disputes, the law provides mediation or arbitration after failed consultation between the parties. Specific types of contracts are provided for, and the major items that should be contained in the contract. The law became effective 1 July 1982, and it is hoped that as a result, economic contracts will be formulated by implementing the principles of equality, mutual benefit, and that neither party will impose its will to the detriment of the other party. Finally, once formed according to the law, the contract has legally binding force without further review by party officials.[170]

United States

The Second Circuit Court of Appeals has ruled that 'boilerplate' successor obligor clauses do not permit assignment of the public debt unless all or substantially all of the assets of the company at the time of the liquidation are transferred to a single purchaser. This was decided in the case of *Sharon Steel Corporation* v. *Chase Manhattan Bank*[171] where the court noted that a successor obligor clause has a two fold purpose: first, to enable the borrower to sell its assets to a successor so that it may enter into a new business free of public debt; and secondly, to protect lenders by assuring a degree of continuity of assets. The purpose of the successor obligor clause is to assure that the principle operating assets of the borrower are available for the satisfaction of the debt. To allow a final sale in liquidation of assets to go to multiple purchasers to be covered by the successor obligor clause would defeat this purpose.

A basic principle of law concerning promissory estoppel is that the plaintiff must establish that his reliance on the defendant's promise was reasonable under the circumstances, in order to recover under this theory.[172] In *RCM Supply Co.* v. *Hunter Douglas, Inc.,*[173] the court found that the plaintiff's expenditure of $951,000 in reliance on an alleged oral promise was not recoverable under principles of promissory estoppel. Officials of the defendant corporation orally promised to provide the plaintiff with their lowest price and an unlimited line of credit for an indeterminate period of time, without regard to the state of the plaintiff's financial condition. The court ruled that the plaintiff's reliance in this situation exceeded the bounds of commercial reasonableness. The plaintiff was allowed to recover only those expenditures specifically made in reliance upon the defendant's promise. In this case, the plaintiff failed to show any evidence of specific expenditures made in reliance on the defendant's representations, and recovery was denied.

The United States Court of Appeals for the Ninth Circuit decided in *Polar Shipping Limited* v. *Oriental Shipping Corporation*[174] that foreign court selection clauses will be enforced in admiralty actions unless the resisting party can show that it is unreasonable, unjust, or otherwise invalid.[175] The case goes a step further and adds the principle that because scope and enforcement of foreign court selection clauses is a matter of contract, the intent of the parties governs the extent to which the nonselected court may exercise its jurisdiction. Under English and United States law, the enforceability of foreign selection clauses is a matter of judicial discretion. The court further stated that where there is a valid and enforceable foreign court selection clause, the court should exercise its jurisdiction only to the extent necessary to ensure that the plaintiff will not be prejudiced by vacating prejudgment security and to ensure that the plaintiff has an adequate remedy in the alternative forum.

Diplomatic Conference for the Adoption of the UNIDROIT Draft Convention on Agency in the International Sale of Goods

The diplomatic Conference met in Geneva, Switzerland, and drafted and adopted the Convention on Agency in the International Sale of Goods on 17 February 1983. The Committee adopted this act out of a desire to establish common provisions concerning agency in the international sale of goods, to account for different social, economic, and legal systems, to adopt uniform rules which govern agency in the international sale of goods, and to promote international trade.

The Convention would apply only when an agent with authority to act on behalf of a principal concludes a contract for the sale of goods with a third party, and the principal and the third parties have their places of business in different states. An agent who acts without authority or who acts outside the scope of his authority shall be required to place the third party in the same position as he would have been in had the contract been made with the proper authority. The agent will not be held liable if the third party knew or ought to have known that the agent had no authority or was acting outside the scope of his authority.[176]

European Court of Justice

Brussels Convention: In a dispute between an employed agent and his employer, the Court ruled that the obligation which characterized the contract is the determining factor. In *Schul v. Inspecteur der Invoerrechten en Accijnzen,*[177] the court allowed the action to be brought in the place where the work is performed, which provides a measure of security for the employee.

(7) Taxation

United States

Domestic International Sales Corporations

On 29 June 1982, at the General Agreement on Tarrifs and Trade (GATT) Council meeting, the Council agreed that the December 1981 Council decision had 'found' the United States income tax provisions regarding the domestic international sales corporation (DISC)[178] to be in 'violation' of GATT.[179] This view is consistent with that of the Carter Administration of 8 June 1979.[180] A DISC is not taxed at the corporate level on one-half of its profits. The untaxed profits regardless of distribution are taxed to the shareholders. The tax on the remaining one-half is deferred until the income is 'actually distributed', the stock of the DISC is transferred, the DISC is liquidated, the DISC requirements are not met, or DISC election is terminated or revoked by the 'shareholder(s)'.[181]

The Reagan Administration in March of 1983 announced a legislative proposal which is intended not only to comply with the GATT rule that allows a territorial tax system, which exempts overseas income, but also to simplify the present DISC rules.[182] During the year alternatives were offered[183] and special interests voiced their recommendations.[184]

On 4 August 1983, the Reagan Administration introduced legislation that would replace the DISC with a foreign sales corporation (FSC).[185] The FSC would be allowed to make export sales from which a portion of the income will be exempt from United States tax at both the corporate and domestic corporate shareholder levels, so long as certain requirements are satisfied. Those requirements being that certain sales activities be performed outside the United States, so as to comply with the GATT understanding which requires tax exempt income to originate from economic processes outside the United States.[186]

To qualify as a FSC, a corporation must have no more than twenty-five shareholders and satisfy four requirements of business presence. The FSC must:[187]

1. maintain an office outside the United States Territory,
2. maintain a summary of its permanent books of account at its foreign office,
3. have at least one director who is resident outside the United States, and
4. hold a distribution license or sales agency agreement with respect to products purchased from or sold on behalf of a related supplier.

To determine the income of the FSC the arm's length pricing method of IRC Section 482 would be utilized. Also, two allocation rules would be available which are 'designed for administrative convenience to approximate arm's length pricing'.[188]

The FSC must also satisfy three categories of foreign presence requirements. Categories 1 and 2 will be allowed to be performed on a contract basis.

Category 1 will require the FSC to participate outside the United States in the 'solicitation, negotiation or acceptance of each sale which gives rise to the foreign trading gross receipts'.[189]

Category 2 will require the FSC to perform activities that account for fifty percent of the direct cost for five activities outside United States Territory. The activities are:[190]

1. processing customer orders and arranging delivery;
2. billing customers and receiving payment;
3. domestic and foreign transportation;
4. advertising and sales promotion;
5. assumption of credit risk.

Category 3 will require the FSC to incur eighty-five percent of the direct costs of certain managerial activities outside the United States. The activities are:[191]

1. meetings of the Board of Directors;
2. shareholders' meetings;
3. maintenance of bank account;
4. disbursement of dividends, legal and accounting fees, and salaries of officers and directors.

Two exceptions will exist to protect small exporters, the small DISC interest charge exception and the small FSC foreign presence exception. The exceptions are designed to provide relief for small businesses that 'may find the foreign economic activity requirement onerous'.[192]

The small DISC interest charge exception provides for the deferral of tax on DISC taxable income derived from DISC qualified export receipts in a taxable year. The small DISC will be allowed deferral of tax on income derived from up to $100,000 in qualified export receipts. The deferred tax will be subject to an arm's length interest charge based on the Treasury Bill rate.

The small FSC foreign presence exception would allow an electing small FSC to be exempt from categories 1 through 3 above. However, income derived from foreign trading gross receipts greater than $2,500,000 cannot

124

be deferred. Also, foreign trading gross receipts from a consolidated group will be aggregated.[193]

State Taxation

In the field of State taxation of multijurisdictional firms, there were three significant United States Supreme Court cases involving the taxation of unitary business enterprise operating in multiple jurisdictions.

The first two held that the states of New Mexico and Idaho's tax legislation was unconstitutional under the due process and commerce clauses. In *Asarco Inc.* v. *Idaho State Tax Commission*,[194] it was held that Idaho could not include within taxable income of a parent corporation doing some business in Idaho amounts received from dividends and sale of stock of a subsidiary corporation having no other contact with the state. *Woolworth Co.* v. *The Taxation and Revenue Department of New Mexico*[195] held that New Mexico may not tax 'gross-up' amounts, fictitous amounts received for foreign tax credits of subsidiary corporations.

The more recent and significant case, however, *Container Corp. of America* v. *Franchise Tax Bd.*,[196] held that California's three-factor apportionment formula was constitutional as it would result in no greater taxation if applied in every jurisdiction than would result if applied to the business in one state. The method California uses is as follows:[197]

$$\left(\frac{\text{In-State Property of All Unitary Corporations Operating in State}}{\text{Everywhere Property of Unitary Group}} + \frac{\text{In-State Payroll of All Unitary Corporations Operating in State}}{\text{Everywhere Payroll of Unitary Group}} + \frac{\text{In-State Sales* of All Unitary Corporations Operating in State}}{\text{Everywhere Sales* of Unitary Group}} \right) \times \begin{array}{c} \text{Combined Total} \\ \text{Net Income* Earned} \\ \text{Everywhere By} \\ \text{Unitary Group} \end{array} = \begin{array}{c} \text{Income Earned} \\ \text{Within Taxing State} \end{array}$$

AVERAGED BY DIVIDING THESE FACTORS BY 3

* All intercorporate transactions are eliminated in this formula.

A system similar to California's is applied in more than twenty states.[198]

The Court held that Container was a unitary business enterprise, rather than merely an investment corporation. The Court found Container and its subsidiaries to be decidedly close in that Container guaranteed approximately fifty percent of the long term loans to its subsidiaries[199] without any indication that the guarantees were negotiated in an arm's length manner.[200] Container provided its subsidiaries with technical assistance and assisted them in obtaining equipment.[201] Furthermore, the subsidiary's capital expenditures required Container's consensus.[202]

Container had objected to the California Administrative Code's 'strong presumption' that corporations involved in the same business are unitary.[203] Further, Container argued that the Court had already adopted the 'substantial flow of goods' test.[204] However, the Court rejected this argument stating that the 'prerequisite to a constitutionally acceptable finding of unitary business is a flow of value ...'.[205]

The Court also concluded that the fourteen percent difference in the apportionment of income between Container's method and California's method was a reasonable error,[206] unlike the 250 percent difference found in *Hans Rees' Sons, Inc.* v. *North Carolina ex rel. Maxwell.*[207]

As the result of threatened retalitory measures by British business and parliamentary officials, Treasury Secretary Donald Regan asked President Reagan to join him in asking the Court to rehear Container. The President refused, but agreed to the formation of a special advisory panel.[208]

Foreign Investment Real Property Tax Act of 1980

The Foreign Investment in Real Property Tax Act of 1980 (FIRPTA),[209] which substantially changed taxation rules on foreign investors in United States realty, was further amended by the Economic Recovery Tax Act of 1981 (ERTA).[210] The purpose of FIRPTA is to impose taxation on the disposition of real property by foreign parties.

FIRPTA also imposes 'broad reporting requirements', which require annual returns to be filed by direct and indirect foreign investors.[211] FIRPTA further requires the disclosure of the names and addresses of the beneficial owners of United States realty without regard for the intervening entities.

The Internal Revenue Service issued regulations interpreting the reporting requirements, which while 'temporary' are also 'comprehensive'.[212] The reporting forms provide for three types of real property investors.

Form 6659 must be filed by a domestic corporation with foreign shareholders if the domestic corporation is a United States Real Property Holding Company (USRPHC) and has one or more foreign shareholders.[213]

Form 6660 must be filed by entities with 'substantial investors' in United States real property. A 'substantial investor' as defined by Temporary Regulations Section 6a.6039C-3(b) is any 'foreign person who holds an interest in a partnership, trust or estate' or any 'person who holds an interest in a foreign corporation, if the fair market value of the person's pro rata share of the United States real property interest exceeds $50,000'.[214] Also note that the Internal Revenue Service will also use the 'look-through' approach where intervening entities are considered.[215]

The Temporary Regulations also provide that a security agreement with the IRS's District Director, Foreign Operations District, can be made in lieu of the reporting requirements. This is considered to be 'one of the most significant items' in the temporary rules.[216]

Subchapter S Revision Act of 1982

The Subchapter S Revision Act of 1982[217] was enacted on 19 October 1982. The Revision Act generally applies to tax years beginning after 31 December 1982, though 'transitional rules apply to certain provisions',[218] The new law removes the former eighty percent limitation on foreign source income.[219] It allows the passing through of foreign tax credits in a method determined by the partnership under Section 1373, so long as the 'substantial economic effect test of Section 704 (b)(2)' is met.[220]

Furthermore, the Revision Act allows excess passive income from pre-'Subchapter 5' years, where under the former law excessive passive income terminated Subchapter S status. Note, however, that excessive passive income is taxed at forty-six percent and the status will terminate if passive income is greater than twenty-five percent of gross receipts for the three consecutive years.[221]

Other notable changes were increasing the maximum number of shareholders from 25 to 35,[222] and allowing S corporation shareholders to carry forward a loss so long as it does not exceed the shareholder's basis in stock and loans to the corporation.[223]

Tax Equity and Fiscal Responsibility Act of 1982

The Tax Equity and Fiscal Responsibility Act (TEFRA) of 1982 was enacted 3 September 1982.[224] Sections 211, 212 and 213 have a notable impact on foreign tax.

(A) Sections 211 and 212: Oil and Gas. TEFRA major changes for the oil and gas industry. While TEFRA will 'liberalize the treatment of foreign taxes on nonextraction oil activities', it will make it 'more difficult for most taxpayers to utilize foreign extraction taxes as credits against United States taxes on foreign extraction income'.[225]

Under I.R.C. Section 907(b) the Commissioner may now determine that foreign oil and gas taxes are not creditable to the extent that they materially exceed other taxes on non-oil related income.[226] However, the rules regarding the carryover of extraction taxes were liberalized by the repeal of the two percent foreign oil and gas extraction income (FOGEI) limitation.[227]

I.R.C. Section 907(c)(2) now defines foreign oil related income (FORI) to exclude FOGEI.[228] Therefore, FORI now includes foreign taxable income attributable to:[229]

(1) the processing of minerals extracted (whether or not by the taxpayer) from oil or gas wells into their primary products;
(2) the transportation, distribution, or sale of the minerals or primary products;
(3) the disposition of assets used by the taxpayer in any of the trades or business of (1) or (2); or
(4) the performance of any other related service.

I.R.C. Section 907(c)(4) was revamped by a new law which provides for the recapture of oil extraction loss on taxable years after 31 December 1982. The recapturing process is effectuated by recharacterizing future FOGEI to the extent of the loss as foreign non-oil and gas related income.[230] 'Apparently' the change does not affect foreign oil and gas extraction taxes under 907(c)(5).[231]

It is important to note that the per-country extraction rule has been repealed.[232] Consequently, a 'net extraction loss in one country offsets extraction income from other countries for the purpose of computing the amount of creditable foreign oil and gas extraction taxes'.[233]

(B) Section 213: Possessions and Virgin Islands Corporations. This provision was enacted because Congress felt that the possessions' tax provisions were being used to transfer nonindigenous intangible assets into possession corporations generating tax free income without creating new jobs.[234]

To achieve that end the percentage of a possession corporation's gross income which must be derived from an active business within the possession will be increased on a graduating scale from the fifty percent 1982 level to the 1985 and after level of sixty-five percent.[235]

The Section provides that income from intangibles is to be taxed to United States shareholders of possession corporations by one of two options, the 'cost sharing' option and the 'fifty-fifty profit split' option.[236]

The 'cost sharing' option allows the possession corporation to earn income from the manufacture of intangibles so long as the possession corporation shares by a cost sharing payment with the parent and has a 'significant business presence' in the possession.[237] The 'significant business presence' test requires a showing that the possession affiliate has added more than twenty-five percent to the value of the end product or that sixty-five percent or more of the direct labor costs were incurred by the possession corporation for services rendered within the possession.[238]

The 'fifty-fifty profit split' option splits the combined taxable income from all products produced within the possession between the United States affiliates and the possession corporation on a fifty-fifty basis.[239] The 'significant business presence' is required for the fifty-fifty option as well.[240]

It is important to note that trademarks, trade names, brand names and other similar intangibles may not be the subject of the election.[241]

Recent Developments in Tax Treaties

Australia

The United States and Australia signed a new income tax treaty to replace the 1953 convention on 6 August 1982. The treaty was reported approved by the Senate on 27 July 1983.[242]

Austria

The Convention between the United States of America and the Republic of Austria for the Avoidance of Double Taxation and the Prevention of Fiscal Evasion with respect to taxes on Estates, Inheritances, Gifts, and Generation-skipping Transfers was signed in Vienna on 21 June 1982, and was ratified by the United States Senate on 29 September 1982.[243] The Convention is similar to the United States model estate and gift tax convention, published by the United States Treasury Department on 8 December 1980, and the estate and gift tax conventions with the United Kingdom (entered into force 11 November 1979) and France (entered into force 1 October 1980.[244]

Article 9 of the Convention, while preserving the United States rule of worldwide taxation of United States citizens and residents, avoids double taxation by allowing a credit for foreign taxes paid on property situated within the foreign state.[245]

3 elgium

The United States and Belgium initialed a treaty on 17 June 1983, that is to replace the 1972 convention.[246] The United States Treasury Department also announced that notices of termination were delivered to certain Belgian Territories.[247]

Canada

The protocol to a new income tax treaty to replace the 1942 convention between the United States and Canada was signed on 14 June 1983.[248]

China

The shipping and aircraft agreement signed on 5 March 1982, was reported approved by the Senate on 27 July 1983, while negotiations were held for an income tax treaty on 1 September 1982.[249]

Cyprus

Cyprus, which has no income tax treaty with the United States, initialed an income tax treaty on 15 June 1983.[250]

Denmark

In Washington, D.C. on 27 April 1983, the United States and Denmark signed an estate and gift tax treaty. The treaty is similar to the United States model estate and gift tax treaty and the Austrian estate and gift tax treaty which entered into force on 1 July 1983.[251]

The treaty provides that the 'country of domicile may tax transfers of estates and gifts and generation-skipping transfers (deemed transfers) on a world wide basis, but must credit tax paid to the country with respect to real property and certain business assets located in that country'.[252]

Finland

The United States and Finland initialed text on 27 July 1983 to replace the 1970 income tax convention.[253]

Ireland

Negotiations have begun to replace the 1949 income tax treaty.[254]

Italy

The United States and Italy initialed text on 30 March 1983, to replace the 1956 income tax convention.[255]

130

Netherlands

Negotiations have begun to replace the 1948 income tax treaty.[256]

Netherland Antilles

Negotiations have begun to replace the Netherlands extension.[257]

New Zealand

The United States and New Zealand signed a new income tax treaty to replace the 1952 convention on 23 July 1982. The treaty was reported approved by the Senate on 27 July 1983.[258]

Nigeria

Nigeria which has no income tax treaty with the United States entered into negotiations in October of 1982.[259]

Sweden

Negotiations have begun to replace the 1939 income tax convention.[260]

Tunisia

The United States and Tunisia, with no treaty now in force, initialed an income tax treaty on 10 June 1983.[261]

INTELLECTUAL PROPERTY RIGHTS

(1) Patents

United States

Law of the Sea Treaty

On 9 July 1982, President Reagan announced that the United States would not sign the convention adopted by the Third United Nations Conference on the Law of the Sea.[262] In a policy statement made on 19 January 1982, regarding the position of the United States on the Law of the Sea Treaty, he stated, 'While most provisions of the draft convention are acceptable and consistent with United States interests, some major elements of the deep seabed mining regime are not acceptable'.[263]

One of the major points of contention is contained in Article 5 of Annex III of the treaty[264] which requires privately owned and developed technology related to the exploration of the seabed and the development and processing of the minerals found there, to be mandatorily transferred to the Deep Seabed Authority and through it to other countries, their nationals and the Enterprise, a supernational mining company to be established by the draft convention.[265]

The definition of 'technology'[266] under the mandatory transfer provision is far more inclusive than any employed in current commercial practice.[267] It is broad enough to include technological information which is normally treated as confidential and proprietary such as defense-related technologies, raising concerns regarding access to, security of, and compensation for loss of proprietary data.[268]

The United States had approached the Law of the Sea Treaty from an essentially economic viewpoint[269] as evidenced by the conflict over the mandatory transfer of privately owned technology provisions of the Treaty.

Part XIV, Section 1, Articles 266, 268 and 274 of the Treaty[270] set out as the basic objectives of the transfer of technology provisions, the encouragement of the development and dissemination of marine technological knowledge with particular emphasis on the transfer of technology to developing states.

Contrary to these stated objectives, the United States fears that the provisions will serve as a disincentive to the development of new technology since any new inventions will be immediately transferred to industry competitors with an accompanying loss of investment potential.[271] This is of special concern to the United States since, through its transfer of technology provisions, the convention compels the sale of proprietary information and technology now largely in United States hands.[272]

The confiscatory nature of the transfer of technology provisions and the concerns which United States business enterprises are voicing, are reflected in the statement made by the Special Representative of the President for the Conference to the House Committee on Merchant and Fisheries on 23 February 1982, 'There is a deeply held view in our Congress that one of America's greatest assets is its capacity for innovation and invention and its ability to produce advanced technology. It is understandable, therefore, that a treaty would be unacceptable to many Americans if it required the United States or, more particularly, private companies to transfer that asset in a forced sale. That is why the problem must be solved'.[273]

The Final Act of the Third United Nations Conference on the Law of the

Sea was opened for signature on 10 December 1982, at the conclusion of the Third United Nations Conference on the Law of the Sea held at Montego Bay. The treaty remains open for signature until 9 December 1984.[274]

The Award of Prejudgment Interest for Patent Infringement

The United States Supreme Court on 24 May 1983, unanimously affirmed the judgment of the Court of Appeals for the Third Circuit awarding prejudgment interest in the patent infringement case of *General Motors Corporations* v. *Deve Corporation, et al.*[275] The decision clarifies the proper standard governing the award of prejudgment interest in patent infringement suits under 35 U.S.C. Section 284. This clarification was necessitated by the Courts of Appeals' inconsistent interpretation of Section 284, governing recovery in infringement actions. The court held that an award of prejudgment interest in a patent infringement suit should ordinarily be awarded under 35 U.S.C. Section 284, absent some justification for withholding such an award. The purpose is to afford patent owners complete compensation for the infringement, where the patent was infringed over the course of a number of years and where the patent owner was not guilty of causing unnecessary delay in bringing suit.[276]

Prior to 1946, the section of patent laws governing recovery in infringement actions made no reference to interest, therefore, the award of prejudgment interest was governed by the common law standard enunciated in *Duplate Corporation* v. *Triplix Safety Glass Company.*[277] The award of prejudgment interest under the *Duplate* standard depended on whether or not the damages were liquidated. Prejudgment interest was generally awarded from the date the damage claim was actually liquidated. In the absence of liquidation, prejudgment interest could only be awarded from the data of infringement, if bad faith or other exceptional circumstances existed.[278]

Damages are considered liquidated if they are relatively certain and ascertainable by reference to an established market value. If the patent holder, had an established royalty fee and damages were determined on the basis of this fee, the patent holder was entitled to prejudgment interest since his damages were considered liquidated. Where damages were based on a court determined royalty fee, however, they were considered unliquidated and prejudgment interest would not be awarded absent exceptional circumstances such as bad faith.[279]

The patent laws governing recovery in infringement actions were amended in 1946, and have since been recodified as 35 U.S.C. Section 284 which states in pertinent part:

Upon finding for the claimant the court shall award the claimant damages adequate to compensate for the infringement, but in no event less than a reasonable royalty for the use made of the invention by the infringer together with interest and costs as fixed by the court.

Some Courts of Appeal have interpreted 35 U.S.C. Section 284 as conferring upon the trial court the discretionary power to award interest either from the date of judgment or from the date of infringement. Other courts have continued to apply the *Duplate* standard of liquidated damages or exceptional circumstances as if it had been incorporated into Section 284.[280]

The United States Supreme Court in *General Motors Corp.* v. *Devex Corp.* put the interpretation controversy to rest by specifically declaring that Section 284 does not incorporate the *Duplate* standard.[281] Instead, Section 284 confers upon the court a general authority to award interest and costs. The award of prejudgment interest, however, is not absolute. Section 284 states that interest shall be 'fixed by the court' and therefore leaves the court with some discretion in the award of interest. 'Prejudgment interest should be awarded under Section 284 absent some justification for withholding such an award, a decision to award prejudgment interest will only be set aside if it constitutes an abuse of discretion'.[282]

The Court's interpretation of Section 284 is based on the underlying purpose of the provision which is to afford the plaintiff full compensation for the infringement.[283] The court 'shall award the claimant damages adequate to compensate for the infringement'.[284] An award of prejudgment interest ensures that the patent holder is placed in the same position he would have been in had the infringer entered into a reasonable royalty agreement with the patent holder since the damages for infringement consist not only of the value of the royalty payments but also the foregone use of the money from the date of infringement to the date of judgment.[285]

Since adequate compensation for an infringement can only be achieved through the award of prejudgment interest, the Court's ruling in the case establishes that the proper standard for the award of interest is not whether circumstances exist to justify an award of prejudgment interest, but rather whether circumstances exist to warrant a withholding of interest.

Canada

Patentability of Microorganisms

The issue of the patentability of microorganisms was addressed by the Canadian Patent Office in the case of *In re Abitibi*. The claims involved a mixed fungal yeast culture that had been acclimatized to spent sulfite liquor.

The acclimatized culture was used to purify spent sulfite liquor from pulp plants through digestion by the yeast culture, thus purifying it. The claim was rejected based on the position that living or viable matter is not patentable subject matter.[286]

The applicant argued that the yeast culture was a man-made product and relied on the United States Supreme Court decision in *Diamond, Commissioner of Patents and Trademarks* v. *Chakrabarty,*[287] which held that a new bacterium produced through human ingenuity and having a distinctive name, character and use, is patentable under the United States patent laws. The *Chakrabarty* decision emphasized that anything is patentable subject matter. Since the new bacterium was not a natural phenomenon, could not be repeated in nature or reproduced in nature unaided by man, it was held patentable under Section 101 of the Patent Act.[288]

The Commissioner of Patents for Canada withdrew the rejection on 18 March 1982, while noting that other Patent Offices, such as Great Britain, Australia, West Germany, and Japan were permitting microorganism patent claims.[289] With this decision, Canada joins these and other countries in recognizing the patentability of microorganisms. Some countries, such as Hungary and Bulgaria, grant patents for new varieties of animals and plants without specifically dealing with microorganisms. Other countries, such as Romania, Czechoslovakia, and the Soviet Union, have passed laws which are directly concerned with the patentability of bacteria or microorganisms. The United Kingdom, Germany, Finland, Columbia and Nigeria have adopted statutory schemes which exclude animals and plants from patent protection while specifically exempting microorganisms from such an exclusion.[290]

The United States decision in *Chakrabarty*[291] was based on the construction of 35 U.S.C. Section 101[292], which defines the scope of patentable subject matter. The courts must rely on this section since the United States does not have laws which specifically address the issue of the patentability of new life forms.

The Canadian decision is expansive in that it is stated to extend to:

(a)   11 microorganisms, yeasts, molds, fungi, bacteria, acinomycetes, unicellar algae, cell lines, viruses or protozoa; in fact, to all new life forms which are produced en masse as chemical compounds are prepared, and are formed in such large numbers that any measurable quantity will possess uniform properties and characteristics.[293]

The decision also made reference to higher life forms by stating that if a new and unobvious insect were created, which was useful and reproducible at will, it would be considered patentable subject matter.[294]

New Uses for Old Compounds

Patent claims for chemical compositions comprised of chemical compounds mixed with an adjuvant, which are useful for plant growth regulation, were presented to the Supreme Court of Canada in the case of *Shell Oil Company v. Commissioner of Patents*. The chemical compounds employed in some of the claims had been previously existing and used compounds while others were new. The court only addressed the claims concerning the use of old chemical compounds for novel purposes.[295]

Shell argued that the invention consisted of the discovery of the novel and new use for the old compound and therefore the composition should be patentable. The Supreme Court of Canada ruled that the patents should be granted and held that a new use for an old compound is patentable. A composition claim is the proper claim form, and may properly present composition claims for newly invented compounds as well as new uses for old compounds.[936]

China

The Chinese Patent Law is now pending formal approval by the National People's Congress.[297] These new laws are part of an effort to promulgate a Western-type patent system in China.

The new laws encompass inventions as well as utility models and industrial designs which are not contrary to public interests, morals, or practices. The minimum periods of protection vary according to the type of work patented. Inventions are granted protection for a minimum of 15 years, utility models for a minimum of 10 years, and industrial designs have a minimum protection of 5 years. Claims are granted on a first-come, first-filed basis.

(2) Copyrights

United States

The rapid development and advancement of technology in audio and video recording equipment has been paralleled by a rapid increase in piracy and counterfeiting of audio and audiovisual works.[298] A representative of the Department of Justice in testimony before the Senate Judiciary Committee, stated: 'Piracy and counterfeiting of copyrighted material, the theft of intellectual property, is now a major white collar crime. The dramatic growth of this problem has been encouraged by the huge profits to be made, while the relatively lenient penalties provided by the current law have done little to stem the tide'.[299]

This rapid increase in piracy and counterfeiting prompted passage of Public Law 97-180, the Piracy and Counterfeiting Amendments Act of 1982. The Act amends Titles 17 and 18 of the United States Code to increase sanctions for record, tape, and film piracy and counterfeiting. Prior to the passage of this legislation, the penalties for infringement were considered inadequate as a deterrent. In a highly-lucrative counterfeiting business, the criminal infringers viewed the potential penalties merely as an incidental cost of doing business.[300] By increasing the sanctions Congress hopes to bring the penalties more in line with the enormous profit being made by criminal infringers. The object is to deter criminal activity, and to encourage prosecutors and judges to view these activities as serious crimes.[301]

18 U.S.C. Section 2318 formerly provided sanctions only for the trafficking in counterfeit labels of phonorecords. The 1982 amendments expand the section to include the trafficking in counterfeit labels of copies of motion pictures and other audiovisual works.[302]

Prior to the 1982 amendments, Section 2318 differentiated between first offenders and repeat offenders with regard to maximum penalties. First offenders faced a maximum penalty of one year of imprisonment and/or a fine of $10,000. Subsequent offenses carried a maximum penalty of two years imprisonment and/or a fine of $25,000. Amended Section 2318 disposes of the difference in penalties for first and subsequent offenses and increases the maximum penalty for any offense to five years imprisonment and/or a fine of $250,000. The penalties would apply to anyone who knowingly traffics in a counterfeit label affixed or designed to be affixed to a record, motion picture, or other audiovisual work.[303]

The requirement of fraudulent intent was also eliminated by the 1982 amendment. It is now sufficient that the offense be committed 'knowingly', i.e., with knowledge that the articles are counterfeit.[304]

P.L. 97-180 also adds Section 2319 to Title 18 of the United States Code, establishing sanctions for the willful infringement of a copyright for the purpose of commercial advantage or private gain.[305] Under Section 2319, the maximum penalties for copyright infringement depend on the type of copyrighted work infringed, whether the infringement is a first or subsequent offense, the number of infringing copies made, and the time frame within which the copies were made or distributed.[306] Penalties range from one year imprisonment and/or a fine of $25,000, up to five years imprisonment and/or a fine of $250,000, depending on the factors enumerated above.[307]

The former penalties for criminal infringement of a copyright were differentiated only on the basis of the type work infringed and whether it was a first or repeat offense. These former penalties were substantially increased by the addition of Section 2319.

Sweden

Also in response to growing piracy activity, Sweden passed amendments to its copyright laws to increase sanctions for copyright infringement.[308] Swedish Courts have characteristically dealt with copyright infringements, in particular, audio and video piracy, with a firm hand.[309] This disposition is reflected in the more stringent sanctions contained in Swedish Statute Book 1982, Nos. 284[310] and 285[311] which relate to the piracy of sound recordings, audiovisual recordings and photographic pictures. These statutes became effective on 1 July 1982.

The amendments include four major changes.[312] The maximum penalty for infringements was increased from six months imprisonment to two years imprisonment; public prosecutors can institute criminal actions without a prior complaint from the injured party; punishable infringements now include attempted or planned acts, in addition to complete acts; and equipment used to fabricate infringing material can now be seized under certain circumstances.

United Kingdom

The United Kingdom is presently considering a Copyright Bill which will amend the present laws concerning sanctions for copyright infringement. The bill will greatly increase penalties for video piracy and other related offenses. The penalty for summary conviction would consist of a fine of up to £1000 and/or two months imprisonment. Conviction on an indictment would carry an unlimited fine and a maximum of two years imprisonment for each offense.[313]

Nigeria

In Nigeria the House of Representatives rejected a bill which would have imposed heavy penalties on pirate recording of tapes, records and cassettes. The opponents of the bill argued that the bill was overly broad and that penalties consisting of prison terms of up to seven years or fines of N500,000 would be applicable to private home recording.[314]

Switzerland: Photocopying

On 12 December 1982, the Swiss Federal Supreme Court ruled that the three conditions contained in Article 22 of the Copyright Act, own use, private use, and not for profit, must be satisfied in order for photocopying to be legal.[315] The case involved the making of 530 copies of an article from Neue Zurcher Zeitung for the post office house magazine. Despite the fact that the copies were not sold, the court ruled that the money saved by reproducing the article 530 times, rather than purchasing 530 copies, was the equivalent of copying with an intent to make a profit.

Japan: Computer Software

On 6 December 1982, the Tokyo District Court rendered the first Japanese decision on the issue of the copyrightability of computer software. The Court ruled, in *Taito* v. *I.N.G. Enterprises*, that computer related software could be considered literary works subject to protection under the Japanese Copyright Law.[316]

United States: Private Noncommercial Videorecording

On 14 June 1982, the United States Supreme Court granted certiorari to review the decision of the Ninth Circuit Court of Appeals in *Universal City Studios, Inc.* v. *Sony Corporation of America*.[317] The Circuit Court of Appeals held that private noncommercial home video recording is not fair use and therefore constitutes copyright infringement. In addition to holding private owners of video recorders liable for copyright infringement, the Court of Appeals held the manufacturers and distributors of video tape recorders liable for contributory infringement since they materially contributed to the infringements.[318]

Upon grant of certiorari, Sony filed a brief on the merits and contended that in-home video recording of copyrighted works constitutes 'fair use' according to 18 U.S.C. Section 107. Section 107, Sony argued, was not intended to restrict 'fair use' to any exact definition but rather enables a case-by-case determination of whether a particular use constitutes a 'fair use'.[319]

Sony further argued that even if in-home video recording is considered direct infringement, the manufacturers of video recorders should not be held liable for contributory infringement since video recorders, like cameras, typewriters and photocopying machines, are staple articles of commerce.[320]

In opposition to these arguments, the copyright owners asserted that the 'fair use' doctrine is limited in purpose and scope. It is only applicable to use by subsequent authors who build on the work of others to create new works. Since video recorder copying involves no independent creativity, the 'fair use' doctrine is not applicable.[321]

The copyright owners countered Sony's 'staple article of commerce' theory by pointing out that this concept is applicable to patents, and that no such concept exists in the area of copyrights. In addition, the articles to which the 'staple article of commerce' theory applies, such as cameras, typewriters and photocopying machines, are used primarily for noninfringing purposes while video recorders have no substantial noninfringing use.[322]

Oral arguments on the case were presented to the United States Supreme Court on 18 January 1983. Six months later, on 6 July 1983, the Court restored the case to the calendar for reargument.[323]

The Ninth Circuit Court of Appeals decision in the *Sony* case, also known as the *Betamax* case, sparked a congressional lobbying war between copyright owners and manufacturers of recording equipment and media, both sides seeking protective legislation from Congress.[324] Seven bills[325] concerning home recording were introduced in the 98th session of Congress, 1982 – 1983. The bills would amend the 'first sale doctrine' which essentially removes any use restrictions on copyrighted material once it is purchased from the copyright holder.[326]

House of Representative bills 175, 1027, 1029 and 1030 closely parallel Senate Bills 31, 32, 33 and 175.[327] HR 1027 and S 32 prohibit the unauthorized commercial rental of record albums. The 'first sale doctrine' in copyright law which permits renting to take place without any role by copyright owners would thus be changed. The Senate Judiciary subcommittee on Patents, Copyrights, and Trademarks extended the provisions of S 32 to require rental permission not only from record companies but from songwriters and publishers as well.[328]

The prohibition on unauthorized rental of copyrighted works under HR 1027 and S 32, would be extended to motion pictures and other audiovisual works by HR 1029 and S 33.[329]

HR 175 and S 175 exempt from liability for copyright infringement, individuals who make video recordings for private noncommercial use, essentially repudiating the holding of the Court of Appeals in the *Sony* case.[330]

Similar exemptions for individuals making private noncommercial audio or visual recordings are contained in HR 31 and S 1030. In addition to the liability exemption, these bills provide for a compulsory licensing system for all audio or video recording equipment and media as well as the payment of royalty fees by the manufacturers and importers of the recording equipment and media. The royalty fees would be distributed to the copyright owners through the Copyright Royalty Tribunal.[311]

All of the bills were sent to the House and Senate Judiciary Committees but none of the proposed legislation made significant progress toward passage, in part due to a desire to wait for the Supreme Court's ruling in the *Sony* case.[332] Now that the Supreme Court has calendared the case for re-argument, the proposed legislation before the 98th Congress will most likely encounter further delay in passage until a final decision is rendered on this highly controversial issue.[333]

Recent Copyright Legislation and Reform

Columbia

On 19 February 1982, the government of Columbia promulgated Law 23 which repealed and replaced the existing copyright law.[334] Law 23 contains major changes and revisions which reform and modernize the previously existing law.

It consists of 260 Sections divided into 19 chapters, incorporating the twenty-three articles of Title XV, Book IV of the Commercial Code which regulated commercial publishing contracts.[335] The incorporated provisions of the Commercial Code have been extended to cover any type of publishing contract, whether civil or commercial. The Columbian legislation also adopts the necessary measures at the domestic level to enable implementation of the rights covered by the international conventions to which it is a party.[336] The new law has also been extended to encompass contracts for cinematographic fixation and phonographic fixation, two areas which were not previously covered.[337]

Barbados

The Barbados Copyright of 1981 – 1982[338] became effective on 1 October 1982. The legislation is an effort to reform and modernize the copyright law. The new Copyright Act repeals the 1905 Act of the Barbados Parliament and provides that the British Act of 1911 ceases to have effect in Barbados.[339] The Act is divided into three parts, copyright proper, neighboring rights, and sanctions and miscellaneous matters.[340]

In addition to the new Copyright Act, Barbados has also enacted a new Patents Act, a new Trade Marks Act and a new Industrial Designs Act. The four new Acts are intended to provide for updated administration of intellectual property rights and to provide the necessary clearance for Barbados to subscribe to the various international organizations for the protection of the owners of intellectual property.[341]

ANTITRUST

United States

El Cid, Ltd. v. *The New Jersey Zinc Company,*[342] decided by the United States District Court for the Southern District of New York, involved a motion for summary judgment by the 'so-called Gulf and Western defendants'[343] based on the 'pivotal' question of whether the intended effects of defendants' action had a sufficiently significant impact upon United States commerce to warrant application of American antitrust laws to adjudicate the extraterritorial dispute.[344] The antitrust claim at issue was based on Section 1 of the Sherman Act, and Section 73 of the Wilson Tariff Act.[345] The Court granted defendants' motion for summary judgment holding that the effect of the alleged conspiracy was at most de minimis.[346]

The case concerned eight gold mining concessions in Bolivia, owned but not presently mined by the defendant Camino Gold Mines Ltd. Plaintiff contended that defendants conspired wrongfully to deprive plaintiff of the concessions. 'The conspiracy is claimed to have affected, among others, the security market and commerce in mining equipment and machinery' in the United States.[347]

The Court granted defendant's motion citing the line of cases beginning with Judge Learned Hand's statement in *United States* v. *Aluminum Co. of America:*[348]

> We should not impute to Congress an intent to punish all whom its courts can catch, for conduct which has not consequence in the United States.

The Court noted that the claimed effects on United States' commerce were at most de minimis, but plaintiff argued that any conspiracy to eliminate a competitor is a per se antitrust violation.[349] The Court disagreed and stated that it had discarded the line of cases holding that such a conspiracy was a per se violation, and instead adopted the rule that such conduct only rises to the level of a Sherman Act violation when it has an anticompetitive effect.[350]

The United States Court of Appeals for the Fifth Circuit considered the extent of the Noerr-Pennington doctrine in *Coastal States Marketing, Inc.* v. *Hunt.*[351] The issue was whether petitioning immunity shielded from antitrust scrutiny the defendants' pursuit of companies dealing in nationalized Libyan oil.[352]

Defendants discovered oil in the concession area in Libya in 1961. They developed the concession until 1971 when the Libyan government nationalized the oil field. Defendants refused to accept the action, and joined others in publicizing their claims of ownership. The defendants also traced the movement of the claimed oil and sent notices to anyone suspected of dealing in it and initiated a number of lawsuits in various countries. Through this legal action and boycott, defendants took joint action to protect their rights.[353]

Plaintiff contracted to purchase the subject oil in 1973, and was warned by an agent of defendant Hunt's eventual co-conspirator, B.P. Exploration Company (Libya), that 'B.P. would be doing everything in their power to hamper the fulfillment of any contract that was entered into for this crude'.[354] Defendants' joint action was taken under the shield of the Noerr-Pennington doctrine for petitioning immunity. The doctrine basically provides that:[355]

> Joint efforts to influence public officials do not violate the antitrust laws even though intended to eliminate competition. Such conduct is not illegal either standing alone or as part of a broad scheme itself violative of the Sherman Act.

The Court in the instant litigation initially established, contrary to Coastal's argument, that petitioning immunity is applicable to boycotts.[356] The Court then confronted the issue of whether petitioning a foreign government should be treated differently than the petitioning of officials in the government of the United States. The basis for such a distinction would be the interpretation of the Noerr-Pennington doctrine as an American constitutional principle as determined in *Occidental Petroleum Corp.* v. *Buttes Gas & Oil Co.*[357] The Court in the instant case, however, rejected the *Occidental* holding that the disputed principle is not confined to efforts to influence domestic officials. The Noerr-Penington doctrine is instead also applicable to joint efforts to influence foreign governments. The Court implied this principle in part from the United States Supreme Court decision in *Continental Ore Co.* v. *Union Carbide & Carbon Corp.*[358]

On 8 October 1982, the Foreign Trade Antitrust Improvements Act of 1982[359] was enacted into law in the United States. The new law was enacted as Title IV of the Export Trading Act of 1982.

The Sherman Act (15 USC Section 1 et seq) was supplemented by the New Act through Section 7 which provides for the following:[360]

> Section 7. This Act shall not apply to conduct involving trade or commerce (other than import commerce) with foreign nations unless –
>   (1) such conduct has a direct, substantial, and reasonably foreseeable effect –

(A) on trade or commerce which is not trade or commerce with foreign nations, or on import commerce with foreign nations; or

(B) on export trade or export commerce with foreign nations, of a person engaged in such trade or commerce in the United States; and

(2) such effect is the basis of the violation alleged under this Act. If this Act applies to such conduct only because of the operation of paragraph (1) (B), then this Act shall apply to such conduct only for injury to export business in the United States

Section 5(a) of the Federal Trade Commission Act (15 Section 45(a)) was also supplemented through the addition of the following paragraph:[361]

(3) This subsection shall not apply to unfair methods of competition involving commerce with foreign nations (other than import commerce) unless –

(A) such methods of competition have a direct, substantial, and reasonably foreseeable effect –

(i) on commerce which is not commerce with foreign nations, or on import commerce with foreign nations; or

(ii) on export commerce with foreign nations, of a person engaged in such commerce in the United States; and

(B) such effect gives rise to a claim under the provisions of this subsection, other than this paragraph.

If this subsection applies to such methods of competition only because of this operation of subparagraph (A)(ii), this subsection shall apply to such conduct only for injury to export business in the United States.

Julian von Kalinowski, a noted commentator on the antitrust laws of the United States, claims that the reason for the legislation was to remedy the existence of conflicting judicial authority which prevented an orderly enforcement of the anti-trust laws that relate to foreign trade. Similar inconsistencies also existed in the views of the United States Justice Department.[362]

Von Kalinowski asserts that the existence of the 'reasonably foreseeable' language is present to further promote certainty in determining the applicability of anti-trust laws to a given situation even if the effect of the actions being excluded is direct or substantial.

European Commission

On 15 December 1982, the European commission condemned Compagnie Royale Asturienne des Mines (CRAM), of France; Rheinisches Zinkwalzwerk Gmbh (RZ), of Germany; Société des Mines et Fonderies de Zinc de la Vieille-Montagne (VM), of France; Société et Métallurgique de Penarroya (PYA), of France; and Société Anonyme de Paryon, of Belgium for implementing a series of restrictive practices.

The Commission found that CRAM and RZ acted together with the purpose of protecting their respective markets from all uncontrolled imports. The two companies included a clause in an agreement with a Belgian wholesaler that specified that goods supplied by the companies would be sold only in a country outside of the specified community. When CRAM and RZ found that the Belgian wholesaler had violated the agreement, they sought enforcement. For this the Commission fined CRAM 400,000 European Currency Units and fined RZ 500,000 European Currency Units.

Three other agreements were never submitted to the Commission for exemptions under Article 85(3) of the EEC treaty. It was the view of the Commission that the agreements would not have been granted exemptions even if submitted for consideration due to their duration. The first of the three agreements was between CRAM, RZ and VM providing that each would supply the other with rolled zinc if one of the parties became unable to produce temporarily. With regard to this agreement, the Commission said that it could not approve agreements that substituted ongoing mutual assistance for the normal risks of competition. The second agreement was between CRAM and PYA. Under this agreement, PYA would have refrained from production, investment, and research in rolled zinc in exchange for an undertaking by CRAM that it would be allowed one third of the French zinc alloy market. The third agreement was between CRAM and Prayon requiring Prayon to obtain its required supplies of rolled zinc from CRAM for fifteen years.[363]

PROCEDURE

(1) Jurisdiction and the Foreign Sovereign Immunities Act

The 1976 Foreign Sovereign Immunities Act (FSIA) codifies as a matter of federal law, the restrictive theory of sovereign immunity.[364] Broadly stated, the FSIA bars state and federal court jurisdiction over a foreign state's purely public acts unless one of the exceptions in 28 U.S.C. Sections 1605 – 1607 applies.[365]

Commercial Exception

Several recent cases illustrate the difficulties which United States courts have experienced in applying the commercial activity exception to sovereign immunity under the FSIA.[366] Section 1605(a)(2) provides:[367]

(a) A foreign state shall not be immune from the jurisdiction of courts of the United States or of the States in any case ...

(b) in which the activity is based upon a commercial activity carried on in the United States by the foreign state; or upon an act performed in the United States in connection with a commercial activity of the foreign state elsewhere; or upon an act outside the territory of the United States in connection with a commercial activity of the foreign state elsewhere and that act causes a direct effect in the United States.

In *Gibbons* v. *Udaras na Gaeltachta*[368], the United States District Court for the Southern District of New York held that the commercial activity exception to the FSIA provided a sufficient basis for statutory subject matter jurisdiction over the plaintiff's claims.[369]

Plaintiffs, United States investors, sued Udaras na Gaeltachta (UG) and the Industrial Development Authority of Ireland (IDA), instrumentalities of the Republic of Ireland for breach of contract and fraud relating to a proposed investment in Ireland. Plaintiffs met with UG and IDA in the United States several times to discuss the investors' plan to build a factory in Ireland to manufacture cosmetic containers. UG and the investors formed a joint venture company (IPC) which was established in Ireland.[370] Several disputes arose between UG and the investors; the investors charging that the leased factory did not meet specifications and that UG withheld scheduled payments of the capital grants it had agreed to provide the investors. IPC went out of business in 1980 and the investors returned to the United States where they filed the instant action against both IDA and UG.[371]

The commercial activity exception only applies to a cause of action where (1) the cause of action is 'based upon' an act performed in connection with conduct that qualifies as 'commercial activity', and (2) the act sued upon and the connected commercial activity bear some relation to the United States as described in either clause 2 or 3 of Section 1605(a)(2).[372] A foreign state's breach of an agreement is necessarily performed 'in connection with' that agreement and is therefore performed in connection with 'an activity carried on by a foreign state'.[373] All of the causes of action against UG and IDA were based upon acts that were performed in connection with their participation in the joint venture agreement.

The commercial character of an activity is determined by looking at the nature of the activity rather than the purpose, (this is known as the Nature of the Act test). Also, if the activity is one in which a private person would normally carry on for profit, such activity is commercial under the FSIA despite the fact that it was intended to serve the most integral or fundamental objectives.[374]

Applying the foregoing principles, the court held that UG's participation in the joint venture constituted commercial activity under FSIA because the joint venture could just as easily have been entered into by a private party and for a pecuniary, rather than a public purpose.[375] IDA, as well as UG, conducted extensive activities in the United States relating to the joint venture agreement. IDA had offices in New York which it used in conducting promotional activities in the United States in bringing about the joint venture agreement. UG also held substantial contractual negotiations with United States investors in the United States and the joint venture agreement required UG to buy goods and services in the United States for use in the factory in Ireland.[376] The Court also denied defendant's motion to dismiss based on forum non conveniens. After weighing the interests of the parties, the inconvenience of litigating in an alternative forum versus the present forum, the Court concluded that the case should be tried in the United States.

In *Gilson* v. *Republic of Ireland,*[377] the United States Court of Appeals for the District of Columbia reversed in part the United States District Court for the District of Columbia which held that it lacked subject matter jurisdiction and that the commercial exception did not apply. Plaintiff, Gilson, filed a complaint against the Republic of Ireland and three Irish corporations for alleged 'commercial misdeeds'.[378] Gilson was allegedly induced by two instrumentalities of Ireland, organized under Irish law, into entering into a commercial venture to develop quartz crystals in Ireland. This venture required plaintiff to move himself and his family to Ireland and to reveal certain proprietary information. Subsequent to the move, Gilson charged defendants with breach of contract, misappropriation of patent rights and proprietary information, and interference with ongoing contractual relations with another Irish corporation.

The Court held that counts three and four which charged defendants with stealing plaintiff's expertise, patent rights and equipment fell within the commercial exception Section 1605(a)(2). This was an action based '... upon an act performed in the United States in connection with a commercial activity of the foreign state elsewhere ...'.[379] The 'act' of enticing Gilson from the United States and the commercial activity was the quartz capital business in Ireland.

In *Alberti* v. *Empresa Nicaraguensa De La Carne,*[380] the Court of Appeals for the Seventh Circuit held that the commercial exception did not apply. Plaintiffs owned stock in defendant corporation, a Nicaraguan corporation in the beef packaging and slaughtering business. The Nicaraguan government nationalized the corporation. Plaintiff had purchased some beef from the corporation, but never paid for it.[381] Plaintiff sued defendant in Illinois District Court for the wrongful conversion of plaintiff's stock, and sought a declaratory judgment approving plaintiff's right to offset the value of his converted stock against the value of the purchased beef. Defendants filed a claim in Florida District Court requesting payment for the purchased beef. Defendants removed the Illinois action to federal court and moved in part to dismiss due to lack of subject matter jurisdiction under the FSIA.

Plaintiffs claimed that because they sought to offset their debt to the Nicaraguan corporation with their loss from the nationalization of their stocks, this action was clearly based on a commercial activity of defendants carried on within the United States. The Court held otherwise, stating that the commercial transaction, the debt over the beef, was not the controversy with which the lawsuit was concerned. The basis of the lawsuit was the nationalization of the Nicaraguan corporation, a purely public act. Because such nationalization was not in violation of international law, defendants did not lose their immunity under Section 1605(a)(3). In part Section 1605(a)(3) states that a foreign state does not lose its immunity from suit 'in which rights in property taken in violation of international law are in issue and that property or any property exchanged for such property is present in the United States in connection with a commercial activity carried on in the United States by the foreign state ...'.[382]

Harris Corp. v. *National Iranian Radio, Etc.*,[383] heard by the United States Court of Appeals for the Eleventh Circuit, held that appellant's sovereign immunity was waived under the commercial exception.[384] Plaintiff, an American manufacturer, sued an Iranian radio and television station and a bank to enjoin payment and receipt of payment on a letter of credit. Plaintiff also sought a judgment declaring that the contract underlying the letter of credit and guarantee was terminated by force majeure as a result of the Iranian resolution and subsequent seizure of U.S. hostages.[385]

One defendant asserted sovereign immunity based on lack of subject matter jurisdiction. The Court held that appellants' demands for payments on the letters of credit did involve the necessary amount of 'direct effect', as required under Section 1605(a)(2), because they 'triggered the entry of a blocked account on Harris' books in Florida'.[386] The letter of credit arrangements, structured according to appellant's demands, had a direct, significant and foreseeable financial consequence in the United States. Thus, the effect was sufficiently direct and within the United States that Congress would have wanted an American court to hear the case.[387] Maintenance of the suit in the U.S. was also consistent with due process as the minimum contacts standard set forth in *International Shoe* v. *Washington* were met.[388] Appellants both conducted business activities in the United States in connection with the letters of credit, therefore, they could 'have reasonably anticipated being subject to suit' in the United States.[389] The Court held that sovereign immunity had been waived because the commercial exception was met, and thus, 28 U.S.C. Section 1330(a) subject matter jurisdiction existed and service of process was proper (discussed infra); consequently the court also had personal jurisdiction. Finally, suit was proper as Constitutional Due Process was satisfied.

Service of Process

To obtain personal jurisdiction over a suit involving a foreign entity, all that is required under FSIA is that subject matter jurisdiction and service of process be satisfied. In *Harris,* supra, the Court found that the service of process was proper despite the fact that Harris had not fully complied with certain technical requirements in serving notice under Section 1608(b)(2).[390] Because notice was actually received by the defendant, this was sufficient and the court had personal jurisdiction over the suit as well as subject matter jurisdiction.

In *Alberti*, supra, the complaint and summons served by mail upon the Nicaraguan Ambassador in Washington, D.C. was improper under Section 1608(3) because the ambassador was not the head of the ministry of foreign affairs.[391] Section 1608(3) states:

> if service cannot be made under paragraphs (1) or (2) by sending a copy of the summons and complaint and a notice of suit, together with a translation of each into the official language of the foreign state, by any form of mail requiring a signed receipt, to be addressed and dispatched by the clerk of the court to the head of the ministry of foreign affairs of the foreign state concerned ...

Jackson v. *People's Republic of China,*[392] involved a suit between plaintiffs, holders of certain railroad bonds, and the successor of the issuer government, the People's Republic of China. Plaintiffs sued to recover payment of the bonds which were in default. Service of process was found proper under Section 1608(4). When the summons, complaint, and notice of suit were transmitted to the Embassy of the People's Republic of China, on 16 May 1980, service was deemed made upon this date of transmittal.[393] Service of process was held valid despite the fact that the embassy returned all of the documents to the Director of Special Consular Services about one month later.[394]

Waiver by Treaty

In *Harris*, supra, plaintiff asserted that defendants also waived their sovereign immunity in an international agreement between the parties. Section 1330(a) permits a district court to exercise:[395]

original jurisdiction without regard to amount in controversy of any nonjury civil action against a foreign state as defined in Section 1603(a) of this title as to any claim for relief in personam with respect to which the foreign state is not entitled either under Section 1605 – 1607 of this title or under any applicable international agreement.

FSIA does not limit waiver of sovereign immunity to those commercial transaction exceptions listed in Sections 1605 – 1607. These exceptions are not exclusive and do not preclude United States courts from obtaining jurisdiction if immunity has been waived by a treaty.[396] The legislative history confirms this stating: 'Significantly, each of the immunity provisions in the bill, Section 1605 – 1607, requires some connection between the lawsuit and the United States, *or* an expressed or implied waiver by the foreign state of its immunity from jurisdiction'.[397]

The Treaty of Amity, Economic Relations and Consular Rights between the United States and Iran[398] specifically states in Article XI, Section 4 that no enterprise of either party shall be immune from suit if it engages in 'commercial, industrial, shipping or other business activities' within the other contracting state.[399] As discussed earlier, this requirement was clearly met, therefore, the Iranian defendants were subject to suit as the treaty effected an express waiver.

Implied Waiver

In *Maritime*, supra, the United States Court of Appeals found that there was not an implied waiver of sovereign immunity as a result of an arbitration agreement. Section 1605(a)(1) states that 'a foreign state shall not be immune in any case in which the foreign state has waived its immunity either explicitly or by implication ...'.[400] The House Report stated, in its explanation of this section, that implicit waivers have been found in cases where a foreign country has agreed to arbitrate in another country or where a foreign state has agreed that a particular country's laws should govern the contract.[401]

Because the contract in this case expressly stipulated that the law of Guinea would be used to interpret the contract, the parties' agreement to submit future disputes to an ICSID arbitration in the United States could not constitute an implied waiver within the meaning of Section 1605(a)(1).[402] Pre-FSIA cases held that agreements to arbitrate in the United States waived immunity from suit in the United States because such agreements could only be effective if the United States courts were considered to have a role in the process by compelling arbitration that stalled along the way. Because this particular ICSID arbitration agreement did not contemplate such a role for the United States' courts, it did not waive Guinea's sovereign immunity despite the fact that the arbitration would occur in the United States.[403]

Foreign States

In *Transportes aeros De Angola* v. *Ronair, Inc. and Jet Traders Investment Corp.*,[404] the District Court for the District of Delaware held that an instrumentality of a non-recognized foreign government was a foreign state for purposes of the FSIA. TAAG, a juridicial entity of the Ministry of Transport of the People's Republic of Angola sued Ronair and Jet Traders, a Florida corporation, for breach of a written contract to purchase a Boeing 707 aircraft. Jurisdiction was based on diversity of citizenship, 28 U.S.C. Section 1332(a)(4).[405]

Defendant, Ronair, moved to dismiss pursuant to Federal Rules of Civil Procedure 12(b)(1), lack of subject matter jurisdiction, on the ground that the TAAG was an instrumentality of a government not recognized by the United States as the true sovereign of the territory it purportedly controls, and thus did not have standing to sue in the United States courts.[406] Ronair argued that the District Court did not have jurisdiction over the dispute and that a contrary holding allegedly '... would eliminate the fundamental political sanction of nonrecognition, and thus undermine the right of the executive branch to control United States foreign policy'.[407]

Courts have construed 'foreign state' to mean a political entity that is recognized by the executive branch of the United States government as a sovereign and independent nation. An entity must be so recognized in order for its citizens or subjects to fall within the scope of diversity jurisdiction.[408] A foreign country not recognized as a foreign state may still fall within the statute under 'de facto' recognition. 'De facto' recognition acknowledges a country, not officially, a 'foreign state' as a foreign state in order to satisfy alienage jurisdiction for various policy reasons.[409]

The Court acknowledged that TAAG was a separate corporate entity and an instrumentality of Angola, but the issue was whether jurisdiction was valid under 28 U.S.C. Section 1332(a)(4) because Ronair argued that TAAG was not a 'foreign state'. According to Ronair, the term 'foreign state' only includes political entities recognized by the United States.[410] 'The obvious purpose of the judicially made rule denying a forum to unrecognized governments is to give full effect to the decision of the executive branch to refuse to receive that government's diplomatic representatives'.[411] In this case, however, the Department of Commerce in consultation with the State

Department, sanctioned TAAG's commercial dealings with Ronair by issuing a license to export the Boeing aircraft to Angola for TAAG's use. Further, the State Department, in response to the parties' solicitations of its opinion, concerning the propriety of the suit, stated that permitting TAAG to have standing in United States' courts would be consistent with the foreign policy interests of the United States.[412]

Therefore, because the executive branch, through the State and Commerce Departments, evinced a definite desire to remove the non-recognition status impediment for TAAG to bring suit in the United States, defendants' motion to dismiss was denied, as the District Court did have jurisdiction under Section 1332(a)(4).

Tort Exception

In *Frolova* v. *Union of Soviet Socialist Republics,*[413] the District Court for the Northern District of Illinois held that the tort exception to the FSIA did not apply. Plaintiff filed suit in the United States against the Soviet Union for its refusal to allow her husband to immigrate to the United States. Plaintiff claimed that the loss of consortium tort fell within Section 1605(a)(5) (the exception to sovereign immunity for tortious acts).

The Court held that the tort immunity exception did not cover plaintiff's loss of consortium claim as the exception was intended to cover ordinary tort claims arising out of foreign states' activities in the United States. 'After reviewing the statute and its legislative history ... it is this court's opinion that the FSIA was not designed to provide jurisdiction over a foreign sovereign in a case such as this'.[414]

Alien Parties

Aliens may gain access to the federal courts through several statutes. The Alienage Jurisdiction Statute is one example and provides that:[415]

> federal courts shall have jurisdiction over actions between citizens of a United States state and citizens or subjects of a foreign state and over actions between citizens of different United States states in which citizens or subjects of a foreign state are additional parties.

Those persons recognized as citizens or subjects of a foreign state come within the scope of alienage jurisdiction under the United States Constitution Article III, Section 2 and the diversity jurisdiction statute 28 U.S.C. Section 1332(a). Foreign jurisdiction exists if a person is recognized as a citizen or subject of a foreign state.[416] The person seeking federal court jurisdiction has the burden of proving that the alien is a citizen or subject of that nation.

Generally, alienage jurisdiction can only exist when aliens are on one side of the controversy. Normally it does not exist if both parties are aliens.[417] In a unanimous decision, however, the United States Supreme Court held in *Verlinden B.V.* v. *Central Bank of Nigeria* that the FSIA authorized a suit by an alien against a foreign state in a Federal District Court, and that such action did not violate Article III of the United States Constitution.[418] 'The Court held that federal interests in foreign affairs and regulation of foreign commerce provide sufficient basis for federal jurisdiction in all cases against foreign states, including those that involve no substantive federal issues beyond the question of sovereign immunity'.[419]

The case involved a contract between the Federal Republic of Nigeria and petitioner Verlinden, a Dutch corporation, for the purchase of cement by Nigeria. Nigeria was to establish a confirmed letter of credit for the purchase price, through Slavenburg's Bank in Amsterdam. However, respondent, Central Bank of Nigeria improperly established an unconfirmed letter of credit payable through Morgan Guaranty Trust Co. in New York.[420] Nigeria had numerous cement contracts with other suppliers and Central Bank unilaterally ordered its correspondent banks, including Morgan Guaranty, to adopt a series of amendments to all letters of credit issued in connection with the cement contracts.

Plaintiff sued Central Bank in United States District Court for the Southern District of New York charging that defendant's actions constituted an anticipatory breach of the letter of credit. Plaintiff alleged jurisdiction under 28 U.S.C. Section 1330 of the FSIA.[421] Section 1330 generally states that District Courts have original jurisdiction regardless of the amount in controversy of any nonjury civil action against a foreign state (as defined in Section 1603(a)) as to any claim for relief in personam so long as the foreign state is not entitled to immunity either under Sections 1605 and 1607 or under any applicable international agreement.[422]

Article III of the United States Constitution provides two sources of authority to grant jurisdiction over foreign states under the FSIA; the diversity clause and the 'arising under' clause.[423] The Court held the diversity clause inapplicable, but stated the 'arising under' clause was broad enough to grant statutory subject matter jurisdiction to actions for foreign plaintiffs under the FSIA.[424] The 'arising under' clause, Article III, Section 2, Clause 1 states in part that 'the judicial power of the United States shall extend to all Cases, in law and Equity, arising under this Constitution, the laws of the United States, and Treaties made ... under their Authority ...'.[425]

The broad scope of Article III 'arising under' was articulated by Chief Justice Marshall in *Osborn* v. *Bank of the United States* wherein the Court stated that 'Congress may confer on the federal courts jurisdiction over any case or controversy that might call for the application of federal law'.[426] In this case, a suit against a foreign state under the FSIA necessarily raises questions of federal law at the very outset because it requires applying the substantive provisions of the Act to determine if one of the specified exemptions applies; hence, it clearly 'arises under' federal law, as that term is used in Article III.[427] The Supreme Court remanded this case to the Second Circuit for a determination as to whether any of the exemptions applied.

(2) Sovereign Immunity Generally

The Organization of American States: Inter-American Draft Convention on Jurisdictional Immunity of States,[428] which was approved by the Inter-American Judicial Committee on 21 January 1983 in Rio de Janeiro is similar to the FSIA in many respects. Article 3 provides states' immunity from other states' jurisdiction for acts performed by virtue of its governmental powers. Immunity also applies to activities concerning property owned and assets used by the State in connection with its governmental authority Section II provides exceptions to jurisdictional immunity including waiver by implication, Article 7(b), action involving real property located in the forum state Article 6(c), tort exception Article 6(e), and counterclaim exception Article 7(c). In contrast to the FSIA commercial exception, the OAS Act limits the exception to provide immunity for claims relating to trade or commercial activities undertaken only in the State of the forum. Trade or commercial activities are defined as the 'performance of a particular transaction or commercial or trading act pursuant to its ordinary trade operation'.

Section III provides in Articles 8 – 15 procedural rules, i.e., notice, service of process, etc., also quite similar to the provision in the FSIA. Section V, Article 17 states that this convention will not apply retroactively to any proceedings initiated prior to the date it enters into force.[429]

Argentine courts likewise have jurisdiction over a foreign state acting in its sovereign capacity. Thus, a foreign state may assert its immunity from suit in Argentina only if the cause of action relates to public acts of a governmental nature. Even though, however, Argentine courts have jurisdiction over a foreign state regarding the foreign state's private acts, appearance in court is optional. A foreign state must consent to Argentine jurisdiction.[430]

Limitation of Action in Scotland

In Publication Report 74, the Scottish Law Commission recommended sim-
plifying present law regarding the time limitations for which claims for personal injuries must be brought. Presently, the law states that such claims
must be brought within three years of the injury or the time when the pursuer
becomes aware of the injury and its extent. In cases where the injury is not
immediately apparent, one of the factors from which to determine when the
time would begin to run should be knowledge of the identity of the person
responsible for the injury.[431]

(3) Act of State Doctrine

A suit brought in a United States court against a foreign sovereign may be
barred by either the FSIA or the Act of State Doctrine (AOS).[432] The AOS
doctrine is a doctrine of judicial restraint rather than a jurisdictional doctrine. 'The AOS doctrine is a policy of judicial abstention from inquiry into
the validity of an act by a foreign state within its own sovereignty ... It also
differs from the FSIA in that the AOS doctrine may be invoked by private
citizens whereas sovereign immunity may only be pleaded by the foreign
state itself'.[433]

Similar to the FSIA, there are several exceptions to the AOS doctrine.
Since the AOS doctrine is discretionary with the court, it does not preclude
United States courts from hearing a case. The Bernstein exception applies
when there has been an express representation or statement from the
Executive department. This is usually a letter from the State Department to
the court hearing the particular case stating that the application of the AOS
doctrine would not advance the interests of American foreign policy. The
commercial exception applies when the foreign state's conduct is private and
commercial in nature. The 'treaty exception' applies where a treaty or other
unambiguous convention establishes controlling legal principles. Finally,
the Hickenlooper Amendment exception, precludes the use of the AOS
doctrine to actions involving expropriations carried out in violation of international law.[434]

Several recent cases have dealt with various questions involving application of the AOS doctrine and its exceptions. In *De Roburt* v. *Gannett Co.,
Inc.*[435] the United States District Court for the District of Hawaii held that
questions as to how and why the government of the Republic of Nauru made
improper and secret loans to the Marshall Island were non-justiciable under
the AOS doctrine.

Plaintiff, De Roburt, President of Nauru (an Island Republic in the

Pacific) sued Gannett Inc. and its subsidiary, Guam Publications, Inc., for libel in connection with stories about loans made by a governmental corporation of Nauru to alleged separatist interests in another foreign state. Defendant moved to dismiss based on the AOS doctrine. Plaintiff, however, claimed that the loan in question placed the case within the commercial exception to the doctrine. Plaintiff's claim was based on the ground that the loan was in fact made by the Republic of Nauru Finance Corporation, not by the Government.

The Court stated that the loan was unquestionably an act of the State covered by the AOS doctrine. The commercial exception was held inapplicable because the corporation's liabilities were guaranteed by the Government, and furthermore, governmental approval of any loan was required. Plaintiff further contended that the AOS doctrine only applied where the legality, motivation, and validity of the act of state in question was the central issue in the case. The central issue in this case was not merely whether De Roburt was involved in making and arranging the loan, but rather the characterization of the loan, whether or not it was legal. This would determine if plaintiff was in fact libeled by a potentially false characterization of the loan.[436]

'... [T]he AOS doctrine extends to situations in which the act of state in question is an element of the claim being made but does not require a direct challenge of the legality of the sovereign act ...'.[437] Plaintiff plead libel and a necessary element of any libel action is that a defamatory statement be published. Thus, the validity, legality, and motivation behind the loan was decidedly an issue in the case. The Court held that the AOS doctrine barred it from deciding the case because resolution of the main issues in the case would undoubtedly cause the court to examine the validity, legality, and motivation of the Nauru government in making the loan to the Marshall Islands.[438] Such an examination was not permitted by the AOS doctrine, its underlying policies and rationale.

In z *illiams* v. *Curtiss-Wright Corporation*,[439] the United States Court of Appeal for the Third Circuit affirmed the lower court. The lower court had held that the AOS doctrine did not preclude it from examining the motives of a foreign government for refusing to buy jet engines and parts from the plaintiff.[440] Plaintiffs and defendants were competitors selling surplus jet engine parts and accessories to foreign governments. Plaintiff sued defendant alleging anti-trust violations in the United States and abroad. Defendant moved to dismiss on the ground that the AOS doctrine prohibits the court from examining the motives of the foreign governments which were no longer buying parts from plaintiff.[441]

In order to determine if the AOS doctrine applies, the court should analyze the nature of the conduct in issue and the effect upon the parties.

The Court held that a private defendant could not avoid anti-trust liability because its illegal scheme involves some acts by an agent of a foreign government. 'The AOS doctrine should not be applied to thwart legitimate American regulatory goals in the absence of a showing that adjudication may hinder international relations'.[442] There was no such showing and further, the Court held that the plaintiff was not challenging the validity of the foreign government's decision to boycott him, but rather, the anti-competitive effects of defendant's activities.

In *Frolova*, supra, the Court held that the Soviet denial of allowing plaintiff's husband to emigrate was an act of state, thus not a subject which the United States courts could properly adjudicate, because under the AOS doctrine a state should not inquire into the validity or propriety of another state's public acts.[443]

In *Compania de Gas Nuevo Laredo, S.A.* v. *Entex,*[444] the United States Court of Appeals for the Fifth Circuit affirmed the United States District Court for the Southern District of Texas' dismissal which held that the AOS doctrine precluded consideration of a tort claim. This case involved a diversity action brought by a privately owned Mexican company, Compania de Gas de Nuevo Laredo, S.A. (CGNL) against an American natural gas exporter, Entex, on a tort and breach of contract claim.

Pursuant to a longstanding contract, Entex exported gas to CGNL which supplied gas to the City of Nuevo Laredo in the Republic of Mexico. Because CGNL could not pass through certain rate increases in the cost of gas to its customers, CGNL became delinquent in its account with Entex. Entex sent letters to CGNL and various officials in the Mexican government threatening to suspend deliveries unless CGNL paid its past debts according to the contract. Shortly thereafter, the Mexican government temporarily took over the company's assets and rights in Mexico.[445]

CGNL filed suit, claiming that Entex unlawfully conspired with Mexican officials to gain control of CGNL's assets. Entex charged that the AOS doctrine precluded an inquiry into the alleged conspiracy. The District Court stated that several factors must be balanced in determining the applicability of the AOS doctrine; '... the degree of involvement of the foreign state, whether the validity of its law or regulation was an issue, whether the foreign state was a named defendant, and whether there was a showing of harm to American commerce'.[446]

Despite the fact that the government of Mexico was not a defendant, consideration of CGNL's charges would have required a determination of the legality of Mexico's conduct in taking over CGNL and the validity of that act under Mexican law. There was no showing that the alleged conspiracy would adversely affect United States commerce. Further, the Court held that the expropriation itself was a governmental, not commercial act; thus, the commercial exception of the AOS doctrine was inapplicable.[447] Contrary to CGNL's claim, the Court also held that there was an implied waiver by virtue of the Mexican government's letter to CGNL which allowed CGNL to prosecute claims before any authority, foreign or national. Even if the letter from a non-litigating foreign government did constitute an implied waiver, it could not operate to deprive a private defendant, Entex, from asserting the AOS doctrine as a defense.[448]

Finally, CGNL claimed that the Hickenlooper exception applied to allow suit in the district court because the alleged conspiracy between Entex and the Mexican government resulted in the taking of CGNL's assets in Mexico without just compensation; thereby violating international and United States law. In an opinion by the Second Circuit Court of Appeals, the judge held that Congress intended for the Hickenlooper Amendment to apply only to cases involving claims of title to American owned property located in the United States, nationalized by a foreign government in violation of international law.[449] In this case, the Hickenlooper Amendment was not applicable since neither the nationalized property nor its proceeds were within the United States.

In *Ethiopian Spice Extraction v. Kalamazoo Spice, Etc.,*[450] the United States District Court for the Western District of Michigan held that because none of the exceptions was found to apply, the AOS doctrine precluded the court from considering the legality for the expropriation of Kalamazoo Spice Extraction Company's (Kal-Spice), shares in the Ethiopian corporation, ESESCO, by the Ethiopian government.[451] Kal-Spice, an American corporation, filed a complaint against the Ethiopian government seeking damages for the expropriation of its interests in an Ethiopian corporation, ESESCO. Ethiopia's nationalization of ESECO's shares held by Kal-Spice was an act of state, as ESESCO was one of a hundred such entities nationalized pursuant to the 'Provisional Military Administrative Council Declaration of Economic Policy' which became effective 3 February 1975.[452]

The Bernstein exception was inapplicable as there had been no statement from the Executive Branch to the court on this case; also the act was a purely governmental one and no facts indicated that Ethiopia was engaged in any commercial activity. The Treaty of Amity and Economic Relations ratified between Ethiopia and the United States did not provide an unambiguous controlling legal standard (stating that property shall not be taken without 'prompt payment of just and effective compensation'). Thus, the Treaty could not be used as an exception to the Act of State doctrine.[453]

The Hickenlooper Amendment exception[454] also did not apply because the expropriated property, ESESCO shares, was not located in the United States. The court followed the general rule that the situs of shares of stock is the place of incorporation, which in this instance was Ethiopia.[455] Thus, because no exceptions applied, the AOS doctrine barred the Court from considering the validity of the Ethiopian government's taking of ESESCO shares from Kal-Spice.

The Department of State expressed its views concerning the AOS doctrine as it related to foreign expropriations in a letter dated 12 November 1982 to the Solicitor General of the United States. The State Department was concerned about the Court's decision in the *Kalamazoo Spice* case to abstain from ruling on the merits of the case because of the AOS doctrine.[456] Specifically, the Court attached major significance to the absence of a letter from the State Department stating that adjudication would not be harmful to the conduct of foreign affairs.[457] Also, the Court felt that the Treaty of Amity and Economic Relations between the United States and Ethiopia was too general and did not define a controlling legal standard which it could apply without conflicting 'with the Executive Branch's assertion of a governing legal standard in the conduct of foreign affairs'.[458] The State Department letter stated that it believed the Treaty did establish a controlling legal standard to apply for compensation for the expropriated shares. Where there is a controlling legal standard for compensation, such as in the expropriation cases, the State Department felt that the presumption should be that adjudication would not be inconsistent with foreign policy interests under the AOS doctrine. Further, the courts should not infer from the State Department's silence in such cases that the AOS doctrine mandates judicial abstention because adjudication would be harmful to United States foreign policy.[459]

(4) Remedies

United States Limits Antitrust Damages for Foreign States

On 15 December 1982, the United States Senate passed an amended version of the Antitrust Reciprocity Act of 1982.[460] The bill had been previously amended by the House of Representatives on 13 December 1982 following approximately four years of study, debate, and consideration.[461] The amendment and act as passed modifies the Clayton Act[462] by limiting the recovery available to injured foreign states in antitrust suits to actual damages and the costs of suit.[463] Prior law allowed any persons injured as a result of antitrust violations compensation in the form of triple damages and costs. The limitation to actual damages, however, is designed to apply only to suits by or on behalf of a foreign government or instrumentality thereof.

The amendment is not intended to apply to entities that conduct primarily or exclusively commercial activities even though owned or controlled by a foreign state.[464]

The Antitrust Reciprocity Act of 1982 was enacted into law in response to the 1978 United States Supreme Court decision in *Pfizer Inc., et al.* v. *Government of India, et al.*[465] In *Pfizer*, it was contended that a foreign government was not a 'person' within the meaning of the Clayton Act. The significance of this argument is that its acceptance would deny a foreign state the ability to collect the treble damages remedy provided under the Clayton Act. The argument, however, was denied by the Court stating:[466]

> A foreign nation otherwise entitled to sue in our courts is entitled to sue for treble damages under the Antitrust laws to the same extent as any other plaintiff.

Chief Justice Burger in a dissent that drew three votes noted the anomaly created by the majority decision. According to the Chief Justice, the United States Government could not recover treble damages under its own antitrust laws, but foreign states that violate those laws under the shield of sovereign immunity were entitled to treble damages.[467] The United States Government's actions against antitrust violators are limited primarily to criminal actions.

The legislative response to the anomalous situation described in the *Pfizer* dissent was the passage of an amendment designed to eliminate the problem while allowing for maximum antitrust enforcement. The solution adopted was the disallowance of treble damages for foreign states. The Clayton Act, however, continues to allow actual damages for foreign states, thus meeting the second stated purpose in allowing for maximum antitrust enforcement. A violator, therefore, cannot profit when the injury is inflicted on a foreign state.[468] Effective enforcement is also maintained since the violator may still face criminal penalties and treble damage actions by the United States Department of Justice and injured domestic parties, respectively. The legislative history gives a third and final reason for the particular solution adopted to remedy the *Pfizer* situation. The single damages remedy for foreign states, according to the Congress, would continue to provide access to American courts, thus promoting harmony among trading partners. The measure would thereby undercut any perceptions that the measure was designed to further protectionist policies on the part of Congress.[469]

The provisions of the Antitrust Reciprocity Act of 1982 do not overrule the *Pfizer* decision that a foreign state is a person within the meaning of Section 15 of the Clayton Act.[470] Subsection (b)(1) limits recoveries by foreign states to actual damages and costs. Subsection (b)(2) excepts from the above limitation foreign entities that would be denied immunity as a result of commercial activities carried on in the United States.[471] This anticipates the otherwise inequitable result of denying a foreign entity sovereign immunity, thus exposing them to treble damages for antitrust violations in the United States, while denying them access to American courts to litigate rights of a similar nature.[472]

Mareva Injunction

The British Court has determined that the use of a Mareva injunction shall not interfere with a bank's right to set-off against the enjoined assets.[473] In the case of *Seawind Maritime Ltd.* v. *Rumanian Bank of Foreign Trade,*[474] the Court granted Barclays a variation of the Mareva injunction placed on the Rumanian Bank's assets held by Barclays. The Court also approved certain language to be used in future similar injunctions as a means of avoiding relitigating the issue.

The question arose as a result of Seawind Maritime Ltd. obtaining a Mareva injunction in September 1982 restraining defendants from removing or disposing of assets within the Court's jurisdiction, unless their value was in excess of $2.19-million. The Mareva injunction is basically a prejudgment remedy employed by the British courts and named after the case of *Mareva Compania Naviera S.A.* v. *International Bulk Carriers.*[475] In the present litigation, Barclays Bank International acted as an intervenor in an effort to obtain guidance on the issue of set-off against a customer's account when the account is subject to a Mareva injunction.

The Court held earlier that a Mareva injunction was not intended to interfere with the rights of third parties.[476] This time the Court held more specifically that Barclays had a right to set-off against its customer's accounts and granted the variation. The Court's approved language to be used in the issuance of similar injunctions is:[477]

> Provided nothing in the injunction shall prevent the (Bank) from exercising any right to set-off it may have in respect of facilities afforded by the (Bank) to the defendants prior to the date of the injunction.

The nature of the Mareva injunction was again litigated in the British Commercial Court in *PCW (Underwriting Agencies) Ltd.* v. *Dixon.*[478] The injunction granted in that case acted to freeze all of the assets held in Great Britain by defendant Dixon. Dixon was allowed under the injunction 100 pounds per week to pay his regular debts. Defendant contested this amount as inadequate. The Court agreed that it was wholly inadequate for the defendant to maintain his lifestyle, and held that the amount was requested by plaintiff in the original injunction as a means of applying pressure on defendant. This was held to be an abuse of a Mareva injunction. Such injunctions were intended to be a means of insuring that defendant could not evade liability by removing his assets from the court's jurisdiction before a judgment was rendered, not designed as a tool to force a settlement.[479]

Foreign Sovereign Immunities Act: Waiver of Prejudgment Attachment

The Foreign Sovereign Immunities Act of 1976 immunizes a 'foreign state' and its alter egos from prejudgment attachment of its assets in the United States.[480] The provision granting immunity under the Act states:[481]

> Subject to existing international agreements to which the United States is a party at the time of enactment of this Act the property in the United States of a foreign state shall be immune from attachment arrest and execution except as provided in Sections 1610 and 1611 of this chapter.

Section 1610 enumerates certain exceptions to immunity from prejudgment attachment including the ability of a foreign state to waive the privilege. A prejudgment attachment under 28 U.S.C. Section 1610(d) may be waived if the property of the foreign state is used in a commercial activity in the United States, the foreign state explicitly waives immunity, and the attachment is not a means of obtaining jurisdiction.[482] In 1982, the United States Second Circuit Court of Appeals held in *Libra Bank Ltd.* v. *Banco Nacional de Costa Rica* that the waiver from prejudgment attachment must be explicit although the words 'prejudgment attachment' need not be intoned.[483] The Court in *dictum*, however, illustrated an occasion similar to the treaty provision in the instant litigation where the waiver was not explicit.[484]

The United States Second Circuit Court of Appeals recently held in *S & S Machinery* v. *Masinexportimport*[485] that the treaty provision that waives 'other liability' was not an explicit waiver of prejudgment attachment immunity. The provision at issue 'can be found in the "Business Facilitation" clause of the subsisting United States-Romania trade agreement'.[486] Similar waivers can be found in numerous other bilateral trade agreements.[487] The issue in the instant litigation was whether the 'other liability' provision was sufficient to constitute an explicit waiver within the meaning of the Foreign Sovereign Immunities Act.

In *S & S Machinery*, the Court ruled directly on the question that they had answered previously by way of dictum in *Libra Bank*. Appellant argued that the bilateral trade agreement between the United States and Romania waived the latter's immunity from prejudgment attachment in the clause purporting to waive 'other liability'.[488] The Court denied this argument, and held that 'other liability' does not waive immunity from prejudgment attachment. According to the Court, 'the phrase "other liability" is ill-suited to encompass prejudgment attachments'.[489]

Libra Bank and S & S Machinery appear to draw a fine distinction between an explicit waiver without the words prejudgment attachment used and an insufficient general waiver. The rule that remains, however, is that the precise words 'prejudgment attachment' need not be used, but an explicit waiver will not exist unless a clear, unambiguous intent to waive liability is expressed.[490] A general waiver of 'other liability' is not a clear intent.[491]

Counterclaims

The Foreign Sovereign Immunities Act denies immunity to a foreign state for a counterclaim in an action initially brought by the foreign state under any one of three circumstances: (1) where the foreign state would not be entitled to immunity under the commercial exception in a separate action; or (2) where the counterclaim arises out of the same transaction or occurence that is the subject matter of the claim of the foreign state; or (3) to the extent the counterclaim does not seek relief differing in kind or amount from that sought by the foreign state.[492] In the normal case, a juridical entity that is separate from the state of its nationality may bring suit in the Federal Court subject to counterclaim in one of the above circumstances. This would normally preclude the separate juridical entity from being subject to counterclaim arising from actions of its national government.

In *First National City Bank* v. *Banco Para El Commercio Exterior de Cuba*[493], however, the United States Supreme Court held that under certain circumstances, defendants in Federal Court may pierce the separate juridical status, and apply a set-off for claims against plaintiff's national government. The facts of the instant case began in 1960 when the Government of the Republic of Cuba established respondent Banco Para El Commercio Exterior de Cuba (Bancec) to serve as an 'official autonomous credit institution for foreign trade ... with full juridical capacity ... of its own ...'.[494] In September 1960, Bancec sought to collect on a letter of credit issued by petitioner First National City Bank (now Citibank) in support of a contract for the delivery of sugar from the Cuban seller to the buyer in the United States. All of Citibank's assets in Cuba were seized and nationalized within days after Bancec made its request for collection on the letter of credit. Bancec brought suit on the letter in the United States District Court, and Citibank counterclaimed for the value of its nationalized assets. The issue addressed by the United States Supreme Court was whether Citibank could obtain set-off, although Bancec was established as a separate juridical entity.

The Court held that Bancec's separate juridical status would be disregarded and allowed Citibank to apply the set-off. According to the court:[495]

> Our decision today announces no mechanical formula for determining the circumstances under which the normally separate juridical status of a government instrumentality is to be disregarded. Instead, it is the product of the application of internationally recognized equitable principles to avoid the injustices that would result from permitting a foreign state to reap the benefits of our courts while avoiding the obligations of international law.

DOMESTIC RELATIONS

(1) General Reform

Greece

Parliament, in January 1983, passed legislation to reform family law and establish full equality among the sexes in the civil code.[496] There are several sweeping changes. The dowry will be abolished and the dowry property vested in the wife. Married women will have freedom to choose their surname, and all legal distinctions between legitimate and illegitimate children will be removed. Divorce will be permissible after four year's separation with consent, or one year's separation with consent in certain circumstances. Maintenance will be payable by either spouse, depending on circumstances, and each will be deemed to have contributed one-third to the increment of the other's wealth after marriage.[497]

Turkey

The Turkish civil law reform commission has proposed a number of revisions in the area of family law.[498] Women will have greater freedom to use their maiden names. Divorce by consent will be easier to obtain, and the minimum period in which a divorce may be sought on grounds of mental illness will be reduced from three years to one year.[499] In addition, husbands and wives will have joint responsibility for maintenance of children and as head of the household.

Nigeria

A newly proposed Marriage Act would create a uniform marriage law for the entire country. It would cover both monogamous and polygamous marriages, and religious and customary marriages.[500]

(2) Divorce/Dissolution

Scotland

A procedure for divorce proceedings to be held without the parties' attendance came into force on 11 January 1983.[501]

Switzerland

The Federal Court recently examined an article in the Civil Code which prohibits the remarriage of a guilty party to a divorce for two years, and three years in the case of adultery.[502] This law was found to be in conflict with the new approach to divorce law which no longer treats adultery as an absolute ground for divorce. The court held that although the terms of the article are imperative and cannot be avoided by the courts, the three year prohibition should not be inflicted on the party unless his or her adultery was unusually grave and had a decisive influence on the break up of the marriage.[503]

(3) Conflict of Laws

United Kingdom

The English and Scottish Law Commissions recently addressed the question of polygamous marriages in Working Paper 83.[504] The Commissions' recommendations are in line with the holding of *Hussain* v. *Hussain*[505] decided 26 June 1982. The court held in that case that a marriage contracted in polygamous form by a man having an English domicile is valid, provided it is not in fact polygamous.

The Commissions believe that their recommendations will give certainty to the law, and also cover certain matters not discussed in the Court of Appeals decision.[506]

France

In a recent French case, *S.M.* v. *S.B.*,[507] the husband possessed dual French-Algerian nationality and started divorce proceedings in Algeria. The wife subsequently started proceedings in France. The French court held on the basis of Civil Code Section 15, that French courts have jurisdiction over obligations undertaken by a French national abroad, even where undertaken towards a foreigner. The husband's contention that the French courts could not intervene once he initiated proceedings in Algeria, was dismissed.[508]

Switzerland

A Swiss court held in *S.V. Department de Justice du Canton du Tessin*[509] that a child born out of wedlock to a Swiss mother and an English father in England, and there registered as the father's son, could not be registered as recognized by him in Switzerland, since the entry into the English register does not constitute recognition of paternity as understood in Swiss law. Because the child, under Swiss law, was domiciled in Switzerland, he had to be registered under the mother's name.[510]

Belgium

In the case of *A.P.*,[511] decided by a Belgian District Court, an Italian born woman and her Belgian husband living in Belgium desired to legitimize her child by adoption. Although the woman acquired Belgian nationality upon marriage to a Belgian national, her child born prior to marriage and recognized by her remained Italian.[512]

Belgian law subjects adoptions between Belgian national and foreigners to all requirements of the parties' respective laws regarding personal status, unless the foreign law is contrary to Belgian international public policy. Italian law only allows such adoptions where the child is under eight years and has been deprived of moral and material support from the parent who recognizes him. Neither of these were true in this case, and the Italian law was not found to be against Belgian international public policy.[513]

Nevertheless, since strict application of the laws would leave a gap, and because the right was recognized by both systems, although by different techniques, the legitimization by adoption was recognized by the Belgian court.[514]

(4) Community Property and Spousal Support

United States

The New Jersey Supreme Court held in *Mahoney* v. *Mahoney*[515] that professional degrees and licenses were not property subject to equitable distribution upon dissolution of marriage.[516] The wife had made a substantial financial contribution to her husband's education while he obtained a master's degree in business administration.[517] The court also held that the wife was not entitled to reimbursement for the contribution she made to her husband's education, because both spouses left the marriage with comparable earning capacities and comparable educational achievements. However, the court stated in dicta that where a wife defers her own further education by reason of the constraints of marriage, she might be eligible for an award of 'rehabilitative alimony'.[518]

In the Wisconsin case of *In Re Lundberg*[519] the wife had supported her husband through medical school. She contributed over $30,000 more to the marriage than the husband, rendered substantial emotional support, and performed the majority of household chores to enable him to devote all his energies to earning his degree.[520]

The Wisconsin Supreme Court held that the trial court was within its discretion in awarding $25,000 to the wife payable in monthly installments.[521] The Supreme Court found that the husband's degree was the most significant asset of the marriage. In addition the Court held that maintenance payments are not to be limited to situations where a spouse is not capable of self-support, but are available as a flexible tool to ensure a fair and equitable determination in each individual case.[522] It would only be fair that the wife be compensated for her costs and foregone opportunities.[523]

The Third Circuit of the Louisiana Court of Appeals held in *Placide* v. *Placide*[524] that the amount awarded for losses from tortious injury occurring during marriage should be considered community property. This amount included all lost wages, medical expenses incurred during marriage, and pain and suffering which were predissolution losses.[525] However, the amount awarded for permanent loss of normal sexual function was the husband's separate property as compensation for post-dissolution losses.[526] The trial court had awarded the wife one-half of the husband's tort recovery from an injury occurring during marriage.[527]

France

The recently enacted Craftmakers' and Traders' Spouses Act provides the spouse of a craftsman or trader who works in the family business as an assistant, an employee, or an associate, additional protection by prohibiting the craftsman or trader from selling or mortgaging the business without consent of the spouse. The non-consenting spouse may seek an annulment of the contract within two years of learning about it, but not more than two years after community property between the spouses had ceased.[528]

(5) Matrimonial Home

United Kingdom

The Law Commission published Law commission Report Number 115 in which it recommends that the legal ownership of the matrimonial home be equally held by the husband and wife as co-owners.[529] This change would aid a creditor of the husband who has a charge against the property, but under the present law, cannot realize it because of the wife's interest in the house arising from her contribution to its purchase.[530]

In the case of *Richards* v. *Richards,* a British court of appeals ordered a husband to leave the former matrimonial home so that the wife could live there with the children. The court reasoned that the needs of the parents were subordinate to the needs of the children.[531]

The Matrimonial Homes Bill, first read in the House of Lords on 27 January 1983, will consolidate enactments relating to the rights of spouses to occupy the matrimonial home.[532] The procedure for registering an interest in the matrimonial home if it is registered land was amended effective 14 February 1983 by Statutory Instrument 1983/40.[533]

France

A wife succeeded in voiding the sale of a home which formed part of the joint property in *Cellerin* v. *Epous Potron.*[534] The court held that neither the wife's passive attitude toward the transaction, nor the husband's claim that he was the administrator of the joint matrimonial property, established the husband's apparent agency. The purchasers still had an obligation to verify the extent of the vendor's powers.[535]

Luxembourg

A Luxembourg District Court, in *Biver* v. *Schuman,*[536] held that there is no presumption of ownership of furniture in the matrimonial home following a court order terminating the joint ownership of the matrimonial property. The claiming spouse must prove ownership. In order to prevent collusion, the law requires more than a spouse's admission to establish ownership over property arrested by the other spouse's creditors.[537]

(6) Child Custody

West Germany

The Federal Constitutional Court ruled that S. 1671 IV 1 of the Civil Code regarding joint custody, is unconstitutional.[538] The code section stated that joint custody may only be granted to the divorcing parents if they are suitable, from the point of view of the welfare of the children, to continue looking after the children. It was held that this offends against the constitutional guarantee of parental rights.

United States

The Oklahoma Supreme Court held in *M.J.P.* v. *J.G.P.*[539] that a custodial mother's open homosexual relationship is a sufficient change of condition to warrant modification of a child custody order. The court reasoned that the child's peer relationships could be disrupted by having to defend his homosexual parent.[540]

In the California Court of Appeal case *Guardianship of Phillip B.,*[541] guardianship of a teenaged child afflicted with Down's Syndrome was awarded to non-parents over the objection of the child's parents. The California Court of Appeal held that, tested by the clear and convincing standard of proof, retention of custody by the parents would cause serious detriment to the child, and that his best interests would be served through a guardianship award to the non-parents. The court stated that the non-parents had become the child's 'psychological parents' through frequent visits at his residential facility. There was evidence of passive neglect on the part of the parents in response to the child's heart condition. In addition, there was evidence that the child would be impeded in his educational and developmental progress if he remained in the custody of his parents.[542]

(7) Paternity and Support

United States

A Texas statute which placed a one year time limit on support claims by illegitimate children was declared unconstitutional by the United States Supreme Court in *Millis* v. *Habluetzel*.[543] The statute required paternity to be established within one year from the date of birth in order to obtain child support. Since legitimate children were not similarly burdened, the statute deprived the illegitimate children of equal protection.

USSR

The Plenum of the Supreme Soviet of the Union Soviet Socialist Republics adopted an ordinance on ascertainment of paternity and questions of maintenance, aiming to secure a more uniform court practice in affiliation disputes.[544]

Belgium

A surviving spouse having need of maintenance out of the estate of the deceased spouse, if it is no longer possible to maintain the lifestyle she/he was accustomed to during marriage, may mortgage immovables of the estate as security for such maintenance.[545]

(8) Parental Rights and Termination

United States

A New York law permitting termination of parental right on a 'fair preponderance of the evidence' was struck down by the United States Supreme Court in *Santosky* v. *Kramer*.[546] The court held that children could not be taken permanently from their parents absent the state supporting its allegations by clear and convincing evidence.[547]

In *In Re J.R.*[548] the Iowa Supreme Court held that because the paternal grandparents had the right to be considered as guardians and custodians of the children following termination proceedings, they had the right to intervene in such proceedings. Further, the best interests of the children required that the grandparents be allowed to adopt them.[549]

The parents had grossly neglected the children and had subjected them to filthy, unsanitary living conditions. The court held that while there was a risk that custody with the grandparents might lend itself to further possibilities of harm if the parents reappeared and took the children, 'the quality of the proposed home ... and the desirability of maintaining an identity with the children's natural family outweigh the benefits of an anonymous adoption'.[550]

(9) Parental Kidnapping

Tort suits are providing a relatively new and growing means of obtaining legal relief in child snatching cases. These suits can be initiated against both the parents who wrongfully abduct, retain, or conceal their children, and people who aid in the initial act or concealment. Among the theories upon which the suits can be based are unlawful imprisonment, custodial interference, enticement, loss of care, custody and companionship, civil conspiracy, and intentional infliction of emotional distress.[551]

The facts in *Lloyd* v. *Loeffler*[552] reveal that custody of the child had been awarded to the father with the mother retaining visitation rights. In July, 1979 the mother and her new husband picked up the child in exercise of the mother's visitation rights. They failed to return the child to the custody of the father, and at the time of the Court of Appeals decision their whereabouts were still unknown. The mother's parents, the Loefflers, actively concealed the whereabouts of the child and her abductors from the father.[553]

The United States Court of Appeals, Seventh Circuit, affirmed the holding of the District Court in awarding $70,000 in compensatory damages for which all the defendants were jointly and severably liable, and $25,000 in punitive damages for which the mother and her husband alone were liable, because of their greater culpability. In addition, the award of punitive damages was to grow by $2,000 per month until the child's return to the custodial father.[554]

In *Wasserman* v. *Wasserman,*[555] the husband removed the three youngest children from the wife's custody during divorce proceedings in 1977. This was allegedly done with the knowing assistance of the husband's present wife, his parents, and the attorneys who represented him in the divorce case. All of these parties were named in the wife's complaint alleging child enticement and intentional infliction of emotional distress.[556] The United States Court of Appeals, Fourth Circuit, held that the case did not fall within the domestic relations exception to federal diversity jurisdiction, and remanded the case to the District Court to decide the substantive issues.[557]

(10) Non-Marital Living Relationships

Switzerland

The Federal Supreme Court of Switzerland recently considered the property entitlement of non-married cohabiting parties. The court concluded that the situation will vary from case to case, that there is no special law to be applied when the parties separate, and that their rights are to be determined according to their agreement.[558]

United Kingdom

Law Commission Report 118 on illegitimacy makes several detailed proposals, including drafting bills to remove all legal disadvantages as they affect illegitimate children. This proposed legislation would replace the Affiliations Proceedings Act and would aim to remove the expressions 'legitimate' and 'illegitimate', using instead 'marital' and 'non-marital'.[559]

TREATMENT OF ALIENS

(1) Asylum

The United States Circuit Courts have experienced a high number of political asylum cases.[560] Current global instabilities, as well as the adoption of the 1980 Refugee Act are cited as major factors causing an influx of immigrants seeking asylum.[561] Recently, several decisions before the courts involve the burden of proof established for 'persecution' which is found in the Refugee Act of 1980.[562]

In *Martinez-Romero* v. *Immigration and Naturalization Service (INS)*[563] the United States Court of Appeals affirmed an INS order deporting a petitioner from El Salvador who was seeking asylum on persecution grounds. Although the brief two paragraph decision did not refer to the Refugee Act in deciding the case, the court concluded that current instabilities in El Salvador were not valid reasons for granting a stay indefinitely on a persecution claim. 'If we were to agree with petitioner's contention that no person should be returned to El Salvador because of reported anarchy present there now, it would permit the whole population of El Salvador, if they could enter this country some way, to stay here indefinitely. There must be some special circumstances present before relief can be granted'.[564] The court did not specifically define what circumstances constitute persecution. The court said that generalized undocumented fears of persecution or political upheaval which affect a country's general populace are insufficient bases for withholding deportation.

In *Raass* v. *Immigration and Naturalization Service,*[565] the Ninth Circuit affirmed *Martinez* in holding that Tongan citizens who are denied rights to land in Tonga because of their lineage, cannot claim persecution, based on economic disadvantage. 'Relief of asylum in the United States depends on something more than generalized economic disadvantage at the destination',[566] said the court.

Conversely, in the case of A-, File A23108407,[567] the immigration judge granted asylum and withheld deportation of a Nicaraguan female who had no documented evidence of prospective persecution if returned to Nicaragua. Prior to the judge's decision, the Bureau of Human Rights and Human Affairs of the Department of State held in an advisory opinion that the petitioner failed to establish a well founded fear of persecution. The facts of A- involve a citizen of Nicaragua, who entered the United States from Mexico without inspection on or about 15 March, 1980. She thereupon applied for asylum under Immigration and Naturalization Act Section 243(h) claiming to have been politically active and associated with the police and military during the Samoza regime. Section 243(h) states 'The Attorney General is authorized to withhold deportation of any alien within the United States to any country in which in his opinion the alien would be subject to persecution and for such period of time as he deems necessary for such reason'.[568]

The immigration judge stated that it was well recognized under the 1951 United Nations Convention and the 1967 Protocol relating to the status of refugees, that 'documentary evidence may be extremely difficult if not impossible to obtain'.[569] Thus, asylum was granted based on a final determination of respondent's account of her life in Nicaragua rather than documentation of persecution.

The Second Circuit Court of Appeals addressed the definition of 'persecution' in *Stevic* v. *Sava,*[570] which is currently pending before the United States Supreme Court. *Stevic* involves a Yugoslavian citizen admitted to the United States in June 1976 as a nonimmigrant to visit his sister, a permanent resident. In January 1977 Stevic, married a United States citizen, which entitled him to petition for an immediate relative visa. Five days after the petition was granted by the District Director, petitioner's wife was killed in an accident, resulting in an automatic denial of the petition.[571]

Stevic appealed to the Board of Immigration Appeals (BIA) on grounds that he feared persecution if deported to Yugoslavia. He cited the facts that since his marriage he had become active in an anti-communist organization and that his father in-law, an American citizen and member of the organization, had been imprisoned while visiting Yugoslavia as a tourist in 1974, resulting in his suicide on release from prison three years later.[572] Additionally, Stevic offered evidence of his involvement in other emigrant organizations and the Yugoslavian government's hostility toward those organizations.[573]

Stevic, instead of surrendering for deportation, moved to reopen the deportation proceedings in order to file an application for withholding deportation under Section 243(h) of the Immigration and Nationality Act of 1952.[574] The BIA dismissed his appeal holding that petitioner failed to make a prima facie showing of a clear probability that he would be singled out for persecution when he returned to Yugoslavia.[575] Petitioner's second motion to reopen deportation proceedings before the BIA was denied for lack of new information not previously available or substantial change in conditions since the first motion was filed.[576]

The BIA regarded the second motion to reopen deportation proceedings as raising essentially the same claims as were disposed of by denial of the first motion to reopen. However, subsequent to the first motion to reopen and before the second motion, the Refugee Act of 1980[577] changed the legal standard of proof for applications for political asylum.[578]

Based on the definition of refugee found in the 1980 Act, read in light of its legislative history, the Second Circuit Court of Appeals held that the 'clear probability' test was no longer the applicable guide for administrative practice under Section 243(h).[579] The 1980 Act defines refugee as:[580]

> [a]ny person who is outside any country of such person's nationality ... and who is unable or unwilling to return to ... that country because of persecution or a *well-founded* fear of persecution on account of race, religion, nationality, membership in a particular social group, or political opinion ... (Emphasis supplied.)

Asylum may be granted and deportation must be withheld upon a showing far short of a 'clear probability' that an individual will be singled out for persecution.[581] Thus, a 'well-founded' fear of persecution replaces a 'clear probability' of persecution as the standard of proof in the Second Circuit.

In *Rejaie v. Immigration and Naturalization Service,*[582] the Third Circuit Court of Appeals rejected the *Stevic* interpretation. The courts and the BIA have consistently held in the Third Circuit that the 'clear probability' standard and the 'well-founded fear' standard mean essentially the same thing and require the same showing.[583] The Court noted further that Congress did not intend to change the substance or procedure of the immigration laws when it acceded to the United Nations Protocol's standards.

The Sixth Circuit Court of Appeals, in *Reyes v. Immigration and*

Naturalization Service,[584] followed the decision in *Stevic*. The Court considered the kind of evidence needed and its sufficiency to support the petitioner's claim for political asylum, requiring some objective evidence concerning the likelihood of persecution, neither desiring the force of the Immigration and Naturalization Service to accept potentially self-serving statements as true nor limiting proof to that of actual persecution after the fact.[585] Petitioner Reyes offered affidavits from relatives, general newspaper and documentary reports concerning general conditions in the Phillipines, a letter from the Director of Mass Media of the Phillipine Catholic Church, in addition to her own testimony. Under the circumstances of the case the evidence presented was held sufficient to bring petitioner within the coverage of the new Act.[586] In the Sixth Circuit a showing far short of a clear probability that the individual will be singled out for persecution is sufficient to withhold deportation under Section 243(h).[587]

The Eighth Circuit Court of Appeals announced its position on the matter in *Minwalla* v. *Immigration and Naturalization Service.*[588] Persecution for purposes of granting asylum to an alien who would be persecuted if deported requires a showing of a threat to one's life or freedom; mere economic detriment is not sufficient.[589]

Resolution of the conflicting interpretation by the various Circuit Courts of the definition of persecution will be resolved during the U.S. Supreme Court's next term. Certiorari was granted in *INS* v. *Stevic* on 28 February 1983.

(2) Corporate Nationality

United States

The issue of corporate nationality under Article VIII(1) of the Friendship, Commerce and Navigation Treaty between the United States and Japan[590] was addressed by the United States Supreme Court in *Sumitomo Shoji America, Inc.* v. *Avagliano.*[591] The issue arose in the context of a Title VII[592] employment discrimination suit against an American subsidiary of a Japanese corporation.

The Japanese corporation claimed an exemption from Title VII based on the provision contained in the Friendship, Commerce and Navigation Treaty (the Treaty) which allows companies of a treaty country operating in the other country to hire employees 'of their choice'.[593]

The United States Supreme Court unanimously held that a United States corporation which is a wholly owned subsidiary of a Japanese corporation is a company of the United States, not a company of Japan, and therefore, cannot invoke the rights provided by Article VIII(1) of the Treaty.[594] This decision is based on a literal interpretation of the Treaty which limits the coverage of the Treaty to foreign corporations operating abroad, i.e. branch operations.[595]

The petitioner, Sumitomo Shoji American, Inc., is incorporated under the laws of the State of New York, and is a wholly owned subsidiary of the Sumitomo Sjoji Kabushiki Kaisha, a Japanese general trading company. Respondents are past and present female secretarial employees of Sumitomo who, with one exception, are United States citizens.[596]

The class action brought by respondents claimed that Sumitomo's practice of hiring only male Japanese citizens for executive, managerial, and sales positions was a violation of 42 U.S.C. Section 1981 and Title VII of the Civil Rights Act of 1964, which prohibits employment discrimination on the basis of sex or national origin.[597]

Sumitomo moved to dismiss on the grounds that Article VIII(1) of the Treaty exempts a Japanese subsidiary incorporated in the United States from the provisions of Title VII by the following language:[598]

> Companies of either Party shall be permitted to engage, within the territories of the other Party, accountants and other technical experts, executive personel, attorneys, agents and other specialists *of their choice*. (emphasis added)

The District Court dismissed the section 1981 claim but refused to dismiss the Title VII claim, holding that Sumitomo was a United States corporation, and therefore, not under the provisions of Article VIII(1) of the Treaty. The question of whether the terms of the Treaty exempted Sumitomo from the provisions of Title VII was certified for interlocutory appeal.[599]

The Court of Appeals for the Second Circuit reversed in part, holding that Article VIII(1) was intended to cover locally incorporated subsidiaries of foreign corporations. These subsidiaries, however, are not completely exempt from American anti-discrimination laws.[600]

The Supreme Court vacated and remanded[601] based on an interpretation of the Treaty language. Article XXII, the definitional section of the Treaty, states in pertinent part:[602]

> As used in the present Treaty, the term 'companies' means corporations, partnerships, companies and other associations ... Companies constituted under the applicable laws and regulations within the territories of either Party *shall be deemed companies thereof* and shall have their juridical status recognized within the territories of the other Party. (Emphasis added.)

Since Sumitomo is 'constituted under the applicable laws and regulations' of the State of New York; Sumitomo was declared a company of the United States and, therefore, precluded from invoking the rights contained in Article VIII(1) of the Treaty. Those rights were interpreted to apply only to Japanese companies operating in the United States and to United States companies operating in Japan.[603]

After noting that both parties to the Treaty support this interpretation, the Court stated that, when the parties to a treaty agree on an interpretation which follows the clear language of the treaty, then the court must defer to that interpretation and give effect to the intent of the parties, absent strong evidence to the contrary.[604]

The Court rejected the argument that literal interpretation of the Treaty language would overlook its purpose because, 'the purpose of the (Treaty) was not to give foreign corporations greater rights than domestic companies, but instead to assure them the right to conduct business on an equal basis without suffering discrimination based on their alienage'.[605] Since the subsidiaries are considered companies of the country in which they are incorporated for purposes of the Treaty; they are entitled to the same rights and subject to the same responsibilities as any other domestic corporation.[606] The Court reasoned that this 'national treatment'[607] assures the accomplishment of the purpose of the Treaty to '... assure that corporations of one Treaty party have the right to conduct business within the territory of the other party without suffering discrimination as an alien entity ...'.[608]

The Supreme Court's decision will have substantial worldwide impact on locally incorporated subsidiaries of foreign corporations due to the fact that the language of Article VIII(1) is nearly identical to the language contained in numerous other Friendship, Commerce and Navigation Treaties. The possibility that foreign governments may reciprocate and subject United States' foreign-incorporated subsidiaries to onerous national employment laws is an issue which will have to be considered by international enterprises in the future.[609]

Notes to Part Two

1. *Financial Times* (London) (3 December 1982), p. 6, as reported in 24 *Bull. Legal Dev.* 258 (1982)
2. Bremer Vulkan Schiffbau und Maschinenfabrik v. South India Shipping Corp. (1981), 2 W.L.R. 142.
3. *Bull. Legal Dev.*, Supra n 1, p. 258.
4. Park and Paulsson, 'The Binding Force of International Arbitral Awards', 23 *Va. J. of Int'l. L.* 253 (1983).
5. Id.

6. Schmittcoff, 7 *Y.B. of Com. Arb.* 162, 163 (1982).
7. Id.
8. William, 'Law Reform: Hong Kong Arbitration', 10 *Int'l. Bus. L.* 317 (1982).
9. Id.
10. Id.
11. Grant, 'Recent Developments in the Far East-Hong Kong', 10 *Int'l. Bus. L.* 292 (1982).
12. 'Swiss Bill on International Arbitration', 17 *J. of World Trade L.* 275 (1983).
13. Id., pp. 278-280.
14. Sanders, 8 *Y.B. of Com. Arb.* 327 (1983).
15. Sperry International Trade, Inc. v. Government of Israel, 689 F.2d 301 (2nd. Cir. 1982).
16. Id., p. 304.
17. Id., p. 306.
18. Maritime International Nominees Establishment v. Republic of Guinea, 693 F.2d 1094 (D.C. Cir. 1982).
19. Id., p. 1100.
20. Id., p. 1104.
21. Id., p. 1108.
22. Id., p. 1109.
23. Gopal, 'International Centre for Settlement of Investment Disputes', 14 *Case W. Res. J. of Int'l. L.* 591 (1982).
24. Id., p. 596.
25. See generally *Int'l. Legal Mat.* (1982), pp. 726, 740, 976.
26. Gopal, supra n 23, p. 610.
27. BOLSA Review No. II/1982, p. 90, as reported in 13 *Bull. Legal Dev.* 142 (1982).
28. Neue Zuricher Zeitung (23/24 May 1982), p. 10, as reported in 11 *Bull. Legal Dev.* 120 (1982).
29. *Financial Times* (London) (20 July 1982), p. 2, as reported in 16 *Bull. Legal Dev.* 175 (1982).
30. *Financial Times* (London) (15 December 1982), p. 2, as reported in 2 *Bull. Legal Dev.* 13 (1983).
31. Proceedings of the European Court of Justice, cases 300 – 301/81, No. 6/83, pp. 4, 5, as reported in 8 *Bull. Legal Dev.* 83 (1983).
32. Memorandum of Understanding, United States-Switzerland, 31 August 1982, reprinted in *Legal Times* (4 October 1982), p. 17, col. 3.
33. Salisbury, 'International Agreements: United States-Switzerland Investigation of Insider Trading Through Swiss Banks', 23 *Harv. Int'l L.J.* 437 (1983).
34. Id., p. 438, note 13.
35. Id., p. 439.
36. Id.
37. Id., p. 440.
38. *Financial Times* (London) (1 October 1982), p. 4, as reported in 18 *Bull. Legal Dev.* 193 (1982).
39. *Financial Times* (London) (6 August 1982), p. 2, as reported in 16 *Bull. Legal Dev.* 171 (1982).
40. Whisenand, 'Interstate Banking in the United States', *Int'l. Fin. L. Rev.* (May 1983), p. 16.
41. Id.
42. Id., p. 18.
43. *Financial Times* (London) (4 March 1983), p. 24, as reported in 7 *Bull. Legal Dev.*. 72 (1983).
44. Press Briefing by Secretary of Commerce Malcom Baldridge on Steel Trading Laws, 21 October 1982, reprinted in 21 *Int'l. Legal Mat.* 1422 (1982).

178

45. 47 Fed. Reg. 49060 (1982) Appendix III.
46. Id., pp. 49058, 49059.
47. Id.
48. 47 Fed. Reg. 35646 (1983); 47 Fed. Reg. 39304 (1982); 47 Fed. Reg. 49058.
49. 47 Fed. Reg. 49061 (1982), paragraph 1 of the Arrangement between ECSC and US.
50. Id.
51. Id.
52. 47 Fed. Reg. 42399 (1982).
53. 47 Fed. Reg. 42393 (1982).
54. 47 Fed. Reg. 44362 (1982).
55. Baldridge, supra n 1.
56. 129 Cong. Rec. 4132 (1983).
57. Id., p. 4133, Title I, Sec. 101(a).
58. Letter from William E. Brock, United States Trade Representative, dated 6/17/82 to Daniel P. Moynihan, Senator, Committee on Environment and Public Works, reprinted in 129 Cong. Rec. 4131 (1983).
59. Id.
60. Id.
61. Id.
62. Id., p. 4132.
63. Id., p. 4133.
64. 20 *U.N. Chron.* 74 (1983). Full text of the GATT Ministerial Declaration is available in 22 *Int'l Legal Mat.* 445 (1983) and 17 *J. of World Trade L.* 67 (1983).
65. *Financial Times* (London) (30 November 1982), p. 1, as reported in 24 *Bull. of Legal Dev.* 262 (1982).
66. United Nations Conference on Trade and Development (UNCTAD) Monthly Bulletin, Number 189 (December 1982).
67. Id.
68. Id.
69. 20 *U.N. Chron.* 118 (1983).
70. Id.
71. Supra n 65, p. 263.
72. United States Senate (98th Congress, 1st Session), Executive Report Number 98 – 1, pp. 1 – 49, (3 February 1983).
73. Montreal Protocol Number 4 to Amend the Convention for the Unification of Certain Rules Relating to International Carriage by Air signed at Warsaw on 12 October 1929, as amended by the Protocol done at the Hague on September 28, 1955 (The Montreal Protocols, 1975). International Civil Aviation Organization Documentation Number 9148 (1975).
74. 49 Stat. 3000, T.S. Number 876, L.N.T.S. 11 (adherence of the United States proclaimed 29 October 1934.)
75. Franklin Mint Corp. v. Trans World Airlines, Inc., 525 F. Supp. 1288 (S.D. N.Y. 1981), Rev'd 690 F.2d 303 (2d Cir. 1982).
76. Supra n 72, p. 2.
77. Supra n 74.
78. Int'l. Civil Aviation Organization Doc. Number 9096.
79. Id.
80. Int'l Civil Aviation Organization Doc. Number 9131.
81. Int'l Civil Aviation Organization Doc. Number 9145 – 9148.
82. Montreal Protocol Number 4. Supra n 73, Article 18, paragraphs 2, 3.

83. Id. at Articles 5 – 16.
84. Id. at Article 22.
85. See generally Franklin Mint Corp. v. Trans World Airlines, Inc., 690 F.2d 303, Maschinenfabrik Kern, A.G. v. Northwest Airlines, Inc., 562 F. Supp. 232 (N.D. Ill., E.D. 1983).
86. Franklin Mint Corp. v. Trans World Airlines, Inc., 690 F.2d 303.
87. Maschinenfabrik Kern, A.G. v. Northwest Airlines, Inc., 562 F. Supp. 232.
88. Id. at 237.
89. Id. at 237 – 238.
90. The SDR was created by the IMF in 1969 to replace gold and foreign currency in the international money reserve markets. IMF banks exchanged SDR's for other convertible currencies as though they were lines of credit against which reserves are borrowed for use in central banks. Methods of calculating SDR's change over time, but currently are calculated in reference to the United States dollar, the Deutsche mark, the French franc, the Japanese yen, and the pound sterling. The amount of any of the five currencies in one SDR is a function of the percentage weights assigned to each currency. The dollar value of one SDR is calculated by adding the dollar value of each currency included based on the daily market exchange rate. SDR's tend to be less prone to fluctuation than the free market price of gold. This relative stability led the Warsaw signatories to propose that the SDR be adopted as the official unit of conversion for the Warsaw Convention (Montreal Protocols).
91. Franklin Mint Corp. v. Trans World Airlines, Inc., 690 F. 2d at 305.
92. Id., p. 306.
93. Id.
94. Id., p. 311.
95. Maschinenfabrik Kern, A.G. v. Northwest Airlines, Inc., 562 F. Supp. at 239.
96. Id.
97. 41 Cong. Q. 465 (5 March 1983).
98. Id.
99. Id., p. 466.
100. Id., p. 465.
101. 41 Cong. Q. 636 (26 March 1983).
102. The Times (London) (31 July 1982), p. 5, as reported in 18 Bull. Legal Dev. 192 (1982).
103. O.J. Eur. Comm., Number L 230, p. 38. (1982), as reported in 17 Bull. Legal Dev. 184 (1982).
104. Financial Times (London) (24 September 1982), p. 2, as reported in 19 Bull. Legal Dev. 208 (1982).
105. O.J. Euro. Comm. Number L. 301, p. 1 (1892), as reported in 22 Bull. Legal Dev. 237 (1982).
106. Polish Steam Ship Co. v. Atlantic Maritime Co., 2 W.L.R. 798 (Q.B. 1983).
107. Id., p. 807.
108. Id., p. 800.
109. Id.
110. Id., p. 807.
111. Afovos Shipping Co. S.A. and Romano Pagnan and Pietro Pagnan, 1 W.L.R. 195 (House of Lords 1983), decision of the Court of Appeal (1982) 1 W.L.R. 848; (1982) 3 All E.R. 18 Aff'd.
112. Id., p. 197.
113. Id., p. 198.
114. Id.

180

115. Id., p. 201.
116. Scandinavian Trading Tanker Co. A.B. v. Flota Petrolera Ecuatoriana, 2 W.L.R. 248 (C.A. 1983), decision of Lloyd J. (1981) 2 Lloyd's L.R. 425, Aff'd.
117. Id., pp. 250, 251.
118. Id., p. 252.
119. Id., p. 251.
120. Id., p. 250.
121. Id., pp. 253, 254.
122. Id., p. 258.
123. The Hollandia, 3 W.L.R. 1111 (House of Lords 1982), decision of the Court of Appeal (1982) Q.B. 872; (1982) 2 W.L.R. 556; (1982) 1 All E.R. 1076 Aff'd.
124. Id., p. 1113.
125. Id., pp. 1113, 1114.
126. Id., pp. 1115, 1116.
127. Id., p. 1114.
128. Id., pp. 1119, 1120.
129. Id., p. 1118.
130. Id., p. 1113.
131. Amoco Transport Co. v. S/S Mason Lykes, 550 F. Supp. 1264 (S.D. Tex. 1982), 1983 AMC 1087.
132. 1983 AMC at 1088.
133. Id.
134. Id., pp. 1091, 1092.
135. Robins Dry Dock & Repair Company v. Flint, 275 U.S. 303, 1928 AMC 61 (1927).
136. 275 U.S., p. 309.
137. Florida Department of State v. Treasure Salvors, Inc., 459 F. Supp. 507 (S.D. Fla. 1978), Aff'd in part, Rev'd in part, 621 F.2d 1340 (5th Cir. 1981), Aff'd in part, Rev'd in part, 458 U.S. 102 S.Ct. 3304, 1983 AMC 144 (1983).
138. 1983 AMC, p. 145.
139. Id., p. 147.
140. Id., pp. 147, 148.
141. Id., p. 166.
142. Id., p. 167.
143. In Re State of Florida, Department of State v. Treasure Salvors, Inc. 689 F.2d 1254 AMC 181 (1983), on remand from the Supreme Court of the United States, 458 U.S. 670, 1983 AMC 144 (1983), Aff'd with directions.
144. 1983 AMC, p. 183.
145. Fojo v. American Express Company, 554 F. Supp. (D.P.R. 1983).
146. Id., p. 1200.
147. Id., p. 1203.
148. Id., p. 1201.
149. Id., citing Article 1054 of the Civil Code, P.R. Laws Ann., tit. 31 Section 3018.
150. Prieto v. Maryland Casualty Co., 98 P.R. 583, 608 (1970).
151. Fojo v. American Express Company, 554 F. Supp. at 1201.
152. Id., p. 1202, citing Green Giant Co. v. Superior Court, 104 P.R. 685, 694 (1975).
153. Day and Zimmerman v. Exportadora, Etc., 549 F. Supp. 383 (E.D.Pa. 1982).
154. Id., p. 386, citing Melville v. American Home Assurance Co., 584 F. 2d 1306, 1311 (3d Cir. 1978).
155. Id., p. 387, citing Schoenkopf v. Brown & Williamson Tobacco Corp, 483 F. Supp. 1185, 1195 (E.D.Pa. 1980), Aff'd, 637 F.2d. 205 (3d Cir. 1980).

156. Id., p. 387.

157. Id., pp. 384, 385.

158. Id., p. 386.

159. Id., p. 385, Gulf Oil Corp. v. Gilbert, 330 U.S. 501, 508, 67 S.Ct. 839, 843, 91 L.Ed. 1055 (1946); Hoffman v. Goberman, 420 F.2d 423, 426 (3d Cir. 1970).

160. Gulf Trading & Transportation Co. v. M/V Tento, 694 F.2d 1191 (9th Cir. 1982), cert. denied, 103 S.Ct. 2091 (1983).

161. Rainbow Line, Inc. v. M/V Tequila, 480 F.2d 1024, 1026, note 5 (2d Cir. 1973).

162. Gulf Trading and Transport Co. v. M/V Tento, 694 F.2d at 1195 – 1196.

163. Fisher v. Agios Nicolas, 628 F.2d. 308, 316 (5th Cir. 1980), cert. denied, 454 U.S. 816, 102 S.Ct. 92, 70 L.Ed.2d 84 (1981).

164. Amin Rasheed Shipping Corporation v. Kuwait Insurance Co., 1 W.L.R. 228 (Court of Appeals 1983), decision by the Queen's Bench Division (1982), 1 W.L.R. 961 Aff'd.

165. Id.

166. 19 Bull. Legal Dev. 204 (1982).

167. Int'l. Fin. L. Rev. (March 1983), p. 28.

168. Int'l. Fin. L. Rev. (April 1983), p. 26.

169. Compagnie Europeene Des Petroles S.A. v. Sensor Nederland B.V., as reported in 22 Int'l. Legal Mat. 68, 69 (1982).

170. 22 Int'l Legal Mat. 300 (1982).

171. Sharon Steel Corporation v. Chase Manhattan Bank, 691 F. 2d 1039 (2d Cir. 1982), cert. denied, 103 S.Ct. 1253 (1983).

172. N. Literio and Co. v. Glassman Construction Co., 319 F.2d 736, 739 (D.C.Cir. 1963).

173. RCM Supply Co. v. Hunter Douglas, Inc., 686 F.2d. 1074 (4th Cir. 1982).

174. Polar Shipping Limited v. Oriental Shipping Corporation, 680 F.2d 627 (9th Cir. 1982).

175. Bremen v. Zapata Offshore Co., 407 U.S. 1, 15, 92 S.Ct. 1907, 32 L.Ed.2d 513 (1972).

176. 22 Int'l. Legal Mat. 246 (1983).

177. Schul v. Inspecteur der Invoerrechten en Accijnzen, Bull. of the E.C. Number 7 – 8/1982 at 92, as reported in 21 Bull. Legal Dev. 228 (1982). 178. I.R.C. Sections 991 – 997 (1971).

178. I.R.C. Sections 991 – 997 (1971).

179. 'DISC Again Under Attack Before GATT Council', 16 Tax Notes 81 (1982).

180. 'Treasury Took View that DISC Violated GATT', 16 Tax Notes 453 (1982).

181. Foreign Sales Corporation: General Explanation, Office of the Secretary of the Treasury (9 June 1983), p. 178.

182. 'Administration Proposes DISC Replacement Plan', 18 Tax Notes 976 (1983).

183. 'Frenzel Introduces Revised DISC Replacement Legislation', 17 Tax Notes 771 (1982); 'Vander Jagt Introduces DISC Revision Act', 18 Tax Notes 852 (1983).

184. 'GE (General Electric Corp.) Proposes FISC Concept as Alternative to DISC', 17 Tax Notes 770 (1982).

185. H.R. 3810, 98th Cong. 1st Sess. (1983); S. 1804, 98th Cong. 1st Sess. (1983).

186. Foreign Sales Corporation: General Explanation, supra n 178, at 8, 9.

187. Id., p. 10.

188. Id., p. 9.

189. Foreign Sales Corporation Proposal: Technical Explanation, Office of the Secretary of the Treasury (14 June 1983), p. 10.

190. Id., pp. 11, 12.

191. Id., p. 13.

192. Foreign Sales Corporation: General Explanation, supra n 178, p. 17.

193. Id., p. 15.

194. Asarco v. Idaho State Tax Commission, 459 U.S. 96, 73 L.Ed. 2d 787, 102 S.Ct. 3103 (1982).

182

195. Woolworth Co. v. the Taxation and Revenue Department of New Mexico, 454 U.S. 812, 73 L.Ed. 2d 819, 102 S.Ct. 3128 (1982).
196. Container Corp. of America v. Franchise Tax Board, 103 S.Ct. 2933 (1983).
197. Whitenack, 'State Tax Litigation After the Container Decision: The Potential Tax Break for Foreign Multinationals', 20 *Tax Notes* 771 (1983).
198. *The Sacramento Bee* (24 September 1983), p. A10.
199. Container Corp. of America v. Franchise Tax Board, 103 S.Ct. at 2944.
200. Id., p. 2948, n 19.
201. Id., p. 2944.
202. Id.
203. Id., p. 2947.
204. Whitenack, supra n 19, p. 774, citing Appellant's brief on the merits.
205. Container Corp. of America v. Franchise Tax Board, 103 S.Ct., p. 2947.
206. Id., p. 2940.
207. Hans Rees' Sons, Inc. v. North Carolina ex rel. Maxwell, 283 U.S. 123 (1931).
208. *The Sacramento Bee*, supra n 198.
209. Pub. L. 96 – 4999 (1982).
210. Pub. L. 97 – 34 (1982).
211. I.R.C. Section 6039(a) – (c).
212. Hickey and Zimmerman, 'Foreign Investment in U.S. Real Estate Reporting Requirements', 14 *The Tax Adviser* 214 (1983).
213. Temp. Regs. Section 6a.6039C – 2(b).
214. Temp. Regs. Section 6a.6039C – 3(e).
215. Id.
216. Goldberg and Hirschfeld, 'An Analysis of the New Temporary Rules on Reporting Foreign Investments in U.S. Realty', 58 *J. Tax'n* 259 (1983).
217. Pub. L. 97 – 354.
218. 'Subchapter S Revisions Charted by Coopers & Lybrand: Subchapter S Revision Act of 1982 – Summary of Changes', 17 *Tax Notes* 475 (1982).
219. I.R.C. Section 1361(b)(1)(A) (1982).
220. Fellows, 'Allocations of Foreign Taxes to S Corporation Shareholders Under the Subchapter S Revision Act of 1982', 61 *Taxes – The Tax Mag*. 404 (1983).
221. Subchapter S Revisions Charted by Coopers & Lybrand', supra n 218, p. 477.
222. I.R.C. Section 1361(b)(1)(A) (1982).
223. I.R.C. Section 1367 (1982).
224. Pub. L. 97 – 248 (1982).
225. Stevens, 'TEFRA Amendments to I.R.C. Section 907 Creates Problems and Opportunities for Corporate Taxpayer', 31 *Oil and Gas Tax Q*. 547 (1983).
226. Pub. L. 97 – 248 Section 211(c) (1982).
227. Pub. L. 97 – 248 Section 211(d)(2) (1982).
228. Pub. L. 97 – 248 Section 211(b) (1982).
229. Orbach, 'The Tax Equity and Fiscal Responsibility Act of 1982 and the Subchapter S Revision Act of 1982: Their Effect on the Oil and Gas Industry', 31 *Oil and Gas Tax Q*. 520 (1983).
230. Pub. L. 97 – 248 Section 211(a) (1982).
231. Orbach, supra n 229, p. 519.
232. 'Senate Finance Committee Explanation of Tax Equity and Fiscal Responsibility Act of 1982', 16 *Tax Notes* 211, 227 (1982).
233. Joint Committee on Taxation, 'Summary of Revenue Provisions of the Tax Equity and Fiscal Responsibility Act of 1982', 16 *Tax Notes* 818 (1982).

234. 69 *Std. Fed. Tax Rep.* Number 36 at Section 303, p. 143 (25 August 1982).
235. Id. Section 302, p. 143.
236. Joint Committee on Taxation, supra n 233, p. 818.
237. Id., pp. 818, 819.
238. 69 *Std. Fed Tax Rep.* p. 144.
239. Joint Committee on Taxation, supra n 233, p. 819.
240. 69 *Std. Fed. Tax Rep.,* p. 144.
241. Id.
242. See 2 *Tax Treaties* (CCH) Number 9015, p. 9018.
243. Gately and Hoffman, 'The United States Estate and Gift Tax Treaty Program and the Post- 1970 Treaties', 15 *N.Y.U.J. of Int'l L. and Pol.* 597 (1983).
244. See 1 *Tax Treaties* (CCH) Number 566N, p. 656.
245. See 1 *Tax Treaties* (CCH) Number 564, p. 653.
246. See 2 *Tax Treaties* (CCH) Number 9015, p. 9018.
247. See 2 *Tax Treaties* (CCH) Number 9941, p. 9919.
248. See 2 *Tax Treaties* (CCH) Number 941, p. 9918.
249. Id.
250. Id.
251. See 2 *Tax Treaties* (CCH) Number 9941, p. 9919.
252. Id.
253. See 2 *Tax Treaties* (CCH) Number 9015, p. 9019.
254. Id.
255. Id.
256. Id.
257. Id.
258. Id.
259. Id.
260. Id.
261. Id.
262. Blommer, 'Washington Letter', *Am. Pat. L.A. Bull.* (July-August 1982), p. 370.
263. Blommer, 'Washington Letter', *Am. Pat. L.A. Bull.* (March-April 1982), p. 179.
264. Final Act of the Third United Nations Conference on the Law of the Sea, reprinted in 21 *Int'l. Legal Mat.* 1331 (1982).
265. Blommer, supra n 262, p. 370.
266. Article 5, Section 8, of Annex III, defines 'technology' as 'specialized equipment and technological know-how, including manuals, design, operating instructions, training and technical advice and assistance, necessary to assemble, maintain and operate a viable system and the legal right to use these items for that purpose on a non-exclusive basis', supra n 264, p. 1332.
267. Larson, 'The Reagan Administration and the Law of the Sea', 11 *Ocean Dev. and Int'l. L.* 297, 311 (1982).
268. Id., p. 311.
269. Jones, 'The International Sea-Bed Authority Without U.S. Participation', 12 *Ocean Dev. and Int'l. L.* 151 (1983).
270. Final Act of the Third United Nations Conference on the Law of the Sea, supra n 264, pp. 1320, 1321.
271. 'Intellectual Property Rights: Draft Convention on the Law of the Sea', 5 *Comp. L. Y. B.* 292, 293 (1981).
272. Larson, supra n 267, p. 304.
273. Blommer, supra n 263, p. 180.

184

274. Final Act of the Third United Nations Conference on the Law of the Sea, supra n 264, p. 1326.
275. General Motors Corp. v. Devex Corp., – U.S. —, 103 S.Ct. 2058, 76 L.Ed. 2d 211 (1983).
276. Id., p. 218.
277. Duplate Corp. v. Triplex Co., 298 U.S. 448, 56 S.Ct. 792, 80 L.Ed. 1274 (1936).
278. General Motors Corp. v. Devex Corp., 76 L.Ed. 2d, p. 215.
279. Id. at n 5.
280. General Motors Corp. v. Devex Corp., 76 L.Ed. 2d at 216.
281. Id., p. 217.
282. Id., p. 218.
283. Id., p. 217.
284. 35 U.S.C. Section 284.
285. General Motors Corp v. Devex Corp., 76 L.Ed. 2d at 217, 218.
286. Kroboth, 'Microbiology/International Law Subcommittee', Canadian Law, *Am. Pat. L.A. Bull.* (January-February 1983) p. 4.
287. Diamond, Commissioner of Patents and Trademarks v. Chakrabarty, 447 U.S. 303, 100 S.Ct. 2204, 206 U.S.P.Q. 193 (1980).
288. Kroboth, supra n 286, p. 84.
289. Id.
290. Intellectual Property Rights: Reflections on Chakrabarty, 5 Comp. L. Y. B. 295, 296 (1981).
291. Diamond, Commissioner of Patents and Trademarks v. Chakrabarty, 447 U.S. 303, 100 S.Ct. 2204, 206 U.S.P.Q. 193 (1980).
292. 35 USC, Section 101 provides that: 'whoever invents or discovers any new and useful process, machine, manufacture or composition of matter, or any new and useful improvement thereof, may obtain a patent therefrom, may obtain a patent therefrom, subject to the conditions of this title'.
293. Kroboth, supra n 286, p. 84.
294. Id.
295. Kroboth, 'Microbiology/International Law Subcommittee, Certain Chemical Composition Claims Now Available in Canada', *Am. Pat. L.A. Bull.* (March-April 1983), pp. 184, 185.
296. Id., p. 185.
297. 'China: Latest Legal Developments', 2 *Int'l L. Newsletter* 5 (1983).
298. Piracy and Counterfeiting Amendments Act of 1982, Senate Report Number 274, 97th Cong., p. 41, reprinted in (1982) *U.S. Code Cong. and Ad. News* 127, 130.
299. Id., p. 130.
300. Id., p. 132.
301. Id., p. 133.
302. 18 U.S.C. Section 2318 (1982).
303. Id.
304. Senate Report Number 97 – 274, supra n 298, p. 134.
305. 18. U.S.C. Section 2319 (1982).
306. Senate Report Number 97 – 274, supra n 298, p. 136.
307. 18 U.S.C. Section 2319 (1982).
308. Olsson, 'Correspondence: Letter from Sweden', 1 *Copyright* 24 (1983).
309. Id., p. 34.
310. 'National Legislation: Sweden', 1 *Copyright* 14 (1983).
311. Id., p. 16.

312. Olsson, supra n 308, p. 24.
313. *London Times* (22 January 1983), p. 4.
314. *West Africa* (11 October 1982), p. 2679.
315. *Neue Zurcher Zeitung* (23 December 1982), p. 21, (20/21 March 1983), p. 17.
316. 'Japan Court Rules Copyright Law Applies to Software', 1 *Int'l L. Newsletter* 3 (1983).
317. Universal City Studios v. Sony Corporation of America, et al., 457 U.S. 1116 (1982).
318. Universal City Studios v. Sony Corporation of America, et al., 659 F.2d 963 (9th Cir. 1981), cert. granted at 457 U.S. 1116 (1982).
319. 'Arguments Before the Court: Copyrights', 51 *U.S.L.W.* 3543 (1983).
320. Id.
321. Id.
322. Id.
323. Sony Corporation, et al. v. Universal City Studios, et al., 51 U.S.L.W. 3938 (1983).
324. Pressman, 'Lobbying "Star War" Flares as Movie Industry Fights Invasion of Video Recorders', 41 *Cong. Q.* 1099 (4 June 1983).
325. H.R. 175, 1027, 1029, 1030, 98th Cong., 1st Sess. (1983); 31, 32, 33, 175, 98th Cong., 1st Sess. (1983).
326. Pressman, supra n 324, p. 1101.
327. 1983 Copyright L. Rpts. Number 57, p. 4.
328. Pressman, supra n 324, p. 1102.
329. Id.
330. Id.
331. 1983 Copyright L. Rpts. Number 56, p. 2.
332. Pressman, supra n 324, p. 1102.
333. Id., pp. 1099, 1100.
334. Plazas, 'Correspondence: Letter from Columbia', 5 *Copyright* 178 (1983).
335. Columbia Law on Copyright, Articles 1 to 71 (Number 23 of 28 January 1982), reprinted in 10 *Copyright* 286 (1982). Articles 72 to 150, reprinted in 11 *Copyright* 324 (1982). Articles 151 to 260, reprinted in 12 *Copyright* 357 (1982).
336. Plazas, supra n 324, p. 178.
337. Id.
338. Barbados Copyright Act of 1981 – 1982, Articles 1 to 29, reprinted in 2 *Copyright* 55 (1983). Articles 30 to 56 and schedules, reprinted in 3 *Copyright* 83 (1983).
339. Hunte, 'Correspondence: Letter from Barbados', 2 *Copyright* 69 (1983).
340. Id., p. 70.
341. Id., pp. 69, 70.
342. El Cid, Ltd. v. The New Jersey Zinc Company, 551 F. Supp. 626 (S.D.N.Y. 1982).
343. Id., p. 627, note 1.
344. Id., p. 628.
345. 15 U.S.C. Section 8.
346. El Cid, Ltd. v. The New Jersey Zinc Company, 551 F. Supp. at 629.
347. Id., p. 627.
348. Id., p. 629, citing United States v. Aluminium Co. of America, 148 F.2d 416, 443 (2d Cir. 1945).
349. See generally the First Circuit's line of cases that follows this per se approach in Albert Pick-Barth Co. v. Mitchell Woodbury Corp., 57 F.2d 96 (1st Cir. 1932), cert. denied, 286 U.S. 552, 52 S.Ct. 503, 76 L.Ed.2d. 1288, later limited by George R. Whitten, Jr., Inc. v. Paddock Pol Builders, Inc., 508 F.2d. 547 (1st Cir. 1974).
350. El Cid, Ltd. v. The New Jersey Zinc Company, 551 F.Sup. at 632.
351. Coastal States Marketing, Inc. v. Hunt, 694 F.2d. 1358 (5th Cir. 1983).

186

352. Id., p. 1359.
353. Id., p. 1360.
354. Id.
355. Eastern Railroad Residents Conference v. Noerr Motor Freight, Inc. 365 U.S. 127, 81 S.Ct. 523, 5 L.Ed.2d 464 (1961), and United Mine Workers v. Pennington, 381 U.S. 657, 85 S.Ct. 1585, 14 L.Ed.2d 626 (1965).
356. Coastal States marketing, Inc. v. Hunt, 694 F.2d p. 1364.
357. Id., p. 1365, citing Occidental Petroleum Corp. v. Buttes Gas & Oil Co., 331 F.Supp. 92 (C.D. Cal. 1971), aff'd per curiam on other grounds, 461 F.2d. 1261 (9th Cir. 1971), cert. denied, 409 U.S. 950, 93 S.Ct. 272, 34 L.Ed. 2d 221 (1972).
358. Continental Ore Co. v. Union Carbide & Carbon Corp., 370 U.S. 690, 707, 82 S.Ct. 1404, 1414 – 15, 8 L.Ed.2d 777, 788 (1962).
359. The Foreign Trade Antitrust Improvements Act of 1982 enacted as Title IV of the Export Trading Company Act of 1982, Pub. L. No. 97 – 290, 96 Stat. 1233 (codified at 15 U.S.C. Section 7).
360. Id. at Section 402.
361. Id. at Section 403.
362. J.O. Von Kalinowski, *Antitrust Laws and Trade Regulations* (1982), p. 10.
363. 44 *Antitrust & Trade Reg. Rep.* (BNA) 244 (1983).
364. Verlinden B.V. v. Central Bank of Nigeria, 103 S.Ct. 1962, 1968 (1983).
365. Id. See generally Kane, 'Suing Foreign Sovereigns: A Procedural Compass', 34 *Stan.L.Rev.* 385 (1982).
366. *Int'l Fin. L.Rev.* (April 1983), p. 41.
367. 28 U.S.C. Section 1605(a)(2).
368. Gibbons v. Udaras na Gaeltachta, 549 F.Supp. 1094 (S.D.N.Y. 1982).
369. *Int'l. Fin. L. Rev.*, supra n 366, p. 42.
370. Id.
371. Id.
372. Gibbons v. Udaras na Gaeltachta, 549 F.Supp. at 1108 – 1109.
373. Id., p. 1109, citing Texas Trading & Milling Corp. v. Federal Republic of Nigeria, 647 F.2d. 300, 311, n. 30 (2d. Cir. 1981), cert. denied, 454 U.S. 1148, 102 S.Ct. 1012, 71 L.Ed.2d 301 (1982).
374. Id., citing Texas Trading & Milling Corp. v. Federal Republic of Nigeria, 647 F.2d. p. 309 and International Association of Machinists v. O.P.E.C., 649 F.2d. 1354, 1357 (9th Cir. 1981), cert. denied, 454 U.S. 1163, 102 S.Ct. 1036, 71 L.Ed.2d 319 (1982).
375. *Int'l. Fin. L. Rev.,* supra n 366, p. 42.
376. Gibbons v. Udara na Gaeltachta, 549 F. Supp. at 1123.
377. Gilson v. Republic of Ireland, 682 F.2d 1022. (D.C. Cir. 1982).
378. Id., p. 1023.
379. Id., p. 1027, note 22.
380. Alberti v. Empresa Nicaraguense De La Carne, 705 F.2d 250 (7th Cir. 1983).
381. Id., p. 252.
382. 28 U.S.C. Section 1605(a)(3).
383. Harris Corp. v. National Iranian Radio, 691 F.2d 1344 (11th Cir. 1982).
384. Id., p. 1351.
385. Id., p. 1349.
386. Id., p. 1351.
387. Id.
388. International Shoe Co. v. Washington, 326 U.S. 310, 66 S.Ct. 154, 90 L.Ed. 95 (1945).
389. Harris Corp. v. National Iranian Radio, 691 F.2d p. 1353, citing World-Wide Volkswagen

Corp. v. Woodson, 444 U.S. 286, 291 – 99, 100 S.Ct. 559, 563 – 568, 62 L.Ed. 2d 490 (1980).

390. Id., p. 1352.
391. Alberti v. Empresa Nicaraguense De La Carne, 705 F.2d p. 253.
392. Jackson v. People's Republic of China, 550 F.Supp. 869 (N.D. Ala. E.D. 1982).
393. Id., p. 873.
394. Id.
395. 28. U.S.C. Section 1330(a).
396. Harris Corp. v. National Iranian Radio, 691 F.2d at 1350.
397. Id.
398. Id., citing Treaty of Amity, Economic Relations, and Consular Rights United States – Iran, 15 August 1955, Article XI, paragraph 4, 8 U.S.T. 899, T.I.A.S. 3853.
399. Id.
400. Maritime International Nominees Establishment v. Republic of Guinea, 693 F.2d 1094 (D.C. Cir. 1982), at 1100, citing 28 U.S.C. Section 1605(a)(1).
401. Id.
402. Id., p. 1103.
403. Id.
404. Transportes Aereos De Angola v. Ronair, Inc., 544 F. Supp. 858. (D.Del. 1982).
405. Id., p. 860.
406. Id.
407. Id.
408. See generally, Rubenstein, 'Alienage Jurisdiction in the Federal Courts', 17 *The Int'l. Lawyer* 240 (1983).
409. Transportes Aereos Angola v. Ronair, Inc., 544 F.Supp. p. 862.
410. Id.
411. Id.
412. Id.
413. Frolova v. Union of Soviet Socialist Republics, 558 F.Supp. 358 (N.D.Ill.E.D. 1983).
414. Id., p. 362.
415. 28 U.S.C. Section 1332(a)(2) and Section 1332(a)(3) as cited in Rubenstein, supra n 408, p. 285.
416. Id., p. 287.
417. Id., p. 300.
418. Verlinden B.V. v. Central Bank of Nigeria, 103 S.Ct. 1962 (1983).
419. Skeen v. Federative Republic of Brazil, No. 82 – 3504 (D.C. Cir., 7 July 1983) (available on Lexis, Genfed library, cases file).
420. Verlinden B.V. v. Central Bank of Nigeria, 103 S.Ct. at 1966.
421. Id.
422. 28 U.S.C. Section 1330(a).
423. Verlinden B.V. v. Central Bank of Nigeria, 103 S.Ct. p. 1970.
424. Id.
425. Id., p. 1964.
426. Id., pp. 1970, 1971, citing Osborn v. Bank of United States, 9 Wheat. 738, 6 L.Ed. 204 (1824).
427. 12 *Int'l. L. News*, Section of International Law and Practice, American Bar Association (Summer 1983).
428. 22 *Int'l. Legal Mat. (1983), p. 292.*
429. *Id., p. 298; Canada enacted its own state immunity act entitled 'Act to Provide for State Immunity in Canadian Courts' which went into force on 15 July 1982. This act also was*

188

closely patterned after the FSIA and has many similar provisions.

430. Onetta, 'Sovereign Immunity under Argentine', *Int'l. Fin. L. Rev.* (February 1983), p. 34.

431. *Bull. of Legal Dev.* (March 1983), p. 40.

432. Frolova v. Union of Soviet Socialists Republics, 558 F.Supp., p. 360.

433. Williams v. Curtiss-Wright Corp., 694 F.2d 300, 303 – 303 (3rd Cir. 1982), citing Mannington Mills Corp. v. Congoleum Corp., 595 F.2d 1287, 1292 (3d. Cir. 1979).

434. *Int'l Fin. L. Rev.* (January 1983), p. 46.

435. De Roburt v. Gannet Co., Inc. 548 F. Supp. 1370 (D. Ha. 1982).

436. Id., p. 1382.

437. Id., p. 1380.

438. Id., p. 1383.

439. Williams v. Curtiss-Wright Corp. 694 F.2d. p. 300 – 305.

440. Id., p. 302.

441. Id.

442. Id., p. 304.

443. Frolova v. Union of Soviet Socialist Republics, 558 F.Supp. at 363.

444. Compania de Gas de Nuevo Laredo, S.A. v. Entex, Inc., 686 F.2d. 322 (5th Cir. 1982), cert. denied 103 S.Ct. 1435 (1983).

445. Id., p. 324.

446. Id., p. 325.

447. Id., p. 326.

448. Id.

449. Id., p. 327; citing Banco Nacional de Cuba v. First National City Bank of New York, 431 F.2d 394 (2d Cir. 1970), rev'd on other grounds, 406 U.S. 759, 92 S.Ct. 1808, 32 L.Ed.2d. 466 (1972).

450. Ethopian Spice Extraction v. Kalamazoo Spice Extraction, 543 F.Supp. 1224 (W.D. Mich., S.D. 1982).

451. *Int'l. Fin. L. Rev.,* supra n 434, p. 46.

452. Ethiopian Spice Extraction v. Kalamazoo Spice Extraction, 543 F.Supp. at 1229.

453. 9 *Int'l. L. Perspective* (January 1983), p. 5.

454. S. 1434 which was introduced in the 96th Congress would repeal the Hickenlooper Amendment and would provide that 'no court in the United States shall decline on the ground of the federal Act of State doctrine to make a determination on the merits in any case in which the Act of State is contrary to international law'. Ethiopian Spice Extraction v. Kalamazoo Spice Extraction, 543 F.Supp., p. 1231, note 6.

455. Id., p. 1232.

456. The views expressed in this letter were submitted to the U.S. Court of Appeals for the 6th Circuit which is hearing the appeal from the district court's ruling in the *Ethiopian Spice* case, 543 F.Supp. 1224 (1982), 22 *Int'l. Legal Mat.* 207 (1983), as reported in 10 *Bull. Legal Dev.* 104 (1982).

457. Frequently, private litigants and foreign governments will request the State Department's opinion on the propriety of the application of the AOS doctrine in a particular case.

458. 22 *Int'l. Legal Mat.* 207 (1983), p. 208.

459. Id.

460. 15 U.S.C. Sections 15(b) – 15(c) (Supp. X 1983).

461. The passage of the current act is a result of efforts of the 95th and 96th Congresses. The bill was initiated in the 97th Congress as a result of the Senate Report of 15 May 1981, Number 97 – 98 (Judiciary Committee), 1982 *U.S. Code & Ad. News* (96 Stat.) 3495, 3498 – 99.

462. Clayton Act, ch. 323, Section 7, 38 Stat. 730, 731 – 32 (1914) (current version at 15 U.S.C.

Sections 12, et seq. (1973 & Supp. X 1983)).

463. 15 U.S.C. Sections 15(b) – 15(c) (Supp. X 1983).
464. 1982 U.S. Code & Ad. News (96 Stat.) 3495, 3506.
465. Pfizer Inc., et al. v. Government of India, et al., 434 U.S. 308, 98 S.Ct. 584, 54 L.Ed.2d. 563 (1978).
466. Id., p. 320.
467. Id., p. 328.
468. 1982 U.S. Code & Ad. News (96 Stat.) 3495, 3500.
469. Id.
470. Id., p. 3501.
471. 15 U.S.C. Sections 15(b) – 15(c) (Supp. X 1983).
472. U.S. Code, supra n 464, p. 3506.
473. *Int'l. Fin. L. Rev.* (March 1983), p. 34.
474. Seawind Maritime Inc. v. Rumanian Bank of Foreign Trade, as reported in *Int'l. Fin. L. Rev.* (March 1983), p. 34.
475. Mareva Compania Naviera S.A. v. International Bulk Carriers, (1975) 2 L.R. 509.
476. 'The Eleftherios', 2 *L.R.* 351.
477. *Int'l. Fin. L. Rev.* (March 1983), p. 34.
478. PCW (Underwriting Agencies) Ltd. v. Dixon, as reported in *Int'l. Fin. L. Rev.* (March 1983), pp. 34, 35.
479. *Int'l. Fin. L. Rev.* (March 1983), p. 35.
480. 28 U.S.C. Sections 1602 et seq. (1973 & Supp. X 1983).
481. Id., p. Section 1609.
482. Id., at Section 1610(d).
483. *Libra Bank Ltd. v. Banco Nacional de Costa Rica*, 676 F.2d 47, 49 – 50 (2d. Cir. 1982).
484. Id.
485. *S & S Machinery v. Masinexportimport*, 706 F.2d. 411 (2d. Cir. 1983).
486. Id., p. 416.
487. See, e.g. Treaty of Amity, Aug. 15, 1955, United States – Iran Art. XI 4, 8 U.S.T. 899, 909, T.I.A.S. No. 3853.
488. *S & S Machinery v. Masinexportimport*, 706 F.2d p. 417.
489. Id.
490. *Libra Bank Ltd. v. Banco Nacional de Costa Rica*, 676 F.2d. p. 49.
491. *S & S Machinery v. Masinexportimport*, 706 F.2d. p. 417.
492. 28 U.S.C. Sections 1601 et seq.
493. First National City Bank v. Banco Para El Commercio Exterior de Cuba, 103 S.Ct. 2591 (1983).
494. Id., p. 2593.
495. Id., pp. 2603, 2604.
496. *The Times* (London) (1 December 1982), p. 8, as reported in 24 *Bull. Legal Dev.* 254 (1982).
497. Id.
498. *Information Bulletin on Legal Activities,* Council of Europe, Number 13 (September 1982), p. 23, as reported in 23 *Bull. Legal Dev.* 244 (1982).
499. Id.
500. Id.
501. *Commonwealth Law Bulletin* (April 1982), p. 662 as reported in 21 *Bull. Legal Dev.* 224 (1982).
502. *Financial Times* (London) (11 January 1983), p. 1, as reported in 2 *Bull. Legal Dev.* 15 (1983).

190

503. *Neue Zurcher Zeitung* (23/24 May 1982), p. 18, as reported in 11 *Bull. Legal Dev.* 112 (1982).

504. 19 *Bull Legal Dev.* 204 (1982).

505. Hussain v. Hussain, (1982) 3 All E.R. 369.

506. *Bull. Legal Dev.* supra n 504.

507. S.M. v. F.B. 11. J.C.P. 19717, as reported in 10 *Eur. Dig.* 165 (April 1982).

508. Id.

509. S. v. Department de Justice du Canton du Tessin, II BGE 236 (1981), as reported in 10 *Eur. L. Dig.* 351 (August 1982).

510. Id.

511. 'A.P.', *Journal des Tribunaux* 603 (1982), as reported in 10 *Eur. L. Dig.* 534 (December 1982).

512. Id.

513. Id.

514. Id.

515. Mahoney v. Mahoney, 442 A. 2d 1062 (N.J. 1982).

516. Id., p. 1069.

517. Id., p. 1064.

518. Id., p. 1072.

519. In Re Lundberg, 318 N.W. 2d 918 (Wis. 1982).

520. Id., p. 920.

521. Id., p. 924.

522. Id., p. 923.

523. Id., p. 924.

524. Placide v. Placide, 408 So. 2d 330 (La. 1981).

525. Id., p. 335.

526. Id., p. 336.

527. Id., p. 330.

528. 'Family Business (Craftmakers' and Traders') Spouses Act', *Journal Officiel de la République Française* (13 July 1982) p. 2467, as reported in 10 *Eur. L. Dig.* 541 (December 1982).

529. *Financial Times* (London) (20 August 1982), p. 6, as reported in 18 *Bull. Legal Dev.* 192 (1982).

530. Id.

531. *The Times* (London) (8 December 1982), p. 2 as reported in 24 *Bull. Legal Dev.* 27 (1983).

533. Id.

534. Cellerin v. Epoux Potron, II J.C.P. 19746 (1982), as reported in 10 *Eur. L. Dig.* 258 (June 1982).

535. Id.

536. Biver v. Schuman, Pasicrisie Luxembourgeoise 65 (1981), as reported in 10 *Eur. L. Dig.* 361 (August 1982).

537. Id.

538. *Recht* (10 – 12/1982), p. 167; *Neue Juritische Wochenschrift* (3/1983), p. 101, as reported in 3 *Bull. Legal Dev.* 23 (1983).

539. M.J.G. v. J.G.P., 640 P. 2d 966 (Okla. 1982).

540. Id.

541. In Re Phillip B., 139 Cal. App. 3d 408 (1983).

542. Id.

543. Mills v. Hableutzel, 456 U.S. 91, 71 L.Ed.2d 770, 102 S.Ct. 1549 (1982).

544. *Rabelszeitschrift* (4/1982), p. 818, as reported in 3 *Bull. Legal Dev.* 25 (1983).

545. V. v. F., Rechtskundig Weekblad 954 (1981 – 92), as reported in 10 *Eur. L. Dig.* 304, 305 (July 1982).

546. Santosky v. Kramer, 45 U.S. 745, 71 L.Ed.2d. 599, 102 S.Ct. 1388 (1982).

547. Id.

548. In Re J.R., 315 N.W. 750 (Iowa 1982).

549. Id., p. 753.

550. Id.

551. Hoff, 'Child Snatching: Getting Legal Relief Through New Tort Remedies', 5 *Family Advocate* 38 (1983).

552. Lloyd v. Loeffler, 694 F. 2d 489 (7th Cir. 1982).

553. Id., p. 491.

554. Id.

555. Wasserman v. Wasserman, 671 F.2d 832 (4th Cir. 1982).

556. Id., p. 833.

557. Id., p. 834.

558. *Neue Zurcher Zeitung* (11 January 1983), p. 9, as reported in 6 *Bull. Legal Dev.* 57 (1983).

559. 1 *Bull. Legal Dev.* 5 (1983).

560. 60 *Interpreter Releases*, (1983) 612 – 13.

561. Id.

562. The Refugee Act of 1980, Pub. L. Number 96 – 112, 94 Stat. 102, 8 U.S.C. Section 1101(a)(42) (1980).

563. Martinez-Romero v. Immigration and Naturalization Service, 692 F.2d 595 (9th Cir. 1982), cert. denied 102 S.Ct. 2129.

564. Id., pp. 595, 596.

565. Raass v. Immigration and Naturalization Service, 692 F.2d. 596 (9th Cir. 1982).

566. Id.

567. 60 *Interpreter Releases*, (1983) 21.

568. Id., p. 28.

569. Id.

570. Stevic v. Sava, 678 F.2d 401 (2d Cir. 1982).

571. Id., p. 403.

572. Id.

573. Id.

574. 8 U.S.C. Section 1253(h).

575. Stevic v. Sava, 678 F.2d at 404.

576. Id.

577. The Refugee Act of 1980, supra n 562.

578. Stevic v. Sava, 678 F.2d p. 404.

579. Id., p. 408.

580. 8 U.S.C. Section 1101(a)(42) (1980).

581. Stevic v. Sava, 678 F.2d at 409.

582. Rejaie v. Immigration and Naturalization Service, 691 F.2d 139 (3d Cir. 1982).

583. Id., p. 144.

584. Id., p. 146.

585. Reyes v. Immigration and Naturalization Service, 693 F.2d 597 (6th Cir. 1982).

586. Id., p. 600.

587. Id.

588. Id.

589. Minwalla v. Immigration and Naturalization Service, 706 F.2d 831 (8th Cir. 1982).

590. Treaty of Friendship, Commerce and Navigation 2 April 1953, United States-Japan, 4

192

U.S.T. 2063, T.I.A.S. Number 2853.

591. Sumitomo Shoji America, Inc. v. Avagliano, 473 F.Supp. 506 (S.D.N.Y. 1979), aff'd on other grounds, 638 F.2d 552 (2d. Cir. 1981), rev'd, 457 U.S. 176, 102 S.Ct. 2374 (1982).

592. 'It shall be an unlawful employment practice for an employer ... to discriminate against any individual with respect to his compensation, terms, conditions, or privileges of employment, because of such individual's race, color, religion, sex, or national origin ...'. Civil Rights Act of 1964, Pub. L. Number 88 – 352, tit. VII, Sec. 703, 78 Stat. 241, 255 (codified at 42 U.S.C. Sec. 2000e – 2(a) (1976)).

593. Article VIII(1), Treaty of Friendship, Commerce and Navigation, supra n 590.

594. Sumitomo Shoji America, Inc. v. Avagliano, 457 U.S. at 181 – 82.

595. Id., pp. 185, 189.

596. Id., p. 178.

597. Civil Rights Act of 1964, supra n 592.

598. Article VIII(1), Treaty of Friendship, Commerce and Navigation, supra n 590.

599. Sumitomo Shoji America, Inc. v. Avagliano, 457 U.S., p. 179.

600. Id., p. 179.

601. Id., pp. 180 – 190.

602. Article XXII(3), Treaty of Friendship, Commerce and Navigation, supra n 590.

603. Sumitomo Shoji America, Inc. v. Avagliano, 457 U.S. pp. 182 – 83.

604. Id., pp. 183, 185.

605. Id., pp. 187, 188.

606. Id., p. 188.

607. 'The term "national treatment" means treatment accorded within the territories of a Party upon terms no less favorable than the treatment accorded therein, in like situations, to nationals, companies, products, vessels or other objects, as the case may be, of such Party'. Article XXII(1), Treaty of Friendship, Commerce and Navigation, supra n 590.

608. Sumitomo Shoji America, Inc. v. Avagliano, 457 U.S., p. 188.

609. 76 *Am. J. Int'l. L.* (1982), pp. 854, 855.